The ABCs
of Soviet Socialism

James R. Millar

University of Illinois Press
Urbana Chicago London

Library of Congress Cataloging in Publication Data

Millar, James R   1936-
   The ABCs of Soviet socialism.

Includes index.
1.   Russia--Economic conditions--1918-
2.   Russia--Economic policy--1917-   I. Title.
HC336.25.M54   338.947   80-24196
ISBN 0-252-00845-6 (cloth)
ISBN 0-252-00872-3 (paper)

*For Gera, Leo, and Mira, whose presence
illuminated whole new worlds.*

Contents

Preface

This book is based upon what I have learned about the Soviet economy over the past fifteen years. It is rooted in the work of other scholars as well as in my own research. I have drawn heavily upon two six-month visits (in 1966 and 1979) to the Soviet Union to conduct my research.

My aim is to present what I have learned in concise nontechnical prose, within a framework of analysis that I have formulated to make sense of my experiences and findings. This text is not intended as a neutral survey of the subject. When my views differ materially from the majority of my colleagues in the field, I so indicate, and I provide alternative readings for those who wish to have the various views detailed. As a general rule, however, the reader should bear in mind that this book has been written by one student of the USSR's economy, not by a group of authors. It represents one person's opinion about a number of unsettled questions.

Introduction

Means Versus Ends

Economists like to think of the economy as a means to an end, not as an end in itself. They regard the institutions that compose the economy as mechanisms by which the economic activities of diverse individuals and groups within the society are coordinated so as to produce the goods and services that are demanded by private individuals, enterprises, government agencies, and other organized groups. If the ends of economic activity are determined by individuals and/or by certain organized groups in society and if institutions such as the market serve merely to communicate these needs to producers and to coordinate production and distribution of goods and services, the economist's job is confined to questions about the efficiency with which coordination takes place.

The study of diverse economic systems reveals, however, that peoples and cultures do act as though certain aspects of the economic structure are ends in themselves, not just means for the satisfaction of wants. It also reveals that the ends of economic activity cannot be taken for granted either. Ends sometimes conflict with one another. The desire for full employment, in capitalist countries today, seems to conflict with the desire for price stability; and many economists in the less developed economies believe that efficiency and economic growth are not entirely compatible goals. Thus the economist finds it unrealistic to confine himself to questions of efficiency. He finds himself mediating between conflicting goals and defending institutions that are not efficient but that are deemed desirable nonetheless.

Since the question of efficiency does not exhaust the issues that occupy the attention of active economists, we shall not confine ourselves to it. We shall be concerned with describing the institutions that coordinate economic activity in the Soviet economy and with explaining the way they differ from institutions elsewhere, especially those that serve as ends and not just as means.

Sources

That Soviet authorities are highly secretive about many aspects of Soviet economic activity is well known. Anyone who purports to know something about the economy of the USSR can and should be asked how he knows what he claims. Those of us who have been in the field a long time are accustomed to such challenges, which are quite appropriate. A great deal of misinformation about the Soviet Union parades as knowledge in the West, and not all of it can be attributed to Soviet propaganda.

Specialists draw upon two primary sources of information about the economy of the USSR. The first consists of Soviet statistical publications. Although little economic data are available for certain periods in Soviet history, much data were published in the 1920s and early 1930s and again since 1957. The fascist menace, World War II, and the Cold War were largely responsible for the extreme measures of secrecy that characterized the period between 1937 and 1959; but the Soviet Central Statistical Administration has also been selective about releasing data on sensitive political, sociological, or economic issues regardless of questions of military security. Statistics on crime rates in Soviet cities are not routinely published as they are in the United States. Information is rarely provided about airline accidents except when foreign passengers are involved. Newspapers do not report the wildcat strikes that occur occasionally in Soviet enterprises. Many more instances could be enumerated. What these cases have in common is the reluctance of responsible authorities to reveal undesirable aspects of Soviet society. To a certain degree the avoidance of sensationalism in official publications and newspapers is a pleasant relief for sensitive souls, but such suppression can also create a misleading impression of Soviet society. Like many other governments the Soviet government does not like to admit to mistakes or misjudgments, which are frequently concealed. The ownership and control of all legal presses by the state make such cover-ups highly effective.

Prohibitions upon what is reportable in the USSR have decreased substantially since Stalin's time. Poor grain-harvests are reported fully today, for example. One can readily find statistics about divorce rates.

In general, however, serious social and economic problems are still not reported in the press or in standard statistical handbooks unless they have become the object of official criticism. Usually Soviet official publications report the successes of the Soviet economy, not its failures or shortcomings.

Sometimes the failure to disclose information about problems actually makes the situation look worse than it actually is. During the severe winter of 1979, when the temperature fell to 40 or more degrees below zero several times, one of the main heating lines which supply all buildings in Moscow, including apartments, failed. Consequently thousands of the residents of Moscow had no central heat for several days. Temperatures inside their apartments fell well below the freezing point, forcing them to huddle together in their coats to keep warm. This problem was never reported on television or radio, which meant that the people affected could not find out readily what was wrong or how long it would take for the heat to be restored. Of course everyone in Moscow knew about the incident from friends or relatives within a very short time, but the reports that circulated, as in the game of Gossip, were encrusted with all sorts of sinister interpretations. Power failures, spillages of dangerous chemicals, and other catastrophes have become almost common in the major cities of the world, and it is difficult to understand Soviet bashfulness in reporting such incidents. Such secrecy is characteristic, however, of the kinds of deficiencies and omissions in data that students of the Soviet economy must overcome in attempting to provide a complete and well-balanced picture of the way Soviet institutions work and of the problems they entail.

Governmental and private specialists in the West have devoted a great deal of time to the evaluation of official Soviet statistical publications. Important time series, such as national income, industrial production, defense expenditures, capital investment, and the like are routinely recalculated and adjusted to ensure meaningful comparisons with data produced in western economies. Verifying the accuracy of Soviet published sources on economic statistics is not difficult in principle, because economic data are all closely interconnected: it takes so much coal and iron ore, for example, to produce various grades of steel; the different uses of grain products cannot exceed total sources; all receipts of money income must equal total payments.

Although outright falsification by the Soviet Central Statistical Administation is apparently not in issue, several basic problems must be considered in evaluating the data. Historically the most common practice has been to suppress data that Soviet authorities do not want known by foreigners. Soviet statistics commonly provoke false conclusions by dint of omission. Direct falsification is rare and would in any case be very expensive to carry out successfully if any data were published.

Second is the failure of official handbooks to provide data in forms useful for the kinds of analysis western scholars like to undertake. Sometimes this is because of a failure to provide precise specification for the series in question. The term *average wages*, for example, may refer to all workers or exclude collective-farm workers. It may be calculated using constant prices, thereby excluding the influence of inflation. Or average wages may include an estimate of the value to workers of free medical care and other benefits such as subsidized apartment rents and free education. Comparison with wages outside the Soviet Union, or over time within the country, cannot be meaningfully interpreted without careful specifications. On other occasions the data are presented as percentage increases over some unspecified base year, which makes it impossible to identify the underlying absolute magnitudes in the absence of some other source. This kind of problem has turned all western Soviet specialists into detectives who must spend much of their time "number hunting."

A third basic problem does involve falsification, but not by the Central Statistical Administration. As in every economy, there are incentives in the Soviet Union which lead individuals and establishments to misreport certain kinds of economic data. Conflicts of interest between private corporations and labor unions in the United States, for example, cause corporations to be very cautious and conservative about reporting on changes in productivity that imply a reduction in the work force or that increase profits relative to the wage bill. Many persons also find it difficult to resist the temptation to underreport their incomes to the IRS. Similar temptations exist in the Soviet Union concerning reports of plan fulfillment, budgeting for annual production needs, and the like. To the extent that such misrepresentations are not discovered and remedied by higher authorities, economic data drawn from these sources will be defective. Little can be done about such problems other than to note the kinds of transactions that tend to be affected by identifying the incentives that induce misreporting.

All economies suffer from problems of data reliability and usability to one degree or another. Some of the less developed countries of the world publish data that everyone knows is completely manufactured. Soviet data and statistical presentations are far superior to what is available today for most countries of the world, and such information has become much more nearly complete during the last fifteen years. Given the elaborate research establishment in the United States, both in academic and governmental agencies, we have developed the basis for a full and reliable description and analysis of the Soviet economic system. We can be reasonably confident, I believe, that we have identified the main problems with which Soviet economists and planners struggle and that we understand at least as well as they do why the economy works as well in some areas and as poorly in others as it does.

The second source of primary information on the way the Soviet economy operates is firsthand reports of western observers. Evaluation of the data provided by firsthand observation is more difficult than for official statistics because most of these observations are never committed to paper. They circulate informally as cocktail anecdotes — or classroom tonics. In general, firsthand observations are highly unreliable sources of information, and accordingly we shall rely upon them partly for color and rarely for generalizations. Personal observation is limited since visitors to the USSR are confined to the large cities for the most part, and contacts between Soviet citizens and visitors are severely constrained — both officially and by natural discretion. Moreover, foreign observers in the Soviet Union tend to find what they are looking for, mainly because the Soviet system excites strong feelings pro or con in most outsiders; and these strong feelings shape not only what people actually see but also the reactions of Soviet citizens to the observer.

Despite these reservations certain aspects of Soviet life could not be discovered by any means other than firsthand observation. The hardships posed by commodity shortages and inadequate space for retail sales, especially for the working woman, are brought home to the observer in a way detailed statistical data could never do. Nor is the importance of "connections" that are strategically located with respect to deficit commodities and services easy to grasp in the absence of first-hand experience. Similarly the privileged place that children occupy in Soviet society is not readily deduced from Soviet data on retail sales or on educational expenditures. Firsthand observation provides the student of Soviet society with qualitative information which no amount of statistics could replace. As such, however, it is much more difficult to evaluate and, when used properly, much richer in what it conveys than cold statistics. A week's observation in a Soviet family or in the highest councils of national defense would reveal much left unrevealed by available numbers on family income and expenditures or on national stocks of missiles. But, as is true even in nuclear physics, the observer invariably influences what he sees by his very presence. Hence the care with which firsthand observation must be conducted and interpreted.

Although it would be difficult to measure with any precision, what we know about the Soviet economy today is several times more inclusive and detailed than it was twenty years ago, and the models that have been developed to analyze and to evaluate Soviet economic performance are much more sophisticated and interesting. There remain certain historical periods about which we have little information even now, such as World War II and the immediate postwar years; and certain important questions remain unanswered, such as how political decisions are taken and get translated into economic directives. In general, however, we have been able to fit together enough pieces of the puzzle to visualize the over-all pattern and much of its detailed complexity.

The text that follows is divided into three unequal sections. The first offers primarily a description of the historical evolution of the institutions that coordinate and guide economic activity in the Soviet Union. The second section of the book provides a description of the way the economy works today. The third provides some hypotheses about the way the Soviet economy operates, and it draws some general conclusions and appraisals concerning the nature and performance of the system. It concludes on a speculative note. The final section also addresses the question of dynamics — that is, where the Soviet economy is going and what problems are likely to confront Soviet economists and planners in the medium-term future. Forecasting economic activity is notoriously hazardous, but it ought to be possible to specify with some confidence the possible paths — and within this set the probable paths — that the Soviet economy will follow over the next five to ten years. Besides, no discipline that has scientific ambitions can afford to evade the responsibility of making predictions.

I

The Soviet Economy
in Historical Perspective

1

The Formation of
Soviet Economic Institutions

Prerevolutionary Development

The industrial revolution, which may be defined as a marked acceleration in the rate of growth of industrial production, arrived late in Tsarist Russia in comparison to Western Europe. The output of industrial products did not compare unfavorably in absolute magnitudes with the leading European economies at the time of Peter the Great's death in 1725. Subsequently, and throughout most of the nineteenth century, Russia fell gradually farther and farther behind the other major European powers in economic development. The sheer territorial size and the large population of Russia relative to other European countries, together with the strategic position of Russia as a potential anvil on the border of Europe, caused Russia to play a role in European political and military life much out of proportion to her level of development. Contact with the more developed powers in the West and involvement in international political, military, and diplomatic affairs led eventually to a conflict, the Crimean War in 1854, which revealed the industrial backwardness of the Russian economy.

The efforts of the Tsarist government to force the pace of economic growth during the last quarter of the nineteenth century is commonly attributed, therefore, to military failure in the conflict with England in the Crimea; but it is recognized widely also that these efforts represented a response to a multitude of social and economic tensions that were troubling Russian society during the second half of the century. Whatever may have been the case politically, the reciprocal economic obligations between the nobility, upon which the state had always relied not only for political support but also for local political and economic administration, and the serfs were no longer working satisfactorily. The economic decline of the nobility had reached a crisis, a situation clearly reflected in the works of many of the great Russian prose-writers of the period, particularly Tolstoy, Saltykov-Shchedrin, and Goncharov. Serfdom was formally abolished in 1861 in an effort to clear away economic, social, and interpersonal obligations that had long since disappeared in Europe under the pressure of modernization, urbanization, and the spread of pecuniary institutions. This effort was not entirely successful, for the government apparently found it difficult to abandon its customary partisanship of the nobility. Most Russian serfs were freed with land, as opposed to the emancipation of American Negroes, and compensation was obligatory; but few peasants received sufficient land to permit severing the traditional reciprocal bonds between the peasant and his former master.

The Tsarist government also initiated a series of measures designed to promote capital investment by both domestic and foreign investors. These measures were essentially successful, and the state also promoted the development of railways directly. The growth of rail connections within European Russia and of the now-famous Trans-Siberian line connecting European Russia with the vast hinterland of Siberia affords a good index of development in the years after 1860. Some seventy thousand kilometers of railway were constructed between 1860 and 1913. The significance of this development for economic growth in Russia can readily be seen with a map, for the principal rivers of European Russia flow southward, away from Russia's traditional European markets, and the greatest, the Volga, flows into the landlocked Caspian Sea. The rivers in Siberia, on the other hand, flow northward into the Arctic Circle. These handicaps are augmented by long cold winters during which all major river systems, and the lakes they feed, freeze solid. Russia's waterways therefore afforded an inadequate basis for industrialization and the development of domestic markets. The coming of the railroads greatly reduced these barriers to the development of the Russian economy.

If measured by the rate of growth of industrial production alone, Tsarist Russia registered a very respectable record of growth after 1860. Estimates for this period of scanty statistical data vary, but the rate of growth was somewhere in the neighborhood of 5 percent per year between 1888 and 1913. The gross national product grew at a slower pace because agricultural output increased only marginally. Although the rate of growth of GNP was about 2.5 percent per year, per-capita growth in GNP was only approximately 1 percent per annum. Moreover the slow pace of agricultural growth and the relatively swift rate of growth of population caused Russia's over-all rate of economic growth to fall behind that of the major powers, notably Germany, Japan, and the United States, where rates of per-capita growth hovered between 2.5 and 3.5 percent per annum.

The Tsarist regime did succeed in reducing the rate at which Russia was falling behind by forcing the pace of industrialization during its last fifty years, but it did not narrow the gap between Russia and the principal industrial countries of the world. At the outbreak of World War I, Russia was the world's fifth largest industrial producer, but ranked only approximately tenth in per-capita income. Russia had, of course, started late. Like Imperial Germany and Imperial Japan, development was fostered by an autocratic, paternalistic, essentially feudalistic political system. Possibly the effort of the state to encourage growth in Russia would have paid increased dividends over time, as happened in the other two imperial powers. The political outcome might also have been similar, which gives one pause. In any event Russia was in the process of modernizing technically and institutionally on the eve of its revolution.

Economic historians have naturally been led to speculate about whether or not the revolutions of 1917 and the rise of the Bolsheviks to power have actually made much difference as far as industrialization and economic growth are concerned. The economy the Bolsheviks assumed control of was already quite large by world standards, and its growth performance was improving as well prior to World War I. Large-scale modern industrial establishments had been established in a number of areas. The necessary basic transportation network was essentially complete, and a permanent labor force was in the making. Moreover the Tsarist regime had introduced measures following the unsuccessful 1905 revolution designed to undermine traditional agricultural institutions, which were deemed resistant to modernization of production, and to encourage establishment of independent farmers. If successful, these reforms would have raised the rate of growth of agricultural output, thereby increasing also over-all and per-capita growth of GNP to rates more nearly equal to those of the major world powers.

The usefulness of such speculation is limited but real. It helps to put the economic achievements of the Bolsheviks into proper historical perspective. Neither the aims nor the means of Bolshevik economic policy were new for Russia, although differences in Tsarist and Bolshevik economics existed. And to a large extent the problems the Bolsheviks faced were the same as well. The search for parallels can, however, become ridiculous in short order. That Tsarist policies amounted to too little and too late is an historical truism, and no hypothetical counterfactual analysis of history can be extended very far in time for the simple reason that there are too many complex variables for it to be a meaningful exercise. An historical model based upon inertia alone is not very sophisticated, and with it one can predict nothing new.

Soviet economic histories of the prerevolutionary period tend to exaggerate the level of development achieved under the Tsars, but not because their authors wish to minimize the contribution of the Bolshevik revolution. On the contrary, they seek to demonstrate that "capitalist" relations of production had been established by 1917. Otherwise no Marxist could accept it as a *socialist* revolution. In deciding to seize the 1917 revolution, Lenin had to persuade himself and his followers that the time was ripe for a proletarian revolution in Russia. It would have been difficult in any case for so dedicated a revolutionary as Lenin to pass up such a promising uprising, but there were Marxists, particularly among the Mensheviks (who had split the Social Democratic party with the Bolsheviks at the turn of the century) who argued that the revolution was properly to be interpreted as being against feudalism; and they were prepared to see bourgeois parties assume political power. Much can be said for such a perspective, both on grounds of Marxist theory and in view of the subsequent history of Bolshevik Russia. In 1917 Russia was still backward compared to England, Germany, and the United States; and the theoretically appropriate constituency of a Marxist political party, industrial and other urban workers, was very small — not more than 10 percent of the total population at the most. The great mass of the population was rural, illiterate, and committed to private agricultural enterprise on a small scale. The Bolsheviks assumed power with neither the economic base nor the political following that Marxist theory and political reality would appear to require. That they succeeded in maintaining political control and in initiating workable economic policies is, therefore, all the more surprising.

War Communism

Bolshevik capture of the revolution in November of 1917 put an end to Russia's participation in World War I, but it also precipitated a civil war, which continued through 1920 and which was won at the cost of an almost complete breakdown of the economy. Industrial output in 1920 was only about one-fourth that of 1913, the last year before the war. The transportation system was in shambles. In the hope of avoiding starvation, many citizens had fled the cities for the countryside. Harvests had been disrupted by movements of the opposing armies and by harsh requisitioning measures applied by all parties to the war. This interlude is called the period of War Communism in Soviet official histories, but the underlying notion — that economic policy and institutions constituted a coherent system — is completely misleading. The label is appropriate only in the sense that there was in fact a civil war going on and that, like most civil wars, it was a fierce contest in which no quarter was given or expected and in which both sides pressed the unwilling as well as the willing into service. The peasantry fought on both sides and was exploited by both sides.

The New Economic Policy

Once the civil war ended, the Soviet Union began a period of extraordinary social and economic experimentation. Certain Bolshevik theorists, notably Bukharin and Preobrazhensky, had argued during the civil war for the prompt liquidation of all pecuniary institutions. Cash, the system of prices, markets, and wages were regarded at that time as distinctly capitalist institutions that could and would be replaced by appropriate "socialist" relations of production as soon as feasible. The inflation caused by civil war, military requisitioning, the closure of many private factories and stores, and the breakdown of the market system generally were viewed as promising developments, as a clearing of the decks for establishing new socialist institutions. Just what these new institutions would be was less clear, and Lenin apparently decided that wholesale modification of the economic system the Bolsheviks had inherited with the revolution was inappropriate and unworkable in the shambles that remained after the civil war. Consequently Lenin used his great prestige to introduce a completely new policy in 1921 to stimulate recovery and to utilize private and public enterprise in tandem to reconstruct the economy.

The New Economic Policy (NEP) recognized, for an indefinite but necessarily transitory period, the coexistence of private and public enterprise in the Soviet Union. The NEP promoted, therefore, what today would be called a mixed economy. The state dominated economic activity from the commanding heights of heavy industry, the banking system and all other financial intermediaries, transportation, and communications. Enterprises that had not yet been nationalized were allowed to operate as before the revolution; certain small-scale industries and stores were denationalized; and foreign entrepreneurs were invited to invest in the Soviet socialist economy.

The NEP accepted the legal existence not only of private industrial enterprises and private peasant farms but also of private middlemen in retail and wholesale trade. For these to be functional economic privileges, the fledgling socialist state also had to grant individuals the right to hire others for profit—that is, according to Marxist thought, to extract surplus value from employees, and to permit private alienation of most forms of property. The NEP was, then, partly a compromise between the aims and beliefs of the new regime and the desire of millions of petty producers, including peasants, for private enterprise in production and sales. In retrospect it was also a sober assessment of the limited capabilities of the new Bolshevik government. The fledgling regime was not strong or secure enough to direct recovery of the economy or to coordinate all economic activity from the center. The NEP also represented an important compromise with the peasantry, who constituted close to 85 percent of the total population and who had been seriously alienated during the civil war by Red Army tactics of requisitioning.

As a result of Lenin's willingness to take a step backward, the economy began a gradual but steady recovery from the damages of war and revolution. This recovery afforded a respite for experimentation with planning methods and with the organization of social and economic institutions. The NEP was an economic success. Industrial and agricultural output regained the 1913 levels by 1927 or so, and private as well as public sectors prospered with rapid postwar recovery. These years also witnessed the most creative period in the history of Soviet arts. Prose, poetry, music, drama, film, and other artistic endeavors blossomed in the revolutionary atmosphere. Economic science also developed rapidly, as Soviet economists sought to establish a functioning Marxist economic science and system.

Despite its apparent success as a recovery measure, the NEP troubled most Bolsheviks. Marx taught that human consciousness is the consciousness of the material conditions of life. It follows that those who devote themselves to producing for and selling in capitalist markets will have their political consciousness shaped by these capitalist relations of production and will, therefore, come to oppose the socialist goals of the Bolshevik regime. The NEP presented, therefore, a definite political risk merely by tolerating the persistence of capitalist relations of production. Bolsheviks were faced also with an ethical problem, for the preservation of capitalist institutions meant the preservation of exploitative relations between private enterprises and their employees. The NEP presented a potential economic problem, too, for the mixed economy of the 1920s allowed direct competition between the private and public sectors of the economy.

The unease of good Bolsheviks about the institutions of the NEP was compounded by the reinstatement of pecuniary institutions and the market. Marx had declined to describe the institutions of the coming socialist society because he regarded such speculations utopian and unscientific, but many of his followers assumed that socialist society would, at a minimum, exclude institutions such as the market which he had scathingly attacked. Thus many Bolsheviks were unhappy to see markets reinstated, the monetary system stabilized, and the systems of money wages and prices reestablished under the NEP.

Lenin went a step further and insisted upon full accounting and budgetary measures on the part of all Soviet enterprises, and the system known today as *khozraschët* was introduced in 1922. Although Lenin probably did not recognize the historical generality of these aspects of the NEP, it had become clear to him that it would be impossible to conduct the transition to socialism without the help of pecuniary institutions. Much has changed since 1921-22 when the NEP was being installed, but the role and significance of money, prices, wages, and other pecuniary institutions in the Soviet socialist economy have not diminished to this day. Indeed quite the contrary is the case.

To a large extent the concerns of the Bolsheviks about the NEP were worries about the peasantry. Marx has often been quoted for his description of the idiocy of rural life, and with considerable justice W. W. Rostow once called him a city boy. The Bolsheviks were city boys too and knew little about either the peasantry or about farming. What they did know about the Russian peasant was not encouraging, given their situation. It was well known that the Russian peasantry was given periodically to mass rebellion. Members of the Bolshevik party would not be likely to have forgotten that the peasantry, prior to the revolution, had joined or supported the Socialist Revolutionary party, and had therefore espoused a form of agrarian socialism, when it had shown any political preference at all. Certainly few peasants had demonstrated an interest in Bolshevism. And it was clear to all that the country was overwhelmingly peasant in composition. Finally the peasantry had demonstrated its uncompromising desire for land and for private cultivation during the revolution. In large part the failure of the provisional government to implement land redistribution and rural reform following the first revolution of 1917 had alienated the peasants and provided the Bolsheviks with the opportunity to seize political control. Thus Bolsheviks tended to be mistrustful of the peasantry as a political force, and they were eager to change the system of land tenure and cultivation that had emerged from the revolution into one of large-scale, cooperative, factorylike enterprises.

The Scissors Crisis

The first crisis of the NEP, which arose in 1923, is known as the scissors crisis. The crisis is less important in and of itself than for the way that it was interpreted and the role this interpretation played subsequently in Bolshevik thinking. Marxist economists of the period were interested in measuring changes in purchasing power of the income of different classes of society. According to their measure, the purchasing power of the income of agricultural producers (the peasantry) was falling relatively to income earned in industrial-urban occupations. The basic fact was that prices of industrial products were rising more rapidly than prices of agricultural products. The impact on purchasing power was measured by dividing an index of agricultural prices by an index of prices of both agricultural and nonagricultural commodities. What it revealed was a sharp decline in the purchasing power of agricultural commodities relative to the purchasing power of industrial commodities. If so, it follows that farmers were getting worse off relatively. Soviet economists also calculated the reciprocal of this index—that is, the ratio of an index of industrial prices to an index of industrial plus agricultural prices, and plotted both curves on a graph, the tracings of which look like an open pair of scissors. Leon Trotsky is credited with the term *scissors*.

The opening of the blades of the scissors measured, therefore, the impact of the adverse change in the terms of trade for the agricultural sector. It was interpreted to have resulted from two factors: the more rapid recovery of agricultural production from the ravages of war and revolution, and monopolistic policies being followed by state-owned industries. Both factors would have tended to reduce the availability of industrial products relative to agricultural, with the consequence being increasingly adverse relative prices for the more abundant agricultural commodities. Many analysts anticipated that the supply of agricultural products would decrease in response, because they expected peasants to withdraw into self-sufficiency as the prices for urban-industrial products increased. Thus the Bolsheviks took steps to close the scissors, and they succeeded by the end of 1924. It has sometimes been claimed that the peasantry did in fact withdraw from the market during the scissors crisis, but there is no evidence to support this claim. What is important is the fact that the Bolsheviks *believed* that the peasantry would reduce sales of agricultural products, and they took action in anticipation to ward off such an outcome. Monopolistic practices were terminated, and the flow of industrial products to rural markets was augmented to justify lower relative prices.

The experience with the scissors crisis left a permanent scar, and that experience figured in an important debate on economic development that occurred in the mid-1920s. Alexander Erlich, one of the first western students of the period, called this the Great Industrialization Debate; and he identified Nikolai Bukharin and Evgenii Preobrazhensky as the principals. We know today that this was merely one of a number of ongoing controversies over the nature of and requirements for economic growth of the Soviet Marxist economy, but it may very well have been the most interesting of them all because of the political prominence and the theoretical sophistication of the two principal participants.

The Industrialization Debate

Bukharin and Preobrazhensky were among those who were prematurely enthusiastic about the destruction of pecuniary institutions during the period of War Communism. This view was advanced in their popular book *The ABCs of Communism (Azbuka kommunizma)*. With the introduction of the NEP, Preobrazhensky attempted to work out an appropriate theoretical basis in his *The New*

Economics (Novaia Ekonomika); but in so doing he ran afoul of his previous collaborator, Bukharin. The controversy that ensued attracted considerable attention at the time because of the theoretical stature of the principals and because Bukharin was the darling of the party and a cynosure of Soviet political life and culture in the twenties.

The crucial issue in the controversy turned on an empirical question about peasant economic behavior: How would the peasantry respond to an adverse change in its terms of trade with the state and the state-dominated industrial sector? The frame of the debate was formed, however, by questions about the application of Marxism in the new socialist state, and this was Preobrazhensky's point of departure. What, he asked himself, ought to be the nature of the relationship between the public and private sectors of the mixed economy of the NEP; and what ought the role of the socialist state be in fostering the transition to communism? The first proposition Preobrazhensky put forward was obvious. The socialized sector of the economy had to grow more rapidly than the private sector, for otherwise the economy would backslide into counterrevolution. A principal task for the state was, then, to ensure the more rapid growth of the public sector.

As the theoretical basis for specification of the role of the state, Preobrazhensky turned to one of the historical chapters in *Capital*, in which Marx had discussed original capitalist accumulation in connection with establishing capitalist relations of production in the transition from feudalism to capitalism. The essence of Marx's presentation is to parody the capitalist apologetics which attributed the rise of capitalism to foresight and self-sacrifice of enterprising types of people. He shows that, on the contrary, the process by which capitalism established itself involved divorcing the yeoman farmer from the land and means of production and thereby forcing him into the market in which he was obliged to sell his labor to the capitalist for mere subsistence wages. The wage contract provided the capitalist with the necessary instrument to extract surplus value in the form of unpaid wages. Thus original capitalist accumulation was defined by Marx as the establishment of the institutions or, in his terminology, the relations of production necessary and sufficient for the existence of capitalism as a mode of production.

Preobrazhensky developed a parallel concept which he called original (or primitive) socialist accumulation that was designed to provide a theoretical basis for establishing the conditions necessary and sufficient to ensure the victory of socialist institutions, or socialist relations of production, in the developing Soviet socialist economy. The concept would appear to be an appropriate extension of Marxist thought, given the circumstances of the Bolsheviks and the character of the NEP. Preobrazhensky applied it so that it involved an interception by the socialist state of surplus value created in the private sector that would otherwise go to the capitalist and finance growth of the capitalist sector. It also called for self-exploitation of the workers in the industrial sector. These two sources of accumulation would be adequate to ensure a more rapid development of the socialist sector, and they would minimize the differential impact of exploitation in the capitalist sector, thereby reducing the conflict of the NEP with the ethical standards of Marxists.

The means Preobrazhensky suggested to capture surplus value created in the private sector involved "nonequivalent exchange," which can be understood as involving disadvantageous terms of trade between the state-industrial sector and the private producer. Given the existence of pecuniary institutions under the NEP, this method was appropriate; and it accords with modern fiscal theory as well because no administrative structure is required to collect the "tax" implied by disadvantageous exchange rates for private producers.

Although Preobrazhensky's approach appears to be consistent with Marx and well suited to the situation in which the Bolsheviks found themselves in the mid-twenties, Bukharin objected strenuously to the proposed system. He argued, first, that the exploitation of the peasantry which primitive socialist accumulation implied was ethically unacceptable and, second, that the peasants would not in any case stand for it. The result would be alienation of the peasantry, withdrawal of peasant producers from the market, and the undermining of Soviet plans for development because of inadequate supplies of food and raw materials in cities and industrial regions.

No one could deny, of course, that the main target of Preobrazhensky's original socialist accumulation was the peasant petty producer and marketeer. Alec Nove may be correct in suggesting that Preobrazhensky would have had better luck in selling his conception had he avoided such loaded words as *exploitation, nonequivalent exchange,* and other terms interpreted as opprobrious because Marx had applied them to the capitalist during the phase of original capitalist accumulation. But there seems to be little doubt that the memory of the scissors crisis helped to undermine Preobrazhensky's argument too, and Preobrazhensky himself seems to have accepted the possible withdrawal of the peasantry from the market as a very likely outcome. His strongest counterargument was that the alternative to his conception was one that "tied Soviet development to a peasant nag" — that is, which determined the rate of development and the rate of socialization of the economy in accordance with the preferences of the peasantry, which was clearly also an unacceptable outcome because it implied too slow a rate of industrialization.

Since neither Bukharin nor Preobrazhensky was able to overcome the objections of the other, Alexander Erlich has described the outcome of the debate as a dilemma, one that Stalin was able to resolve by thinking the unthinkable: expropriating and thereby divorcing the peasant producer of agricultural products from control over the production and marketing of his products. Where Preobrazhensky had worked out a model and drawn policy recommendations from an analysis of the model, Stalin called for a frontal assault on the peasantry as a class and a radical change in the material conditions of their existence. Life and work on collective farms would presumably alter the peasant's consciousness and turn him into suitable material for building socialism.

The evidence we have today does not support Erlich's hypothesis. In all probability Bukharin was wrong in thinking that the peasantry would withdraw from the market if the terms of trade were turned against agricultural products. Evidence on the Russian peasantry that was collected prior to the revolution and analyzed in the mid-twenties by A. V. Chayanov suggests that peasant farms usually react to adverse changes in their terms of trade by increasing both production and marketings. Preobrazhensky was therefore on firm ground in suggesting taxation of the peasantry to finance development. But Preobrazhensky was apparently wrong in the basic formulation of his argument also. As a Marxist Preobrazhensky was naturally inclined to assume that surplus value, or the potential source of accumulation, was a direct function of population size. Thus the rural population was expected to yield quantitatively the largest amount of surplus value because it comprised over 80 percent of the total workforce. As we shall see when we come to consider collectivization in the 1930s, this led to a mistaken conclusion about the necessity to force a flow of resources out of the agricultural into the nonagricultural sector.

The debate, among other factors, helped to condition Bolshevik thinking about the problems posed by development and the obstacle represented by the peasantry. Thus, when a grain crisis began to develop in 1928, many were ready with an interpretation that placed blame upon the peasantry and the agricultural sector. Grain marketings dried up in 1928, despite reports of a good harvest. Many were led to conclude that the peasants were holding their grain off the market, an action which, if successfully carried out, would undermine the first five-year plan. Peasant agriculture was regarded as hopelessly backward by comparison to large-scale factory farms in any case. Thus a hostile Bolshevik response to the decline in marketings was almost inevitable.

Erlich's presentation of the industrialization debate as a dilemma offers a considerable degree of rationality for the decision to collectivize, and Alec Nove sees Stalin's solution as necessary, given the very limited understanding the Bolsheviks had of the problem. Once again the evidence that has accumulated since Erlich published his interpretation supports neither an economic rationale for Stalin's decision nor an assumption that a decision to collectivize was in fact taken until long after the process was underway. The emergency measures that Stalin introduced in response to the grain crisis were extremely harsh and harked back to the pitiless requisitions of War Communism during the civil war. Gangs of ruffians and angry townspeople invaded the countryside in search of hidden stores of grain, taking whatever they found, including seed grain. The emergency measures apparently escalated into collectivization, possibly without anyone actually deciding to collectivize agriculture. And the struggle turned into a preemptive war on the peasantry, leaving a much depleted but collectivized agriculture.

There is good reason to think that the basic problem in 1928 resulted from Soviet efforts to keep the price of bread low in urban areas. As the price of bread, and thus of grain, was held down artificially, peasants were induced to feed grain to their animals since prices of animal husbandry products were not controlled. Moreover livestock herds had not regained prewar prerevolutionary levels even by 1928 and meat was dear. Therefore, feeding grain to livestock was completely rational behavior by the peasantry. As a Soviet economist, Iu. Luria, pointed out at the time, the peasantry had always regarded homebrewed alcohol and livestock as their "banks." When grain prices were low, they invested in their banks instead of selling grain. This appears to have been the case in 1928. The solution to the grain crisis of 1928 would have been, then, to change relative prices of grain, livestock, and alcohol so as to favor grain. Certainly the peasants at that time did not have the facilities to store grain except for relatively short periods, and there was no way to store significant quantities for longer periods because they did not have space. It now appears, therefore, that the Bolshevik leadership (and Erlich subsequently) mistook a response to changing *relative prices* of agricultural products for the response they (wrongly) expected from the peasants in reaction to adversely changing *general terms of trade* with nonagricultural sectors.

There were economists in Russia in the 1920s who knew a great deal about peasant agriculture, but few of them were consulted about the problem. The analyses presented by champions of the peasantry, like Chayanov, were not appreciated. The result was perhaps the greatest mistake the Politburo ever made, aside from the expectation that the Germans would not attack in 1941; and the legacy of its mistake is obvious today. The destruction of the NEP had other consequences than agricultural, but the effects were greatest for this large sector of the economy. The termination of open experimentation with styles of life, literature, economic methods, film, and other aspects of culture followed in the van of the violence of collectivization and the fever of rapid industrialization. Soviet society was caught up in the serious business of purposive development, and an excess of determination, exaggeration of capabilities, and unwillingness to acknowledge human limitations swept all along a path that increasingly departed from reality and humanitarianism.

The Origins of the Soviet Planning System

Once the civil war had been brought to a successful close, efforts began at once to develop a system for planning the economy. Marx is unambiguous in his writings about the importance of conscious control and direction of economic activity under socialism, for he sees the principal advantage of socialism in avoidance of the periodic crises and depressions of capitalist society. In keeping with his own strictures against utopian speculation, however, Marx does not spell out the way in which economic activity would be directed and coordinated under socialism. The Bolsheviks and their (temporary) allies were obliged to work out a system of planning by trial and error. Marx's writings and Marxist thought at that time nonetheless importantly influenced the system of planning that eventuated, as did the peculiar institutions of the NEP, the relative backwardness of the Soviet economy, and the character and traditions of prerevolutionary Russian economic science.

Soviet planning inherited from Marxist thought a primary concern with distributive justice, the notion of a model that focused on economic growth, and a strong distaste for pecuniary and financial institutions. Conception of an optimal economic plan, of wages and prices as "signals," of profitability as a measure of and incentive to efficiency at the enterprise level, and of markets as allocative mechanisms were not part of Marxist or socialist thought at that time. Insofar as questions of allocation were addressed, they were confined to the division of national income between accumulation (investment) and consumption and reflected a distinct preference for equality in wages and earnings.

The development of central planning in the context of the NEP no doubt heightened planners' mistrust of markets, of prices, and of decentralized decision making. These were identified with the private sector and were destined to be liquidated along with it when the time was ripe. The relative backwardness of the economy of the 1920s caused economists of the period to concern themselves with questions of growth, particularly with the rate of accumulation. The controversy between the superindustrializers — Preobrazhensky, Trotsky, and others—and those who urged caution—Bukharin and his allies—is a case in point. The controversy focused upon the feasibility of achieving a high rate of accumulation under the institutional arrangements of the NEP. That is, it turned on the question of whether or not the peasantry could be forced to save by means of taxation, by adverse changes in the terms of trade, or by other indirect ways. Naked use of force would, of course, have required dismantling the NEP. Once it became clear that, for the foreseeable future, revolution was not to be expected in the leading capitalist countries, accumulation, growth, and the feasible rate of voluntary domestic saving became even more critical issues.

The development of central planning in the Soviet Union was also shaped by the history of Russian economic science. From a theoretical standpoint, prerevolutionary economic thought was derivative: it reflected the main schools of contemporary thought in the West.

Marxism, the German historical school, Ricardian classical economics, and even the new and modish neoclassical thought of Marshall were all represented among Russian economists prior to World War I. The strongest and most original aspect of Russian economic science was, however, its heavy emphasis upon the collection and analysis of statistical data. The prewar economy had been richly documented and analyzed, including careful detailed studies of peasant households and production. This tradition carried over into economic practice in the 1920s. Data were assembled by young economists on every conceivable question. It is not surprising to learn, therefore, that the first serious effort to create an actual plan document was an assemblage of statistical data called the "control figures." The idea at this early stage was not to produce a plan but to assemble and organize the data along lines required by a plan. The notion of a central plan as a document in which all important categories of economic activity would be prefigured stems directly from the development of control figures in the early 1920s. This became a new sort of social accounting system, and planning has to this day been conducted within the framework of a logically organized set of balancing accounts for enterprises, for branches, and for each higher level.

In consequence of these various influences, the fundamental Soviet concept of economic planning was hammered out in the 1920s. A plan would be a specific document, based upon actual economic data of the most recent period and specifying as comprehensively as possible planned targets for each category of data. The plan evolved as a statement of material sources and uses of resources, specified for each administrative level down to the enterprise. It provided no formal discretion at these lower levels, over and above the role played by lower echelons at the plan formulation stage. Finally the principal question of allocation addressed by the plan was conceived as an issue in political feasibility: maximization of the rate of investment (and of saving) subject to a political constraint (what the peasant producer and consumer would bear). The plan itself contained no explicit reference to optimization. Thus even today Soviet planners and economists call for simultaneous "maximization of output" and "minimization of costs," without realizing that these are conflicting instructions and are not tantamount to optimization, when costs are minimized for a given level and composition of output (or, alternatively, when output is maximized for a given quantity and composition of inputs).

The most arresting theoretical question that arose during the 1920s concerning the nature of economic planning was essentially philosophical in character, and the outcome of the polemic had an important and enduring effect upon the nature of Soviet economic planning. The issue went directly to the heart of the very possibility of economic planning. Was the central planning agency constrained by economic laws or other fixed economic regularities in its activities, or could the planners operate to shape the future according to their own preferences? Two main schools of thought developed. The proponents of one, that came to be known as the geneticists, argued that it was necessary to base plans on careful study of the economic laws and regularities that necessarily constrained any outcome that might be planned. This view highlighted the overriding importance of historical forces. The other school, the teleologists, argued that planners should and could set their objectives independently of such constraints. They stressed, therefore, the importance of goals in determining outcomes. The argument became quite heated, and both sides developed extreme positions that carry no weight today. The degree of freedom allowed planners by extremist geneticist arguments was miniscule, and it appered that economic planning would involve little more than predicting the data required by the cells of the control-figure document. Historical carryover variables determined nearly everything. The degree of power that the teleologists insisted upon was almost total. Historical constraints were almost dismissed. One silly result, for example, concerned the appropriate fraction of total output that agricultural production should occupy. The geneticists claimed that the share was fixed and immutable. The teleologists took exactly the opposite view.

As a formal philosophical question, the issue of the degree to which conscious planning can affect the future — that is, change the outcome (as teleologists claimed) — is not readily resolvable. Empirically the question must always contain untestable counterfactual elements. The question parallels an historical question that was raised above. How rapidly would the Russian economy have developed in the absence of the Bolsheviks and of their interpretation of Marxism? In the broadest sense it can be argued that the geneticists' position — that setting targets cannot affect outcome — is either wrong or irrelevant. If it is wrong, the teleologists are correct. If the position is true, however, the teleologists could act no differently, *and could do no harm*, by assuming that they are able to shape the future. Like the infant Napolean in Tolstoy's characterization, who imagines that he makes his baby carriage move by tugging on a tassel, planners could at least gain satisfaction from the illusion of power.

The teleologists carried their side of the argument to absurdity also. It is obvious, for example, that the force of gravity affects the activities of men on the surface of the earth and beyond. Gravity does not, of course, prevent men from flying airplanes or building elevators, but it is also true that not just anything will fly. Planners can obviously defy the laws of supply and demand in a similar sense, but not every attempt to do so will result in a desirable outcome. In the end the teleologists were loath to admit any such constraint upon their activities in a socialist economy, and this misconception contributed an element to the idea of economic planning that evolved in the 1920s and persists to this day in the form of overcommitment planning, and that wreaked considerable havoc as "voluntarism" in Stalin's time.

It is easy to see that, at the most fundamental level, the issue of planning versus forecasting may be resolved into the age-old question of free will versus determinism; and it is not surprising, given the energy, enthusiasm, and optimism of the Bolsheviks, that the teleologists won the argument in the end. Given the issues involved, the teleologists had the better case, too. And their victory had an important positive consequence for Soviet planning—the willingness of planners to push beyond conventional boundaries and definitions of production possibilities. As Lord Keynes wrote in an analogous context, human society has probably lost more from the timidity of investors and their underestimates of possible returns than from excessive optimism and bold adventurism. Yet the refusal of teleologists to recognize technical or other nonpolitical constraints created conditions in which no one could call for a sense of proportion in setting targets, a situation in which common sense became suspect. Accordingly the targets of the first five-year plan, which were initially specified in "maximalist" and "minimalist" variants, were escalated by means of bureaucratic competition to levels that eventually had no relation to reality or to one another. Questions of feasibility, consistency, and efficiency were all jettisoned in a wild scramble to set the most outrageous targets for oneself and one's subordinates. Such competition continues to undermine realistic planning to this day.

Here it is important to note merely that the victory in the controversy went to the most extreme of the teleologists, thereby removing the question of economic feasibility from the realm of economics and making it instead a test of political loyalty and therefore a criterion for political advancement.

The first five-year plan, adopted in 1927, represented a major accomplishment of Soviet economic science despite these criticisms. It is fair to say that the Soviet experiment with economic planning opened a new door in economic practice; and perhaps, in the long run, it did so in economic theory as well. Being the first to try economic planning, however, the Soviets have had to pay a penalty for taking the lead. (I paraphrase Thorstein Veblen's remark from another context.) The penalty of taking the lead has been paid for attempting an excessively comprehensive and detailed plan, for overcentralizing economic decision-making generally, for disregarding questions of efficiency, for ignoring the functional usefulness of pecuniary institutions, and for establishing a habit of setting overly ambitious targets at all levels and thereby politicizing formulation as well as fulfillment of plan indicators.

Soviet planning is, however, far from a failure. After planning was introduced, the Soviet economy enabled victory over Germany in the most devastating war of modern times. Moreover the Soviet economy is today the second largest in the world, and it sustains what may now be the largest military establishment. The situation is vastly different from that of 1917, when the Bolsheviks accepted Lenin's policy of defeatism and withdrew from World War I at great territorial cost.

Mass Collectivization and Rapid Industrialization

Most Western specialists on Soviet history regard the 1930s as the crucible in which the economic and political institutions that are generally regarded as typical of the contemporary Soviet political and economic system were formed. The events of the early 1930s have been described as the second Bolshevik revolution, with Stalin's role analogous to Lenin's in the first. Four developments of the 1930s are critical for an understanding of the importance of these years. The first was the implementation of planning and successful rapid in-dustrialization. Second was the abolition of the NEP through mass collectivization of private and peasant enterprise. The third was the rise of the cult of Stalin, considered as a dual process of concentrating political power within the Communist party and, within the party, in the hands of Stalin and his close associates. The fourth and culminating development constituted a reign of terror and the liquidation of all actual and potential resistance to the cult of Stalin. These four developments define the Stalinist system.

Both the success of industrialization and the violence of collectivization contributed essential ingredients to formation of the cult of Stalin, and both economic processes presupposed a conception of economic activity and planning that was congenial to Stalin and his close allies. The establishment of the cult of Stalin made possible the destruction of his political enemies and potential competitors, and the sclerosis of the soul that acceptance of the brutality of collectivization brought about among members of the Bolshevik party also helped to make the purges and Stalin's reign of terror possible. In the process critical evaluation of any policy that had been implemented became impossible, and this was (and remains) particularly true for mass collectivization of Soviet agriculture.

The rate of growth of industrial production that was in fact achieved in the Soviet Union in the 1930s remains a matter of intense dispute, despite repeated attempts to resolve it by recourse to independent remeasurement. Soviet claims are extremely high, reaching almost 20 percent per annum. Western recalculations invariably have lowered this figure, but the differences among western estimates are substantial. One very large-scale reexamination of the issue, by Warren Nutter for the National Bureau of Economic Research, asserted that the rate of growth achieved by the USSR in the 1930s was not exceptional when compared to spurts of growth that had occurred in developing countries either in the nineteenth or in the early twentieth centuries. Although this more modest evaluation was fiercely disputed when first published, recent reevaluations suggest that this is a view that will prevail in the long run. In fact a recent reexamination of the issue of economic growth by Steven Rosefielde in the *Slavic Review* (December 1980) suggests that Solzhenitsyn's much lower estimate of true growth, which presumes the elimination of waste, exaggeration, and padding of reports, may inspire further downward revision.

Even if Soviet growth is shown, however, to have been no more spectacular than the growth rates achieved by countries such as

England, Japan, or the United States, which developed earlier under very different economic systems and conditions, it remains an example of successful growth, which is truly rare enough to be worthy of careful study. Study shows, in fact, that Soviet rapid growth was peculiar in several respects, the most important of which was the extreme differential rates of growth (and development) of the industrial and the agricultural sectors. Soviet industrial-urban growth was substantial by any measure, but agriculture stagnated and very nearly failed.

Throughout history, agricultural systems have rarely changed radically. Experimentation is hazardous, and the margin for error is usually not very great. Mass collectivization of agriculture in the Soviet Union in the 1930s is the most dramatic experiment with reorganization of agricultural tenure and production in modern times, and it proves the rule, for the experiment clearly failed. That Soviet students of the period have claimed this obvious failure as a success is ironic, and for years western students followed their lead despite evidence to the contrary.

Collectivization of agriculture appears in retrospect to have been the culmination of increasingly severe emergency measures in the face of rising resistance by peasants to the harsh and inequitable methods applied. Although many scholars have referred to a decision to collectivize agriculture in the Soviet Union, there is little evidence that any such decision was taken until the process was well under way, and certainly there is no evidence to show a weighing of pros and cons. The internal logic of the process was provided by Bolshevik preferences, and by the interpretation of the grain crisis as sabotage by the peasantry of the industrialization drive. It was also viewed as a sign that the historical limit on small-scale, private agriculture enterprise had been reached.

Stalin was not an economist by any stretch of the imagination. In any case it is not clear that any economist of the period understood the grain crisis as an economic phenomenon — as a problem resulting from relatively low prices paid to peasants for grain for urban consumption (and for export) and the higher prices available for animal-husbandry products. In any event to solve the grain crisis Stalin used the means that he understood best and that he personally controlled—the party bureaucracy. Similarly it is not surprising that the ultimate solution involved bureaucratization of all economic relations with the countryside. The simple alternative, raising grain prices relative to prices of animal products, was in all likelihood never considered.

Until quite recently Soviet claims for the success of collectivization were generally accepted by western students of Soviet history. The basis of the claim is the increase in both grain marketings and in the share of the harvest garnered by state procurement agencies afterwards, but nothing could be more misleading than these grain statistics taken by themselves. Overall, in both the long and short run, mass collectivization proved to be an economic mistake; and the cost that it imposed on all parties exceeds the gain of any one or of all taken together, including the state.

The increase in grain procured by the state was a by-product of a major and unexpected failure of collectivization. The peasants slaughtered and sold or ate their livestock rather than have their animals converted into cooperative property. This action was the main form that peasant resistance to collectivization assumed. Only compromise by the central government, in the form of a promise to allow collective farm members in good standing to keep a small number of animals and to hold a small plot of land as a kitchen garden, put an end to the destruction. Compromise came too late, however, for the peasants had already destroyed one-third of the capital stock of the agricultural sector. The loss was not made good in available tractive power or in livestock numbers until long after World War II. Since peasant animals had been fed grains, the increase in state grain collections reflected merely the reduction in feed requirements. This was not a desirable outcome.

The loss of tractive power crippled production, and the loss of animal-husbandry products set Soviet output composition back several decades. Thus, although the state paid very low prices for most of the grain it collected from collective farms (*kolkhozes*), this is not the same as collecting grain on the cheap. *A principal result of collectivization was to raise the real resource cost of agricultural products.* The analytic level of discussions defending the logic of collectivization may be seen in the popularity of the Russian proverb: You can't make an omelette without cracking eggs. An equally ancient and more relevant proverb points out, however, that you can't expect to get an omelette and a chicken from the same egg.

Compromise with the peasantry concerning private plots and private husbandry allowed the persistence of very small-scale private production, and it implied retention of private marketing of these products on a free market. This market is called the collective farm market, the CFM, (or, more simply, the *rynok* [the market]), and it plays an important role in the supply of food products to this day. Collectivization was incomplete, therefore, and the coexistence of small-scale private agriculture and of very large-scale socialized agriculture has proved a permanent feature of the Soviet economy. Ironically, at the time of the emancipation of the serfs when the modernization drive under the Tsarist regime began, many peasants received "hungry plots," by which contemporaries referred to plots of land too small to live on but too big to refuse. Hungry plots helped to preserve mutual dependencies between landlords and serfs which existed before emancipation. The private plot of Soviet agriculture re-created the hungry plot and similar mutual dependency between collective and collective farmer.

The rural sector was depecuniarized by collectivization as well. Pay for work on the collective was calculated in an artificial unit known as the workday (*trudoden'*). Each job on the collective was given a rating in terms of workdays. The lowest skilled job, such as cleaning barns, was rated as one workday per working day. Other jobs, such as driving a tractor, were rated higher, perhaps as high as five workdays per working day. Total compensation was determined as a residual claim on the income of the collective farm, and each individual's share was proportional to the number of workdays that he or she had accumulated during the year. At the end of the year each worker's workdays were totaled; all were then added together and divided into the total of money and products the farm had left over after meeting all of its commitments and allotting seed for the next year. Earnings from the collective until well into the 1950s were primarily in kind, which was particularly important as a source of feed for private animals. Total compensation was rarely sufficient, however, to maintain an individual and his family for the year.

Determination of peasant earnings as a residual claim on the income of the kolkhoz provided a means by which year-to-year fluctuations in farm output could be shifted to its members, for the state took its fixed share first. This system was also useful in counteracting the adverse impact of peasant resistance upon the output of agricultural products. The decline in total production of agricultural products during collectivization forced the peasantry to continue private agriculture on their small plots in order to survive. The private collective farm market provided the main avenue by which kolkhozniks could earn cash with which to finance purchases of processed and industrial products. Consequently, although the physical volume of trade on the CFM was never large, it was critical for both rural sellers and urban purchasers; and persistent shortages of food products caused prices to skyrocket in the early 1930s and again during and after World War II.

The Structure of Collectivized Agriculture

By the end of the 1930s the structure of Stalinist agriculture was in place, and it remained essentially the same until 1958. The *sovkhoz*, or state farm, which was organized along the same lines as the state enterprise, with paid employees and state-financed investment outlays, worked only a trivial proportion of all agricultural land in the Soviet Union until the 1950s. Thus the system of agriculture that emerged from collectivization consisted of the *kolkhoz*, the state agricultural procurement system, and the private plot of the kolkhoznik. All capital of the kolkhoz was contributed to an indivisible fund, and it is called thus to this day because no member may claim any portion of it should he elect to withdraw from the collective—despite the fact that all members of the kolkhoz collectively "own" the capital stock. Unlike the state farm the kolkhoz has always been obliged to finance all investment in the farm out of earnings or through long-term, interest-bearing loans from the state bank (*Gosbank*, or, prior to 1959, *Sel'khozbank*). The level of investment is determined as a fixed share of income and is not actually a result of deliberations by members, although each farm is legally empowered to elect its own leadership (the kolkhoz chairman) and to make its own decisions.

As I have indicated, one deleterious consequence of the way collectivization took place was the destruction of one-third of the capital stock of agriculture. As a result most kolkhozes began existence with a serious capital shortage. They had too little draft power to plow and cultivate the land, and they were seriously short of means of transportation as well. The state consequently was obliged to purchase tractors and trucks and to put them at the disposal of collective farms. A system of stations, called machine tractor stations (MTS), was developed for this purpose. Each was staffed with personnel who operated the equipment for the kolkhozes it served for an in-kind rental charge. Each station served several kolkhozes, and each was responsible for maintaining the equipment. The development of the MTS system required much more agricultural equipment than had been called for in the first five-year plan, and acquisition of tractors involved spending precious foreign exchange.

Government procurement of agricultural products involved four principal channels once the entire system was in place. The MTS system, which persisted until 1958, was a creature of the state budget; and the in-kind payments it received from kolkhozes represented an important procurement channel. Norms based on size and fertility of available land were established by government procurement agencies for each farm, and all were obliged to deliver fixed quantities of various products at very low prices. These deliveries were called obligatory deliveries. Once these targets and MTS rental payments had been met, collective farms were allowed to sell the remainder of their crops either to the government for prices considerably higher than for obligatory deliveries (this was called the *zakupka*), or to sell their surplus on the CFM at whatever price they could command. Most farms were located too far away from major cities, of course, to make the CFM a viable alternative. Finally, certain crops could be sold directly to state enterprises — such as those producing sugar beets or flax, for example — for prices negotiated in advance. This channel was called *kontraktatsiia*.

The government's sources of agricultural products included, therefore, these four channels, plus an in-kind tax on the products of private agriculture. The bulk of procurements was in kind, and this reflected the general depecuniarization of agriculture that was effected by collectivization. The average price received by collective farms for their products was below cost of production, a fact which led many superficial observers to conclude that the government was acquiring agricultural products on the cheap, and from which it seemed to follow that collectivization had been an economic success. That the standard of living of the peasantry fell as a result of the establishment of the collective farm and the predatory state procurement system persuaded these observers that industrialization was made possible by the "pumping of resources out of agriculture."

There is no question but that, taken together, the collective farm system and the state procurement system formed an effective device for forcing output out of the agricultural sector. The entire system was not in place, however, until well into the 1930s, and it was very costly to establish. In addition it was a system that depended more upon disincentives than upon incentives, and it was never able to stimulate productivity, efficiency, or even reliability in agricultural production. The notion that collectivization was initiated in order to create this particular system, which we shall henceforward call Stalinist agriculture, is without foundation. It is far more accurate to see the system that evolved by the end of the first five-year plan as one designed *to minimize the cost of collectivization,* to staunch the arterial loss, than to see it as the end which shaped a decision to collectivize. The evidence that we have on the contribution of agriculture to Soviet rapid industrialization shows that resources flowed on a net basis *from nonagricultural sectors to the agricultural sector* and not vice versa, as so many have assumed was the case during the first five-year plan.

Collectivization cost more to establish than it yielded. The loss of capital stock and the consequent sharp decline in total agricultural production was not made good until the end of the 1930s. State investment in the MTS system and in the development of state farms required a large flow of capital into the agricultural sector, but the state received no net return for it because even this large, unanticipated flow of capital failed to replace what had been destroyed in peasant anger. The transport of millions of peasant farmers (*kulaks*) to Siberia was also damaging, because the best farmers were the most likely to be singled out. Finally the compromise that allowed the persistence of private farming on tiny hungry plots and that permitted private sales of products on the CFM left open a channel through which the peasants could shift a substantial proportion of the cost of collectivization to the urban population. The rise in prices on this market, and the flow of goods through it, even though of small physical volume, ensured that the terms of trade would turn *in favor* of the agricultural sector, rather than the other way around as Preobrazhensky had proposed and Stalin claimed to have effected. The CFM tail wagged the dog during the 1930s.

In economics, unlike a poker game, *everyone can lose* from a mistake. Collectivization was an economic policy mistake in the short run, and the evidence we have on the long run suggests the same. Mass collectivization produced losses without anyone, including the state, deriving a benefit. The idea that all of the suffering, the famine, the brutality, and the grief that collectivization occasioned went for naught is more than many students can understand, but the evidence suggests clearly that this was the case. There are those who claim that collectivization, at the least, ensured an adequate flow of labor into urban areas for industrialization, but this is mere grasping at straws. As measured by the Bolshevik government, there was considerable unemployment in 1928 in the major cities of the Soviet Union. Moreover, nowhere in the literature of the period does any evidence of concern about labor shortages appear. In fact the experience of other under-developed countries which have succeeded in raising the rate of growth is that the flow of labor to the cities is ordinarily excessive and must be regulated. No one has even attempted to show why the Soviet experience would have been different without collectivization.

The system of collectivized agriculture remained essentially unchanged from the middle 1930s until the middle of the 1950s, and in many ways it represented the keystone of the Stalinist economy. It became an article of faith, and I believe that its importance for Stalin and others who might be called Stalinists today was threefold. First the system put an end to private enterprise in the form that Bolsheviks most distrusted — peasant private enterprise. Second the system of collectivized agriculture represented a large, essentially depecuniarized sector, and it appealed to those like Stalin who believed that the future of the Soviet system was one in which "commodity relations" and "commodity production," which western economists call markets and pecuniary institutions, ought to be eliminated. Third, by structure and operation the sector reflected the state's preferential treatment of the worker and its predilection for industrial production. As a result of collectivization the rural population was isolated from the developing sectors of the Soviet economy and its economy and population became even more backward relative to the urban-industrial than had been the case in 1928. The social, educational, and technical backwardness of both the people and the enterprises in the Soviet rural sector persists to this day and does not appear to be diminishing rapidly.

Where Did the Resources Come From?

If, as seems to be the case, collectivized agriculture absorbed more resources than it provided to the industrial sector, the old explanation of rapid industrialization will not do. Little research has been done on the subject to date; and partly, of course, the reason is that the old story was easy to understand, easy to explain to students and, therefore, persuasive. In addition to being wrong about the direction of the net flow of resources between agriculture and industry, the old argument was based on a confusion of two questions. One question concerns financing economic growth in the strict sense: "Where did the money come from?" The other involves the matter of where the *real* resources originated to support the growth that occurred in industrial production. The traditional view argues that the peasantry both financed growth *and* provided the real resources. Yet these two questions are separate and deal with completely different aspects of growth, and they must therefore be answered separately.

When economists seek to discover where the real resources were raised to support an expanding output, the question is based on a highly technical conception of economic activity. Final output of the economy is related to the inputs (land, labor, and capital) used in its production in an essentially technological sense. So much labor, so much coal and iron ore, and so much machinery are required to produce a ton of steel. If steel output increases 10 percent, the increase can be explained by an increase in the use of inputs and/or by an increase in the effectiveness with which these and other inputs are utilized in the production process. Increased productivity is a form of getting something for nothing—that is, better management or a new production technique can serve to "stretch" existing resources.

Soviet growth in the 1930s can be explained in substantial part by increased effectiveness in resource utilization generally. Many people who had been unemployed or underemployed previously, either voluntarily or otherwise, were able or obliged to go to work once the state decided to pursue an ambitious program of growth. Many machines and even whole factories that had been underused, or unused, were put into operation full time; and twenty-four-hour-shift work allowed a substantial once-and-for-all leap in weekly output. As a result of strong feelings and dedication many workers apparently decided to work harder as well. These changes alone would have been sufficient to raise total output of the industrial sector substantially.

A decline in real wages, partly because of the disaster that collectivization produced in the supply of food, caused many women, youths, and older members of the population to seek employment in order to maintain the family's annual income. Thus the primary explanation of rapid growth of industrial production in the USSR during the 1930s lies in the fact that men, women, and machines were put to work either for the first time or more effectively.

Another factor contributing to the Soviet growth in the 1930s was the concentration of resources on heavy industry and the construction of productive facilities. Consequently housing accommodations became increasingly scarce and dilapidated as construction materials and manpower were devoted to the production of industrial facilities. This sytem of priorities has guided Soviet output ever since—favoring industrial production over agricultural production, heavy industry over light industry, investment over consumption. The only major modifications of the system have been the very high priority for military needs during and since World War II and improved priority for consumers since the mid-1950s.

Two factors explain early Soviet rapid industrialization, therefore: an increase in the rate of utilization of existing resources and a redefinition of available resources as, for example, the change that has led practically every ablebodied woman in the Soviet Union to engage in full-time employment. There has also been a third important source, and this is borrowing (and, to a lesser extent, developing) new production techniques which afford more efficient production as well as new products. When we turn to the question of how this growth was financed in a pecuniary sense, we shift from a concern with where real resources came from to a question of equity: Who bore the cost of industrialization and who reaped the benefits?

The bulk of capital investment during the 1930s was financed through the state budget (*Gosbiudzhet*). The state developed three main sources of funds. The first, and the most important throughout the 1930s, was the turnover tax, which was levied primarily on sales of consumer goods. Food products, fresh and processed, provided the main source of turnover tax revenues. Because collective farms were paid low prices by state procurement agencies, sales of these same products in state retail stores generated turnover tax proceeds that represented a tax on consumers only in part. The remainder reflected a tax on agricultural producers. The turnover tax produced the largest share of total revenues of the state budget during the 1930s, and therefore it was the most important way in which investment expenditures were financed. It is not easy, however, to determine the relative incidence of the turnover tax on rural and urban populations. Moreover the CFM provided a valve which tended to equalize the effective burden between the two groups, for peasants were able to charge very high prices for their own products, and urban dwellers, as opposed to the enterprises for which they worked, had little to sell in return.

A second source of funds, one that increased steadily throughout the 1930s, was state-enterprise profits. The state collected most net revenue by a kind of profits tax on all state-owned enterprises. Since collective farms were excluded, and because state farms rarely earned positive profits, this tax was collected primarily from enterprises producing industrial consumer goods.

The third source of funds during the industrialization drive of the 1930s was government borrowing from the population. Bonds were sold by subscription at place of work, and pledges were collected by payroll deduction. Hence the urban population bore the brunt of government bond campaigns. Since these bonds were not redeemed at face value and since many failed to pay promised rates, bond purchases by the population represented merely another form of taxation in the end. Bond revenues constituted between 5 and 13 percent of all state budget-revenues during the 1930s.

Over-all the pattern of development finance in the Soviet Union during the industrialization drive was typical of developing countries, regardless of political and economic systems. The population was induced, or obliged, to work more, longer, and harder for a proportionally smaller reward. The state ensured that the real savings thus generated were used to finance investment, not devoted to consumption. The role of indirect taxation, in this case the turnover tax, increased sharply during the early part of the 1930s and then began to decline as a share of total government revenues late in the decade as direct taxes became more important.

Little can be said with any precision about the relative incidence of taxation for rural and urban populations—or among various income classes in Soviet society. A mechanism did exist which would have tended to equalize the burden of urban and rural tax rates, which was the opportunity that peasants had to sell their own products on the CFM at free market prices. Many peasants would not, of course, have found the CFM accessible because of remote geographical location, and these peasants may have borne the largest proportional burden of the cost of industrialization. Direct taxes were minor sources of funds and were not progressive.

In general the industrialization campaign was financed in the pecuniary sense by indirect taxation, direct taxes, and government borrowing, in that order of importance. The unusual feature about the financing of Soviet industrialization in the 1930s is that it relied little upon foreign capital or foreign trade. Development was self-financed in both senses of the term. Resources and funds came overwhelmingly from within, and, of course, the population taken as a whole paid the cost. Although agriculture did not provide a net flow of real resources for industrialization, members of that sector in all probability paid dearest for industrialization. This occurred because they suffered first and most severely from the mistake of collectivization. The unfortunate fact is that much of this suffering was to no avail economically. Had transformation of the countryside been peaceful and based upon the support of the peasantry, Soviet development could have proceeded either at the same pace with less suffering, or at a higher pace with the same cost.

SELECTED READINGS

Carr, E. H. *A History of Soviet Russia.* 10 vols. New York: Macmillan, 1950-78: *The Bolshevik Revolution* (1917-23), 3 vols., 1950-53; *The Interregnum* (1923-24), 1954; *Socialism in One Country* (1924-26), 3 vols., 1958-64; with R. W. Davies, *Foundations of a Planned Economy* (1926-29), 3 vols., 1969-78.

Cohen, Stephen F. *Bukharin and the Bolshevik Revolution: A Political Biography, 1888-1938.* New York: Alfred A. Knopf, 1973.

Dobb, Maurice. *Soviet Economic Development since 1917.* 6th ed. London: Routledge & Kegan Paul, 1966.

Erlich, Alexander. "Stalin's Views on Economic Development." In *Continuity and Change in Russian and Soviet Thought,* ed. Ernest J. Simmons. Cambridge, Mass.: Harvard University Press, 1955, pp. 81-99.

Goldsmith, Raymond. "The Economic Growth of Tsarist Russia 1860-1913." *Economic Development and Cultural Change* 9, no. 3 (April 1961), 441-75.

Lewin, Moshe. *Russian Peasants and Soviet Power: A Study of Collectivization,* Trans. Irene Nove with the assistance of John Biggart. Evanston: Northwestern University Press, 1968.

Millar, James R. "A Note on Primitive Accumulation in Marx and Preobrazhensky." *Soviet Studies* 30, no. 3 (July 1978), 384-93.

Millar, James R., and Bahry, Donna. "Financing Development and Tax Structure Change in the USSR." *Canadian Slavonic Papers* 21, no. 2 (June 1979), 166-74.

Millar, James R., and Nove, Alec. "Was Stalin Really Necessary? A Debate on Collectivization." *Problems of Communism* 25 (July-August 1976), 49-66.

Nove, Alec. *An Economic History of the U.S.S.R.* Harmondsworth: Penguin Books, 1969.

Nutter, G. Warren. *Growth of Industrial Production in the Soviet Union.* Princeton: Princeton University Press, 1962.

2

The Stalinist
Economic System on Trial

By the end of the 1930s the main institutions of the Soviet economy had been established and were working as an integrated whole. Industry had been fully nationalized and had assumed a stable organizational structure. All state economic enterprises were obliged to operate according to the principles of khozraschët. This meant that they had been required from 1922 on to allocate costs, to maintain a balance sheet detailing their assets and liabilities, and to determine their net-income positions at the end of each accounting period—that is, to determine the amount of net profit or loss for the period. Khozraschët came to include the preparation of budgets for future periods on capital and current accounts.

The role of labor unions in state enterprises had been hotly debated during the late 1920s, but with the initiation of the industrialization drive, labor unions and the principal leader of the movement, Tomskii, increasingly lost power and authority. Consequently by the end of the 1930s the principle of one-man management was firmly established, and participation of labor or its representatives in the management of Soviet enterprises has never again been raised seriously.

Agriculture was fully collectivized by the end of the 1930s, and private plots and socialized production had already become heavily interdependent. Peasants used their plots to supplement their own diets and to specialize in labor-intensive, high-value products for sale to the urban population. Total agricultural output had recovered from collectivization by 1940 to approximately the level of 1928, but per-capita production of animal-husbandry products still lagged significantly behind. The state-farm sector remained small, but was regarded as a model for developing collective farms.

By 1940 the third five-year plan had gotten well underway with its characteristic quality of a campaign. The central planning agency, *Gosplan*, had assumed control of both short-term (annual) and long-term (five-year) planning. Fulfillment and overfulfillment of detailed targets, specified mainly in terms of physical volume, had been established as the principal criteria for awarding premiums to enterprise management, staff, and workers. Collective farms fitted into central planning differently than state enterprises, for their plans were detailed in terms of government procurements rather than total output, and premiums were not awarded for fulfillment or overfulfillment of targets. Financial flows in the economy as a whole were monitored by four agencies: (1) the Gosbank to keep track of current wage payments, interenterprise transactions, and short-term borrowing; (2) Gosbiudzhet (the state budget) to collect and disburse revenues of the state including borrowing; (3) the *Stroibank* to monitor the flow of capital funds from the budget to enterprises; and (4) the Sel'khozbank to provide long-term loans to help finance investment by collective farms.

Despite a clear preference for physical units of measurement, for barter transactions, and for nonmarket relationships, the Stalinist model that emerged at the beginning of the 1940s continued to feature pecuniary institutions and markets. The Stalinist model represented a sharp contrast with the high point of the NEP. Private enterprise had all but been eliminated from the formal structure of planning and production, and the role of markets and monetary institutions had been severely restricted, especially in the agricultural sector and for the rural population. But enterprises operated within a framework of financial as well as a physical-volume plans. Workers were paid most of their earnings in cash, and they were obliged to purchase most of their needs in state-owned retail outlets or on the CFM. The peasant, on the other hand, was linked with the main Soviet money circuit by means of the CFM and a small amount of cash earnings from the collective farm. Moreover, in the countryside and city alike, earnings were differentiated by type of employment. The principal basis for the determination of wages in the Stalinist model was the quantity and quality of the individual's contribution, not need. Egalitarian goals had been postponed. Thus, even at this high point of the Stalinist model, the Soviet economy remained an economy composed of a mixture of state and private enterprise, of nonmarket and market transactions and of centralized and decentralized decision-making. It may be fair to say that the aspiration of the moment was to move ever more decisively away from the private, the market, and the decentralized characteristics of the model; but, if so, the aspiration was not destined to be fulfilled.

By the end of the 1930s the Soviet economy clearly exhibited certain conditions that have since become chronic problems of the institutional structure of the system. Overambitious target-setting led to shortfalls in the production of many goods, particularly of goods slated for sale to low-priority sectors such as households and to the farms and enterprises that serve them. Shortages of skilled labor in the tight conditions of economic campaigning for overfulfillment of unrealistic targets caused wage inflation, and retail prices were rising sharply too. The problem of excessive competition for skilled labor led, in fact, to labor legislation in late 1940 that restricted individuals' leaving their positions. Housing was scarce. The many shortages of consumer goods were evident in the long queues in retail stores and in the creation of special stores to allow "queue jumping" by certain privileged individuals and as a reward for important individual or collective contributions to socialist construction or its defense. Persistent deficiencies in the supply of many highly desirable goods and services served as an invitation to speculation, black marketeering, and the illegal appropriation of state property both in urban and rural communities.

The structure of the economy, however, was compatible with the political and administrative structure that emerged as Stalin rose to supreme political power in the system. The various bureaucracies— such as the military, the administrative, the economic, and the party— all assumed pyramidal structures, with power concentrated at the apex of each. The Communist party permeated all of these pyramidal administrative structures, and its apex, the Politburo, functioned therefore as the overriding control for all of the systems taken together, including, of course, the centralized structure of state security (the KGB).

The "cult of personality," which was originally and more accurately called the "cult of Stalin" in the Soviet Union, has two historical aspects. One refers to what is essentially an historical phenomenon: the fact that Stalin dominated these formative years of the Soviet system and must accept blame as well as credit for what happened. The other aspect is political in the sense that the cult of Stalin represented a system of political control. By penetrating each bureaucracy the Communist party provided the eyes, ears, and leverage to insure respect for party decisions at all levels. The Central Committee represented the penultimate administrative level of the party, at the top of which stood the Politburo, which Stalin personally dominated. The highly centralized structure of the various economic ministries — for transport, industry, or agriculture, for example — which reported to the Council of Ministers at the apex of the economic bureaucracy, fitted nicely into the over-all administrative structure of political control. Thus the highly centralized nature of economic decision-making that emerged under Stalin reflected the political and administrative preferences of Stalin and his colleagues as much or more than their understanding of the needs and character of economic activity.

The Economic Effort in World War II

It would be difficult to imagine a sterner test of the Stalinist political and economic system than was provided by the German invasion in June 1941. The war years and the period of postwar recovery, however, remain largely unexplored periods of Soviet economic history. Treatments of the development of the Soviet economy have typically skipped directly from a discussion of the creation of the Stalinist model in the 1930s to the post-Stalin period of the 1950s with little more than a paragraph by way of transition. This is unfortunate because it has created the impression that these years are not essential to an understanding of the way in which the Soviet economy works today. This is very unlikely. The war and postwar years are skipped because we know so little about them, not as a result of a reasoned decision about their consequentiality for understanding the Soviet system.

It is clear that an understanding of the contemporary problems and successes of any other major participant in World War II, such as Great Britain, Japan, Germany, or the United States, would be incomplete in fundamental respects were we to omit consideration of the impact of the war. The spectacular rise of the Japanese and West German economies during the last three decades reflects both the outcome of the war itself and the nature of the postwar settlement which forbade substantial defense establishments. The long period during which the American dollar dominated the postwar world economy, which has only recently diminished, and the social turmoil of the postwar years both domestically and internationally cannot be understood apart from consideration of the domestic impact of the war and of the relative economic position of the United States at its close. Postwar politics and economic policies in England, France, and Italy were obviously shaped in large measure by the different impact of the war on each of these countries.

It is therefore unreasonable to assume that World War II did not substantially affect the economy, politics, and fundamental structure of the nation that suffered most severely of all the participants in World War II. The impact of the war could not have been less than that of the rapid industrialization and mass collectivization of the 1930s, and it merits much more attention than it has received. Fortunately data are now becoming available and serious analysis is for the first time becoming a possibility. Let me, therefore, present and draw some tentative conclusions from these data concerning the impact of World War II upon the Soviet economy and people and upon Soviet economic institutions.

The Soviet economic effort in World War II was unique in two important respects. First, unlike any other major participant in the war, except France where formal military resistance collapsed immediately, the Soviet economy suffered severe damage at the outset of the war, and a long and bitter contest had to be fought with less than prewar economic capacity. A second, and related, fact is that the magnitude of total war costs was undoubtedly greater for the Soviet population than for any other population, both absolutely and on a per-capita basis.

Operation Barbarossa, Hitler's surprise offensive, was launched on June 22, 1941. For reasons that have yet to be fully explained, permission from the Soviet headquarters to counterattack was slow in coming, and troops in the field received little guidance for several weeks. The battlefield stretched over a thousand miles in length, and German formations penetrated hundreds of miles through confused, unprepared, and demoralized Soviet positions. A large amount of Soviet military equipment, especially tactical aircraft and tanks, was destroyed without the Russians imposing a countervailing cost upon the advancing German armies. The evidence suggests a breakdown in the Soviet military command at the critical level, the top; and stories circulate about a two-week period of vacillation by Stalin himself. Whatever the case, the delay in providing clear orders to the troops was costly in trained manpower, in equipment, and in territory. Territory was the only resource the Soviets could spare.

A great deal of disagreement among historians of the immediate prewar years exists concerning the failure of France, England, and the USSR to close ranks against fascist Germany. Stalin blamed the western powers for their capitulation at Munich, which permitted the destruction of Czechoslovakia without resistance; and the West blames Stalin for insincerity in his protestations on the Czechs' behalf. The Nazi-Soviet pact, it is claimed, is proof that Stalin did not intend to honor his pledge to Czechoslovakia in any case; and the subsequent brutal expansion of the USSR into the small Baltic states, the embarrassing savage war with Finland, and the partition of Poland are all put forward as evidence. Soviet historians claim that the USSR was buying time in this way to build up a defense against anticipated German aggression. It is true that the years 1938-41 witnessed a sharp increase in Soviet military spending. There is, however, evidence to the contrary, such as the risk Stalin assumed in conducting a purge of the Red Army command in the face of possible invasion. Whatever may have been the case, it is possible that even Stalin was taken aback by Hitler's perfidy and was unable for several weeks to assimilate the facts of the invasion and to act upon them.

In the first six months of fighting, German forces occupied a large part of European Russia. Prior to the war some 40 percent of the Soviet population had lived in this territory, and 32 percent of the labor force and 33 percent of the capital stock of all state enterprises in the USSR had been located there also. The German army moved steadily forward, surrounded Leningrad—with the intention of starving the population to death—and approached Moscow. A thrust to the south, toward the valuable oil fields of Baku, delayed the attack on Moscow. By December 2, when the "last heave" of the German army's advance toward Moscow failed, Soviet economic capacity had been reduced by at least one-third, and the precipitous fall in vital economic indices had yet to be reversed.

Marshal Zhukov's hasty and desperate defense of the city of Moscow dealt the German army its first strategic defeat of the war in any theater, and the respite that this setback afforded the Soviet Union permitted the economic mechanism to begin to rebound. By the beginning of the German offensive of the summer of 1942, the Soviet economy was already well on the way to being fully converted to a war footing. Some fifteen hundred industrial plants and their employees had been evacuated ahead of the German advance, and the output of essential

industries had begun to rise sharply as priorities shifted to the production of armaments and as plants and equipment evacuated to and
beyond the Urals began to come back on line. By the fall of 1942 the
revamped Soviet economy was more efficiently geared to war than the
German, and many vital outputs already outpaced those of Germany,
which was to begin total war mobilization in earnest later under the
direction of Albert Speer.

The strategic balance in the war shifted gradually in favor of the
USSR. Lend-Lease assistance from the United States and England
ensured eventual superiority, and in the short run Soviet industry was
rapidly recovering and its output of war materials was rising. Success in
holding Stalingrad, where Germany recklessly spent troops and
equipment to no advantage, meant that the USSR would have
numerical superiority in all important categories of military supplies;
and the German defeat in the battle of the Kursk salient, the world's
greatest tank battle, demonstrated that Soviet military leadership had
mastered the art of tank warfare. From this point the sheer weight of
Soviet forces, in manpower and equipment, would result in the eventual
defeat of Nazi Germany.

Although it is not easy to measure the cost of the war meaningfully,
the cost of war to the Soviet people was almost certainly greater than for
the Germans. An extraordinary commission was established by the
Politburo as the war ended to estimate the material damage the war had
caused in Soviet territory with an eye to reparations. The commission
arrived at a sum—excluding the "cost" of human life and limb—of 184
billion rubles for material damage attributable to the war. By itself, of
course, this figure is not very helpful in trying to come to an
understanding of the magnitude of these costs to the Soviet people. We
can, however, determine how many years the 1940 labor force would
have had to work without pay to replace the damage done by the war.
The cost of the war per employed person in 1940 can be calculated at
2551 rubles. Dividing by the average annual wage, 346 rubles, the
answer we obtain is that it would have required approximately seven
years merely to replace material losses occasioned by the war. It is
possible to check this number using other data that are available on the
Soviet economy during the war years. The result is a range from about
three years' earnings to six. Given the problems of estimation and the
fact that our estimates do not include human costs or estimates for costs
that continued into the postwar years, the higher end of the range is

probably the more nearly applicable. The material cost of the war was large therefore, when measured as the expenditure of human effort.

In addition to the material costs of the war, the country lost 20 million in population, almost equally divided between military personnel and civilians. This incredible number is attributable to three factors. First many millions of Soviet citizens were transported to Germany to work in factories or to be exterminated. Second the eastern front was a war of no quarter, and frequently the troops on both sides refused to take prisoners. This brutality was reinforced by propaganda each side utilized to persuade its own soldiers that surrender would be more terrible than death. Moreover Soviet soldiers were instructed not to surrender under any condition. The third factor was the seeming profligacy with which Soviet commanders utilized troops. Thus, although many women lost their lives during the war, the impact was disproportionately large upon the male population of combat age.

We have no statistics concerning total Soviet casualties. The rule of thumb for the Allied powers in the generally less bitter campaign on the western front against Nazi Germany was the recovery of one wounded soldier for every death. In the Soviet case this would imply a casualty total of 40 million — or 20 percent of the 1940 population. This figure is probably too high, but total casualties could have been hardly less than 30 million. These are losses that no one has attempted to place an economic value upon. Soviet economists believe that it would be a dishonor to attempt to do so, but it is nonetheless clear that such enormous casualties would have had a highly deleterious effect upon the postwar capacity of the Soviet economy and that they must be considered in any attempt to assess the impact of World War II upon the Soviet system.

Such enormous casualties meant that few families could have escaped loss or serious injury to at least one family member, which helps to explain why World War II remains vivid in the memories of Soviet citizens today. The loss of 20 million members of the Soviet population, plus an additional 10 million or so who survived their wounds, imposed a large economic burden on the able-bodied who survived, for the incidence of casualties fell hard upon the working-age population. This increased the ratio of dependents to workers in most families and for society as a whole. Care for invalids and those who became chronically ill as a result of the war must have imposed a still greater burden on those of working age.

There can be little question that the material cost of World War II to the Soviet people exceeded that of any other participant. My own best guess is that material costs to the USSR exceeded that of the country next hardest hit, which was probably Great Britain, by a factor of two. The loss of human life and total casualties of the Soviet population also exceeded that of any other participant. The country nearest to the USSR in total casualties was Germany, with about half as many in casualties. No nation or state in modern times has withstood such terrible costs in war and survived intact as a political and economic system. Political leadership did not change during or after the war in the USSR. Stalinist political and economic institutions proved their stability, flexibility, and durability in World War II. The roots of contemporary Soviet political and economic conservatism feed, no doubt, upon the successful wartime performance of these institutions.

The nadir of Soviet strategic fortunes occurred some time in midwinter 1941-42. Most Soviet war historians divide it into two periods. The first runs from the June invasion in 1941 through July of the next year. The second runs from the middle of 1942 to the end of the war. The economic indexes that are available for the war period support Soviet practice (see table 2-1). By stopping the German advance just outside of Moscow, the Red Army won an important psychological victory over the hitherto unchecked German war machine, and the pause that followed in military activity allowed time for the economy to rebound. Reports suggest that the main economic indexes ceased to fall and began to rise again during the summer of 1942.

Where did the real resources come from to meet the enormous costs imposed by the war? The cost of increasing war production in these years may be seen, in part, in the rapid rise in war production despite drastic decreases in national income, gross industrial production, and the average annual number of workers (table 2-1) in 1941 and 1942. The cost of increasing war production is also evident in the decline in capital investment and in retail turnover. The high proportion of gross industrial production that was absorbed by war production during 1942-44 reveals the effective operation of the powerful system of priorities in Soviet planning and management. The fall in national income and gross industrial production in 1945 reflected the relaxation of war priorities as production lines began to be reconverted to peacetime products and as labor controls were decompressed.

TABLE 2—1: Principal Economic Indexes, 1941-45.
             (1940 = 100)

	1941	1942	1943	1944	1945
National income	92	66	74	88	83
Gross industrial production	98	77	90	104	92
Of which: War production	140	186	224	251	173
Percent of gross industrial production	n/a	63.9	58.3	51.3	40.1
Gross agricultural output	62	38	37	54	60
Average annual number of workers and salaried officials	88	59	62	76	87
Capital investment (nonkolkhoz)	86	53	53	72	89
State and cooperative retail turnover (constant prices)	84	34	32	37	45

SOURCE: *Istoriia Velikoi Otechestvennoi voiny Sovetskogo Soiuza 1941-1945 gg.*
(Moscow, 1961), T.6, p. 45, and G. S. Kravchenko, *Ekonomika SSSR v gody
Velikoi Otechestvennoi voiny* (Moscow, 1970), p. 35l.

The real human cost of war is borne by those who endure it and carry its scars afterward. The economic cost of war represents a subset of this cost, and it is measured as the difference between the greater economic effort war requires and the smaller economic reward individuals receive for this greater effort, plus the economic sacrifices that are imposed upon current and future generations as a result of wartime destruction of capital stock, the labor force, and irreplaceable national treasures. The change that took place in the allocation of (the smaller) national income during the war is presented in table 2-2. Capital investment declined from 19 percent in 1940 to a low of 4 percent in 1942, and prewar rates of capital investment were not regained until after the war. Consumption fell also as a share of national income, but the share could not fall far because the absolute decrease in national income was so large (see table 2-1). It follows, therefore, that war outlays, exclusive of military consumption, rose at the expense of investment and consumption and reached a high of 33 percent in 1943. If military consumption is included, the share of war outlays reached 44 percent in

1943. But even this high share of war outlays underestimates the share of real national income that was devoted to the war effort, for many war-related expenses were not recorded as military — such as certain construction activities, air defense of major cities, and research and development efforts. According to an official source, total "war needs" absorbed 55 percent of Soviet national income in 1942, as compared to 15 percent in 1940.

TABLE 2—2: National income by shares, 1940, 1942-45
(percent of total in each year)

		1940	1942	1943	1944	1945
A.	Capital investment	19	4	7	15	13
B.	Consumption, including military personnel	74	67	60	61	69
C.	War outlays, excluding consumption of military	7	29	33	24	18
D.	Military consumption	4	11	11	11	n/a
E.	Total C + D	11	40	44	35	n/a

SOURCES: M. L. Tamarchenko, *Sovetskie finansy v period Velikoi Otechestvennoi voiny* (Moscow, 1967), pp. 50-51; Ia. E. Chadaev, *Ekonomika SSSR v period Velikoi Otechestvennoi voiny* (Moscow, 1965), p. 350; Kravchenko, pp. 228, 125.

The real resources to support the war effort, therefore, were obtained by a greater economic effort of the population and at the expense of investment, consumption, and nonmilitary government outlays (in that order). When one considers the tautness of the prewar economy and the effort that had been required in the prewar decade of industrialization and collectivization, the wartime sacrifices of the Soviet people are all the more impressive. A contrast with the industrialization drive of the 1930s is to be found mainly in the difference in relative priorities of investment and military expenditures and in the fact that much of war production was intended for destruction or had little future civilian use. The war effort may also have benefited from broader popular support than the efforts of the 1930s.

Financing the war effort, in the strict sense of the word (that is, where the money comes from), comprises the ways in which people and organizations may be induced to cooperate in making the sacrifices that war requires. As long as the central government controls the banking and currency system, the problem of financing the war does not consist in finding funds with which to pay for domestically produced war materials and for additional military personnel, but in avoiding or minimizing the negative consequences of spending the huge sums that warfare on the scale of the Soviet-German conflict requires. Financing war also involves the way in which the fiscal burden of the war is allocated among and influences the behavior of the various individuals and classes of society, present and future. The objective is to find a combination of tax and financial instruments that is optimal with respect to the incentive response of the public.

An examination of the main sources and uses of funds in the Soviet state budget reveals that the sharp increase in defense outlays occasioned in the first four years of the war was financed primarily by increases in direct taxes, by collections from the population, and by extraordinary recourse to borrowing. As defense outlays tapered off in 1944, so did these three sources of funds. The increase in wartime expenditures was also financed in part by the declines in nondefense budget spending, such as on social welfare measures and on nonmilitary administrative needs. These latter categories of government expenditures, however, closely followed the pattern of traditional sources of state budget funds (the turnover tax and the withdrawal of profits from state enterprises).

The reallocation of resources to the war effort was financed, therefore, primarily by new taxes, expecially a "war tax" on personal income, and by borrowing. It is clear, however, that every effort was made to restrict borrowing to a minimum. Although deficit finance played a more important role during the war than at any other time previously other than in 1932, a critical year of rapid industrialization and mass collectivization, deficit finance was a far less significant source of funds to the Soviet government than it was for either the British or the United States treasuries. This reflects a persistent trait of Soviet finance, for Soviet financial policy remains highly conservative today.

Traditional sources of funds declined for obvious reasons during the war. As sales of consumer goods declined, turnover-tax receipts declined also, and enterprises were concentrating on war production, on which no or very low turnover taxes were collected and which generated smaller profits as well, especially in the early years of the war. Scarcities of consumer goods necessitated rationing in all major cities, and an effort was made to allocate rationed goods equitably, in order to gain patriotic support for the war.

The war reversed three prewar trends in government receipts and outlays. First, the share of central government expenditures in total governmental outlays increased, which reflected the increased priority of military outlays that the central government predominently financed. Second, the role of deficit financing increased sharply; and, third, the ratio of direct to indirect taxes increased sharply. All three indicators returned to prewar levels shortly after the war ended. These reversals revealed the preferences of central authorities in peacetime for a greater degree of decentralization of government expenditures, for indirect (as opposed to direct) taxation on the population, and for avoiding deficit finance wherever possible.

Raising real resources and raising money to finance the war effort are related mainly through the systems of pecuniary incentives that operate within the economy—that is, the wage system, the system of prices, and the other institutions that provide money rewards for economic participation and for efficient conduct of economic activity. Although the Soviet economy had relied heavily upon direct controls over resources and directives to organizations and individuals from 1928 onward and did so even more heavily during the war, a serious effort was made to preserve pecuniary incentives and institutions even during the height of the war effort. Presumably the usefulness of these institutions had been demonstrated prior to the war. The aim of financial policy was not to increase the rate of saving of the population, for that rate was determined elsewhere by directives and by direct allocation of resources to the war effort. The aim instead was to avoid a breakdown of incentives to work and to contribute efficiently to the war effort. This meant seeking to provide an equitable distribution of goods available during the war and creating the presumption that wartime saving would retain purchasing power afterward.

This presumption was not borne out, however. Inflation in both final prices of products and in money wages did occur during the war. By and large, retail prices on nonrationed goods rose more rapidly than money wages, which increased turnover-tax receipts and inflated profits of state enterprises as consumer goods became more available toward the end of the war. The greatest impact of inflation was, of course, upon the collective-farm market and upon the black market. Inflation in these markets tended to redistribute the financial assets of the population from buyers to sellers, and thus predominantly from urban to rural dwellers.

A monetary reform was introduced in 1947, which eliminated by confiscation a large part of the value of financial assets that were thus accumulated during the war. It affected differentially hoards of hand-to-hand currency, and it was justified as a tax on war profiteers. Insofar as speculators and other war profiteers would have been inclined to avoid savings accounts, war bonds, and other forms of savings that were less heavily taxed by the reform to avoid detection, the incidence of the monetary reform was appropriate; but it also fell disproportionately upon the rural population, which was more inclined to hold its savings in cash than was the urban population.

Following the 1947 monetary reform, prices in state retail stores were reduced by more than one-half in a series of steps between 1948 and 1953. This also worked to the disadvantage of the rural population because these price decreases were not justified by a corresponding increase in the supplies available or in the procurement prices paid to collective farms for their products. An effort was made to reduce procurement prices as a way to justify decreases in retail prices. The urban population gained relative to the rural because of the inefficiency of the rural distribution system for these goods and because of the better access of urban dwellers to queues for these goods in the cities. Thus the rural population was treated as a whole as though it were composed predominantly of war profiteers, which reflected Stalin's customary preference for industrial workers and the urban population.

An over-all evaluation of the performance of the Soviet economy and of those persons who planned and managed it must be highly favorable. Although the Soviet Union did receive assistance from the United States and Great Britain via Lend-Lease, no one has argued, or could argue, seriously that the outcome of the war on the eastern front would have been reversed in its absence; and the same conclusion holds for whatever contribution British and American strategic bombing in Germany made. The Soviet economic system worked effectively to concentrate resources for military use, and the main institutions of the economy worked without serious problems. The nature of the demands placed by the war on the economy were compatible with the structure of the prewar Soviet system. England and the United States, for example, introduced mechanisms not unlike certain Soviet institutions for the duration of the war. Scarce materials were directly allocated. Military procurement carried the force of law, and needed goods were requisitioned. Price controls were effected, and consumer goods were rationed. Toward the end of the war ablebodied citizens, both male and female, were obliged to work in England; and in both the United States and England plans had been worked out, but were never implemented, for the direct allocation of civilian labor. The organization of the prewar Stalinist economy was therefore advantageous to meet the demands of the war. If so, this must be regarded as an advantage of the Stalinist system in World War II.

On the other hand both England and the United States had considerable excess economic capacity when the war broke out, and the war served as a stimulant to economic activity and full employment. In contrast the Soviet economy was taut as a bow string at the outbreak of the war, and little slack existed with respect to productive capacity or potential labor force. Resources switched to the war effort had to be subtracted from other current uses, and this was a serious disadvantage by comparison with England and the United States. Thus, for example, the agricultural sector was drained of a large proportion of its ablebodied male workers and of its horses and trucks. Agriculture during the war was conducted by women, pensioners, and children; and they had to make do with far inferior tractive power than had been available immediately prior to the war. In the industrial sector, low-priority factories and industries either shut down altogether because of shortages of manpower, fuel, and materials, or they worked only spasmodically as available inputs permitted.

Given the sparseness of the data, it would be even more difficult than for the 1930s to assess the incidence of the cost of World War II concerning urban versus rural population, industrial worker versus peasant, soldier versus civilian, and so forth. The 1947 monetary reform that was discussed earlier suggests that Soviet economists and planners believed that the peasants profiteered during the war, because the reform did not provide for differentiating between the cash hoards of peasants and those of speculators. That the peasants were able to produce and sell products at very high prices on the collective farm market seems to be the primary evidence of peasant profiteering, but it is important to note that only a small fraction of the peasantry would have been able to benefit from this free market. In general, however, the fact that the German invasion forces came to be regarded with great hostility by the majority of the Soviet population eased the task of mobilizing resources for the war and minimized the undesirable financial consequences.

Thus, although no new permanent economic institutions were created in response to the war effort, the war tempered those that had been formed during the 1930s. Success in the war effort also created a presumptive case for the superiority of the economic institutions that were formed in the 1930s. The postwar years witnessed as a consequence the reconstruction of the institutional as well as the material base of the Soviet economy.

The Economic Consequences of the War and the Reconstruction of the Stalinist Model

The war had important qualitative as well as quantitative consequences for the USSR. The Soviet Union concluded World War II with an economy smaller by almost 20 percent than it had been at the outset. In contrast the United States economy was more than twice as large in 1945 as it had been at the outbreak of the war. The relative size of the Soviet economy in 1950 was calculated by an American intelligence agency to be 33 percent of the size of the U.S. economy. Crude projection suggests that it was no more than 25 percent at the close of the war. Even so, as a result of the loss of economic capacity by the other participants in the war, it had become the second largest economy in the world. And, by virtue of the buildup for military victory over Germany, the Soviet Union disposed of the most powerful ground forces in the world. Sole possession of the atomic bomb and a proven ability to deliver it, however, ensured the United States the leading position in the world as a military power. Conflict between the two over the regions of Europe that they had occupied during the war escalated into what is known as the Cold War.

Victory in World War II, therefore, thrust the Soviet Union into world politics as a major force; and occupation of the countries that it had defeated or liberated had turned the Soviet Union into an international presence. Yet Soviet military might and international presence were based upon a slender economic base that did not regain the prewar level of national income in 1940 until about 1950. Full recovery of agricultural production was not achieved, in fact, until at least 1952. Even then per-capita production was less than it had been in 1928 according to Soviet data. Prior to the war the Soviet Union had not been considered a military power of the first rank. Insofar as the USSR had been regarded a threat to capitalist nations, the threat was in the nature of a bad ideological example for the workers of capitalist countries. Hence the war produced a qualitative change in the relative economic, political, and military position of the USSR on the world scene; and maintenance of this position in the postwar world has been costly to the Soviet population. Unlike prewar development, postwar recovery had to be carried out while the country maintained a relatively high burden of defense spending. Russia's failure to participate in the Marshall Plan was also costly in lost opportunities, although it is not clear whether joining was a real possibility for the USSR.

Agricultural production had been reduced the most severely of any economic sector by the war, and the failure of many ablebodied males to return from the war, plus the absence of those who survived but elected to stay in urban areas, greatly diminished the agricultural labor force in postwar years. The loss of tractive power during the war, and the low priority assigned to the agricultural sector afterward, increased the difficulties with which agricultural production struggled. Consequently agricultural output increased more slowly than industrial production. The slow recovery of agricultural production delayed the recovery of household real income as well, for over 60 percent of family budgets was devoted to food products at this time. The decrease in retail prices in state stores that Stalin insisted upon between 1948 and 1953 only made matters worse. It did not reflect an increase in supply, and it led to an attempt to reduce procurement prices offered to producers in justification. Reportedly Stalin was restrained from increasing taxes on the agricultural sector by a total of two billion rubles only by learning that the tax would exceed total cash income of all collective farms.

The Stalinist system of industrial management and of central planning resumed prewar priorities, with the notable difference that military spending competed with investment for resources. By 1950 the recovery of industrial production was proclaimed, and the Stalinist system had been successfully reconstructed. The Soviet economy stood approximately where it had in 1940, but the international responsibilities and the cost of maintaining a competitive military establishment in the chilly climate of the Cold War meant a slower recovery of individual living standards than for the economy as a whole.

In general the war proved the workability and the reliability of Soviet centralized economic institutions. It offered opportunities for the expansion of Soviet influence in both the West and the East, and it created a climate of mutual mistrust that led to an escalation of military preparedness on both sides of the Iron Curtain. If the 1930s can be described as the decade during which Soviet economic and political institutions took shape, then the war was the period of their testing. The postwar years were years of conservatism, therefore, not of experimentation, especially with respect to economic institutions.

When Stalin died in 1953, the economic system had been reconstructed according to the prewar pattern; but it was creaking with the stresses and strains of several decades of incredible sacrifices by the population, the weight of undelivered promises, excessive centralization, and growing inconsistencies that unbalanced growth had created over three decades. The social, economic, and technical backwardness of the agricultural sector had become a serious drag on attempts to increase the standard of living. Stalin's policy had contained a contradiction, for it is impossible to discriminate for long in favor of the urban-industrial consumer and worker while discriminating simultaneously against the primary producer of consumer goods, the peasant agricultural producer. In addition the conservatism of the Soviet planning system was becoming evident in its failure to promote development of new industrial processes and products.

The Soviet Economy Without Stalin

Stalin's death nearly coincided with completion of the task of postwar reconstruction. It is, therefore, possible that major changes would have ensued with or without him. Moreover certain developments were incubating in the years immediately prior to 1953. Several hundred Soviet economists had convened in Moscow in 1951 under the leadership of Academician Konstantin Ostrovitianov, director of the Institute of Economics of the Academy of Sciences of the USSR, to discuss preparation of a new definitive economics textbook for use in Soviet higher education. The conference led to a broadening of the concerns of economists and to greater latitude in economic discussion. In a similar vein two agricultural economists proposed sometime in 1950 that the MTS system ought to be sold to collective farms because of conflicts between the interests of the two types of organizations. Stalin shortly rejected their argument, but it reflected nonetheless a quickening in the economics profession and a desire to move from the realm of pure theory toward policy concerns.

Whatever the case may have been, pressures were building for change. There were compelling reasons to increase the flow of goods to Soviet consumers. The needs and standard of living of the Soviet household had been deferred for decades—first was recovery from World War I, the revolution, and civil war. Then industrialization absorbed all available resources. Moreover collectivization led to stagnation in both rural and urban consumption. The outbreak of World War II caused consumption to fall sharply, and the drive to reconstruct the economy during the second half of the 1940s required the population to do without again. By the early 1950s the time had come for all of this hard work to begin to pay dividends. For most Soviet households the expansion of consumer benefits meant improved provision of food products, improved housing conditions, and the satisfaction of similar basic needs. In order for the state to meet increased dietary expectations, however, something had to be done to achieve significant increases in agricultural output. Improvement in the housing supply would also require a change in investment priorities. Even today Stalin's name is so associated with sacrifices imposed upon the population that it is difficult to imagine just how he would have gone about changing economic priorities to favor the household sector had he lived longer.

Stalin left a legacy of sacrifice, of victory in World War II, of priority for heavy industry and military hardware, of terror, of a highly centralized political, economic, and administrative system, and of one-man rule. Stalin's was an act that could not be easy to follow, but there were many communist leaders prepared to try. The first step of his successors was to remove Lavrenti Beria, the hated chief of state security, from contention. He was arrested in a dramatic confrontation with guns drawn in a meeting of the Presidium (now once again known as the Politburo) of the Central Committee of the Communist Party, the highest and most powerful political unit in the USSR. Later Nikita Khrushchev and Georgi Malenkov competed for power, with each offering substantial benefits to peasants and to urban households in the process. It is interesting to note that all major indicators of consumer welfare reveal this 1953 power struggle.

In the end Khrushchev rose to dominance. He appeared to many at the time as the more conservative of the two men, but the evidence from the period of his hegemony does not correspond with this early estimate. Economists, who prefer simple psychological theories, like to divide the human race into two types of personality when it comes to decision-making: those who seek risks for the sake of excitement and the enjoyment of winning on a long shot, and those who avoid risk, for whom uncertainty affords only disutility. Whether or not there is any validity to this dichotomy as a general psychological proposition, Nikita Khrushchev appears in historical perspective to have had an unusual tolerance, and perhaps even a certain love, for taking risks. Soviet domestic policy was far more conservative during the last years of Stalin's rule and has been more conservative subsequent to Khrushchev's rule as well.

The most serious domestic problem that Stalin's heirs faced was the slow pace of agricultural development. Khrushchev moved rapidly on this front, assuring collective farmers that state procurement agencies would observe "socialist legality," which meant simply that obligatory delivery norms would not be revised upward in good years as had become practice, and that the rules governing the operation of collective farms and the size and rate of taxation on private plots would be observed by all government agencies. The tax rate on private-plot income was decreased. New emphasis was placed upon material, as opposed to moral, incentives to work on the collective. Shortly thereafter Khrushchev initiated the virgin lands program, which brought new lands in remote and marginal agricultural regions of the USSR into cultivation to increase agricultural output dramatically in a short time. Between 1954 and 1957 an area equal to the total cultivated area of Canada was plowed up, and grain output doubled. Not all of these marginal lands could be retained in production for long, but it was a gamble Khrushchev took in order to buy time for intensification of agriculture in traditional growing areas.

Still not satisfied, Khrushchev in 1958 initiated the most thoroughgoing reform of agricultural institutions since collectivization, the full implications of which have yet to be realized. These reforms abolished the MTS system and the old four-channel procurement system. Taken together with the virgin lands program and renewed emphasis upon material incentives, the 1958 reforms are still acting to destalinize Soviet agriculture.

Khrushchev also introduced reforms in the structure of central management, but these reforms proved of less consequence. His attempt to reorganize Soviet industry along territorial, as opposed to functional, lines was unsuccessful and had to be abandoned. In a similar vein Khrushchev's attempt to split local administration into rural-agricultural and urban-industrial subunits created resentment and confusion among local party officials and contributed significantly to his removal in 1964. Leonid Brezhnev, Alexi Kosygin, and Nikolai Podgorny subsequently rescinded this reform.

More significant was the reform of enterprise management and central planning that was announced by Kosygin almost a year after Khrushchev's removal. The Kosygin reforms of 1965, however, were an outgrowth of economic discussions that began in 1962, and the entire period from Stalin's death in 1953 to the present is essentially Khrushchevian. Thus Khrushchev created the framework of the current system, and he cleared away much of the Stalinist residue to make way for it. Those who have followed Khrushchev have taken no comparable dramatic steps. Instead Brezhnev and Kosygin moved quietly and cautiously forward, accelerating certain changes initiated under Khrushchev, slowing others, and reversing a few. The over-all climate since 1964 has not involved the heady excitement of experiment and headlong change of the mercurial Khrushchev, but the staid conservatism of men who fear to risk too much and who therefore must sacrifice radical improvement to avoid a possible radical worsening of their problems. The voluntary resignation of Kosygin for reasons of health in October 1980 was accompanied by no significant change in the cautious conservatism of the government.

SELECTED READINGS

Erickson, John. *The Road to Stalingrad.* New York: Harper & Row, 1975.
Hart, B. H. Liddell. *History of the Second World War.* New York: G. P. Putnam's Sons, 1970.
Millar, James R. "Financing the Soviet War Effort." *Soviet Studies* 32, no. 1 (January 1980), 106-23.
Millar, James R., and Linz, Susan J. "The Cost of World War II to the Soviet People: A Research Note."*Journal of Economic History* 38, no. 4 (December 1978), 959-62.
Voznesensky, N. A. *The Economy of the USSR during World War II.* Washington, D.C.: Public Affairs Press, 1948.
Werth, Alexander. *Russia at War 1941-1945.* New York: Dutton, 1964.

II

How Does the
Soviet Economy Work?

3

Government and the Economy: The View from the Top

Introduction—A Methodological Note

Economists ordinarily conceive of an economy as composed of aggregate sectors. Each sector is represented by the transactions that it deals in, for the transaction is the basic unit of economic analysis. We seek to explain why and how the transactions of the various sectors change over time. The four aggregate sectors that are ordinarily identified for analysis include: households, governmental units, enterprises, and a fourth sector that encompasses all foreign transactors. These sectors may be broken down into smaller constituents. As a general rule, for example, it is useful to distinguish the activities of enterprises in producing and selling goods and services on current account from their transactions connected with the financing and purchase of capital goods. In the Soviet case we shall also find it necessary to consider state enterprises and collective farms separately because of the different legal status of each. In the chapters that follow I seek to describe and explain the structure and functions of these aggregate sectors of the Soviet economy.

These sectors form a mutually interdependent system. No single sector can be fully understood without reference to all of the others, for no one sector is logically anterior to the others. Economists like to think of the household sector as the ultimate sector for which all economic activity is conducted, but this is a prescriptive and not a descriptive judgment. The interdependence of all transactors in a capitalist economy like ours, or a planned economy like that of the Soviet Union, has led economists to favor representation of economic activity by a system of simultaneous equations—that is, by a system in which everything affects everything else. Obviously there can be no fully satisfactory starting point for describing any such system. Wherever we start, we shall have to backtrack a bit, and the conclusion will have to overlap the beginning. After we have considered the main sectors and subsectors of the Soviet economy, I shall bring them all together into an analysis that presents the economy as a functional whole and that will allow the reader to obtain an intuitive grasp of the economist's conception of an economy as a set of simultaneous interrelationships.

It is useful to begin, however, by organizing the description in terms of two partial perspectives: the view from the top and the view from the bottom. Although all sectors are aggregates of transactors, some transactors, such as the central (all-union) government and its agencies such as Gosplan, have a broad panoramic view of economic activity. Others, such as the household sector, are composed of transactors who conduct their economic activities within very narrow confines, whose perspective on the economy is restricted to a window over the sidewalk. We shall begin with the view from the top because it provides the broadest perspective of the economy.

In addition to describing the establishments and agencies that conduct economic activities in the Soviet economy, I shall be concerned with what have sometimes been called economic institutions. The term *institution* receives in this context a more restricted definition than is the case in current popular usage. It is useful, however, to have some way of distinguishing between an organization such as the government budget or a state enterprise, which can be conceived as making decisions according to some sort of rule, such as fulfillment of plan targets, and fundamental social control devices, such as freedom of calling or the use of money in economic transactions, that have evolved historically to shape and articulate the interaction of economic transactors.

To put the matter differently, institutions exist in society because children born into it are socialized to respond to certain kinds of stimuli. Children in the Soviet Union, like children in the United States, are conditioned from an early age to respond rationally to prices, money wages, and the discipline of the factory system. Soviet children are also inculcated with respect for the institution of private property, although Soviet laws define the content of the institution differently than it is defined in the West. To give another example, the Soviet central bank is organized differently than central banks in Europe, and it differs even more substantially from the commercial banking sector, or the Federal Reserve System of the United States; but pecuniary institutions impose similar constraints on all of these banking systems.

Certain economic institutions have a very long and very pervasive history in the western world, and the Soviet economy shares many of these institutions with the capitalist economies of the West. Specific economic organizations, establishments, and agencies differ much more; but these are of a different order and have far shallower historical roots. As we have seen in our brief survey of Soviet economic history, for example, many Bolsheviks expected the abolition of pecuniary institutions in the new socialist state. These expectations were disappointed, however, for experience demonstrated the difficulties, and perhaps even the impossibility, of running a modern economic system with such institutions.

The point is not that economic institutions are immutable—only that they represent time-tested devices for organizing economic activity, devices that are instilled by childhood socialization and are therefore difficult to eradicate on both functional and habitual grounds. Certain "capitalist" institutions have been nearly eliminated in the Soviet Union, but most traditional western economic institutions have merely been modified or constrained. Private property and private enterprise are among the most highly modified institutions in contemporary Soviet society.

Government and Central Planning

In the main the Soviet economy is characterized by public enterprise. What private enterprise remains is narrowly confined and regarded as an "historical survival" scheduled for eventual displacement. Public ownership determines the distribution of net income from production, and it affords the institutional basis for central management of all important economic activity.

State enterprises are managed by public servants who serve at the pleasure of the Council of Ministers, which stands at the apex of the economic bureaucracy. Public ownership of economic enterprises has been interpreted in the Soviet Union to mean that the enterprise manager represents the interests of society, as formulated by the economic bureaucracy in formal plans, and not the interests of his workers. Workers do not participate in decision-making at any level above the shop floor, and their interests are represented by the local trade-union (*profsoiuz*) leader in any (legal) conflict with management. The chairman of a collective farm represents a legal exception to this rule, for he or she is formally selected by farm membership. In point of fact the exception is more apparent than real. For all intents and purposes the collective farm chairman is subordinated to the formal economic bureaucracy, much as is the manager of a state farm, and therefore that functionary is not an exception to the hierarchial organization of the economic bureaucracy.

Soviet industry is organized along functional lines. Enterprises producing coal, for example, are grouped together administratively at each territorial level into increasingly larger administrative units. For industries of nationwide significance, such as coal, iron, rail transportation, or the chemical and petroleum industries, the chain of command runs upward from the enterprise, through a republic-level ministry to the all-union ministry in Moscow, which in turn reports directly to the all-union Council of Ministers. Where the industry is primarily of local significance, the territorial principle overrides the functional, and republic councils of ministers represent the terminus of the chain of command for all routine issues.

The Structure of Soviet Planning

The hierarchial structure of the Soviet economic bureaucracy has led many western scholars to describe the Soviet economy as a command economy — that is, as an economy modelled on the pyramidal command structure of a military bureaucracy. The concept of a command economy, however, is a better approximation of the way in which Soviet high-level planners and policy-makers would like to have the economy operate than it is of the way the economy actually functions. The notion is attractive because a command structure would ensure that decisons made by political leaders at the top could be implemented directly by merely sending out directives to enterprise managers and their regional supervisors. A command economy would not require decision-making by enterprise managers or within other subordinate levels of the economic bureaucracy. Enterprise managers could be instructed to fulfill central directives precisely, and failure to do so could be regarded as insubordination or incompetence.

When one considers what would be required to make the idea of command economy operational, it quickly becomes apparent that such a concept represents an unrealistic objective for any planning system. It would be impossible to collect, assimilate, and formulate sufficient data of the degree of accuracy that would be required to plan economic activity down to the last nut and bolt. No foreseeable advance in computer technology or in data processing is going to make command planning feasible. This conception of global, detailed economic planning represents a kind of planner's dream, and it influences the reality of Soviet planning practices only as an aspiration to minimize decentralized economic decision-making. It represents a prescriptive rather than a descriptive economical model, much as the perfectly competitive model serves western economists and policy makers. The operational significance of either model is to shape the approach of the economist to economic problems. The typical attitude of an American economist is to presume that an unfettered market is the best solution unless he has good reason to think otherwise. The Soviet planner, imbued with the concept of command planning, presumes that the best solution is one that is consciously determined by central authorities, unless he has good reason to believe that this would prove ineffective or otherwise unsatisfactory.

The Soviet economy has also sometimes been described in the West as a form of war economy, and this characterization has a certain validity. Precisely because every detail of the input needs and output capabilities of enterprises cannot be specified in advance, especially not in the exact temporal order required, Soviet planners have tended to rely heavily upon the use of a priority system to allocate scarce resources. Certain industries or subsectors of the economy have traditionally been ranked as high-priority producers or consumers and given preferential access to inputs that they require or the products that they desire. Military procurements and the space program represent two sectors that have exerted priority demands upon economic activity during the last several decades. Priority ensures these sectors relatively high-quality products, good design, adherence to product specifications, and relatively prompt fulfillment of orders. Similarly the enterprises that produce high-priority products—such as steel, aluminum, and machine-tool industries—derive priority-ranking from the status of their customers. Because central plans are ordinarily inconsistent and infeasible, low-priority industries usually fail to meet their targets, and their customers suffer shortages. Industries designated as critical usually fulfill or exceed their output plans. This is the sense in which the Soviet economy has operated like a war economy, for the use of similar priority-systems has been characteristic of the large economies that have engaged in major wars of this century.

From the initiation of formal economic planning in 1928, until well into the 1950s, certain sectors of the Soviet economy were treated as low-priority sectors. The consumer sector and the industries serving it—that is, agriculture and light industry—had to make do with what was left over after higher-priority sectors had satisfied their needs. There are, however, some serious deficiencies with the concept of a war economy for understanding the way the Soviet economy works. First the war economy model actually represents a model for decision-making; it does not offer a model that describes the structure of the economy. By contrast the command-economy model portrays how decisions are implemented, but says nothing about how decisions are taken. Consequently the command-and war-economy notions should be conceived of as complementary and not as alternatives. Second the priorities of a true war economy are very different from those of the Soviet economy in peacetime. Investment as well as consumption is sacrificed in wartime. Finally, when the enemy is at the gates and the majority of the population supports the war effort, as was the case in the USSR during World War II, it is much easier than it is in peacetime to persuade individuals to accept sacrifices and to increase their economic effort at the same time. The war-economy notion offers no comparable explanation of the willingness of the population to accept sacrifices in peacetime.

There is a certain validity and thus usefulness in both the concept of a war economy and that of a command economy as models of Soviet economic planning. A powerful priority-system has been imposed throughout the time since planning was initiated, with attendant and very considerable sacrifices by the population. Similarly planning efforts have aspired to a degree of comprehensiveness that would exclude decentralized decision-making if it could be obtained. Both concepts, however, imply a degree of central control and of general compliance of subordinate economic units that does not obtain in the Soviet economy. The existence of a number of important but relatively open (that is, relatively unregulated) markets, particularly the labor market, the state retail-sales market, and the collective-farm market as well as the limited capacity of the central planning apparatus to assimilate economic data and technical production possibilities together ensure a large sphere of de facto discretion for individual households and for managers of state enterprises and collective farms. The Soviet economy *is* highly bureacratized because so many decisions are made administratively rather than through the interaction of immediate transactors in markets, but markets do exist in the Soviet economy, and the impact of these various markets is pervasive and cannot be ignored when administrative decisions are taken.

The significance of both legal and illegal types of informal economic behavior has been recognized recently in the western literature (by the economists who first adopted the command- and war-economy conceptions) in the development of the idea of a second economy. No one has yet defined the second economy of the USSR to everyone's satisfaction; nor has anyone worked out the relationship of the second economy to the first. Thus the conception of a second economy has not yet remedied the problems presented by the use of a military-warfare model for the centrally planned economy. We shall explore these problems at greater length. It is generally agreed, in any case, that the notions of a war- and of a command-economy are misleading, and I shall henceforth avoid use of the terms for this reason. In my opinion it is more correct and more neutral to describe the Soviet economy as a mixed economy, as an economy characterized by public as well as private enterprise, by nonmarket as well as market-influenced economic behavior, and by centralized as well as decentralized decision-making. The mixture leans heavily toward the first term in each pair of characteristics, which reflects the fact that the economy is centrally managed as well as centrally planned.

The Plan

Operationally, the fundamental instrument of planning is the annual plan, which is broken down into quarterly and monthly variants for each enterprise. Each plan (*tekhpromfinplan*—technical-industrial-financial plan) at each level is made up of targets that are to be fulfilled (or exceeded) subject to a set of constraints. For example the enterprise is ordinarily required to attain certain levels of physical-volume outputs subject to certain maximum levels for wage payments, materials consumption, bank borrowing, and so forth. Operational plans are very detailed documents. They not only specify the various outputs the enterprise is to produce but give very detailed specifications for each product as well. Plans specify in addition the inputs the enterprise is to receive from other enterprises and the labor force to be used during the plan period, and these items are both described in detail. Certain output-input ratios are given too, as either targets or constraints, such as labor productivity targets, fuel-consumption rates, and maximum rates of rejection (a measure of quality). The plan also describes all flows of funds and all borrowing. Finally enterprises' annual and shorter-period plans include the dates on which inputs are to be received and outputs delivered to users. An annual tekhpromfinplan for a single multiproduct enterprise is, therefore, a long, complex, and comprehensive document prescribing the performance of the enterprise in the plan period as extensively and minutely as possible.

Gosplan (the State Planning Committee) seeks to exert central direction over the coordination of essential economic activity by means of the specific directives contained in annual, quarterly, and monthly plans. The annual plan is itself a component of a longer-term plan or plans. With few exceptions long-term planning in the Soviet Union has been conducted since 1928 in the format of five-year intervals. The precise functions of long-term planning in the Soviet Union have never been entirely clear, and some critics claim that they are window dressing of no operational consequence. It is assumed by most students of Soviet planning, however, that the five-year plan has served primarily as a vehicle for stamping the priorities and preferences of the political leadership upon the planning process as a whole.

Fundamental economic parameters, such as the share of investment in national income, the proportion of the state budget that will be devoted to military spending, or the relative priorities of the consumer and the agricultural sectors, are not set by planners in the Gosplan or the bureaucrats in the Council of Ministers but by the highest political authority in the USSR — the Politburo. These decisions are presumably embedded in long-term plans and thus in the annual plans that are built into their framework. Although the Politburo is not an official organ of government, respect for decisions of the highest party leaders is ensured by the fact that the Communist party controls all important positions in the economic, governmental, military, and police bureaucracies. Party members represent the arms and voice of the leadership as well as the eyes and ears, and they are expected to take a leading role in enforcing economic and other preferences of the Politburo.

Economic Planning

On economic issues it is the central economic administration that seeks to fulfill the expectations of the political leadership. At the apex the Council of Ministers serves more or less as an economic "cabinet" for Soviet leadership. Two kinds of agencies report to, and are represented in, the Council of Ministers. First are the nonsectorial specialized committees and agencies, each of which, like Gosplan or the central bank, Gosbank, exercises general responsibility for over-all planning, coordination, or supervision of the activities of enterprises, trusts, and other line units. Second are the various ministries that report to the Council of Ministers, which are divided by sector of the economy (industrial, agricultural, transportation, and communications). Some (all-union) ministries have sole responsibility for the activity in question, such as petroleum and natural gas; others, such as electric power generation, share responsibility with parallel ministries at the republic level (union-republic ministries).

The different nonsectorial committees, notably Gosplan, Gosbank, and *Gossnab* (State Committee for Material and Technical Supply) work jointly with the various ministries to plan, administer, and control production, the supplies of restricted and other centrally allocated scarce commodities, and capital construction. Gosbank and Stroibank, which channels investment funds allocated from the state bank to state enterprises, are particularly important supervisors of moneyflows among enterprises, between enterprises and their employees, and between the state, the enterprise, and the household. Economic plans are written both in physical units — that is, in number of man hours, machine hours, the number and weight of output and so forth, and in monetary terms. Gosbank and Stroibank monitor the monetary flows and verify reported expenses. Gossnab allocates and monitors the actual physical flows of resources in tight supply. Each nonsectorial committee or agency has a comparable responsibility over some general aspect of planning, reporting of results, setting wages, and so forth. The Central Statistical Administration, for another example, is responsible for collecting, verifying, analyzing, and publishing economic statistics; and *Gosstrakh* (the State Committee on Insurance) receives premiums, verifies claims, and pays out funds in connection with both enterprise and individual insurance policies.

Each enterprise falls under the supervision of some ministry, and it is subject to the direct supervision of the appropriate state or republic committees. Preparation of an annual plan for an enterprise involves a complex process of interaction between state committees, the various levels of the appropriate ministry (all-union or union-republic), and the enterprise. In May of each year broad directives (still known as control figures) are drawn up by Gosplan. They incorporate the priorities of the long-term plan, actual achievements of the most recent quarter, and any changes in priorities or in direction that have been passed down from higher political reaches. Individual ministries, in conjunction with the enterprises they supervise, adjust the provisional plans that they have prepared in expectation of the devolution of the control figures, and they scale their tentative claims on essential centrally allocated resources up or down accordingly. This process involves considerable two-way communication between enterprises and the various levels of the ministries, and much depends upon the success of an enterprise in negotiating a "good plan." A good plan can be fulfilled or exceeded, thereby ensuring everyone associated with the enterprise bonuses, special premiums, and the aura of success. These negotiations must be completed by late August or early September, when revised plans are due at Gosplan. Upon receipt of the plans of the various ministries, Gosplan is required to strike a balance between the material requirements and production possibilities they represent and to fit together the component parts of a consistent national plan.

The magnitude of the task rules out any kind of sophisticated technique for balancing input needs and output projections at the economy level, such as an input-output matrix. Gosplan's technique involves a crude comparison of availabilities and needs, followed by the paring down of input requests, of petitions for allocation orders, and of estimates of production-run time on the one hand and the stretching of output targets on the other to eliminate padding. Continuous negotiations go forward throughout October among enterprise managers, the heads of ministry divisions, and representatives of the Gosplan, as each seeks to wring maximum advantage or to protect a margin of error from the other side. Each side knows what is at stake, and the fact that the process is repeated every year affords considerable experience in negotiations to all parties. Enterprise managers know that the ministry and Gosplan will seek to cut fat out of their plans, and they set target levels accordingly. Gosplan and ministry workers know that managers try to protect a margin of error and add fat that can be cut, and they revise targets so as to cut beyond the obvious fat into the reserves against uncertainty. But managers know that Gosplan knows that they know that Gosplan will cut a bit more than the obvious fat, and so the game goes in infinite regress, in what is a form of bureaucratic guerrilla warfare that is well known in the West wherever budgets are negotiated between administrative units.

Once negotiations are closed, the presumption is that a reasonably consistent set of directives exists. The national plan is adopted, and the various ministries disaggregate their portions of the plan for distribution to the enterprises for which they are responsible. Not infrequently the difficulty of reconciling differences is so great that this last step is completed only after the actual plan year has begun. It is also not uncommon for an enterprise to petition during the year for redress of an impossible plan, and the evidence suggests that these petitions are sometimes successful. A contemporary Soviet movie, entitled "Premia," suggests that enterprise managers are sometimes successful in getting targets scaled down even where it is not justifiable, in which case employees and managerial staff receive bonuses despite inefficient and wasteful economic performance. No one outside the higher reaches of the Soviet economic bureaucracy knows the frequency of unjustifiable target reduction during the plan year, and even the bureaucracy's estimates may be very poor. What is well known is that basing significant monetary incentives on plan fulfillment creates as an undesirable side-effect a quest by managers for good plans and for grounds to scale down difficult targets. Because the Gosplan cannot know precisely, and sometimes it cannot know more than approximately, what the various target levels ought to be, there has been a tendency for planners to err on the high side in order to undermine the advantage that the manager has with respect to knowledge of the performance capabilities of his enterprise.

From the outset of central planning in the USSR, plan targets function in two ways. Targets should provide the basis for central direction of the economy, and as such they are not discretionary for managers of state enterprises. Targets are also supposed to spur managers and workers to deliver a maximum effort. That is, targets are set high in order to motivate management to strive mightily to attain them, and fulfillment or overfulfillment is rewarded through the use of powerful material and moral incentives. The need to measure the degree of success of enterprises and individuals in achieving plan targets has created an entire industry in the USSR dedicated to such measurements, and it contributes to the apparently insatiable appetite of Soviet planners, managers, and workers for statistics. That plan targets tend to be set high, both to serve as an incentive and to compensate for the tendency of managers to build "safety factors" into the plan, means that as a matter of course enterprise plan targets cannot all be fulfilled. Thus the second function of plan targets often conflicts with the first, with the result that managers must exercise some degree of discretion over output and input decisions even though no formal provision is made for it. At a minimum a good manager must decide which targets to slight. A good manager from the standpoint of the top is one who knows the correct ranking of priorities. A manager both is good and is popular with his workers if he succeeds in winning premiums despite the inevitable inconsistencies of the plan.

The institutionalization of numerous controls has ensured that Soviet enterprises do observe the priorities established by Gosplan, the Council of Ministers, and higher political authorities; and in this respect Soviet central planning and central management must be classified as successful. High average annual rates of economic growth of priority sectors have been sustained over a long period of time, helping to reduce the gap between the USSR and the USA both for specific product outputs and in relative size of economy. The military and strategic aims of the Soviet state were also met sufficiently well to defeat Nazi Germany and later to discomfit the United States, the largest and most powerful military power on the face of the earth, in the ongoing Cold War. Low-priority sectors, especially those producing and purchasing consumer goods and services, have been obliged to bear the sacrifices imposed by the planners and political leaders' preferences for growth and for military security. It is obvious that the sacrifice has been large. What is not obvious is the extent to which these priorities have accorded with the preferences of the population at large. Looking at the matter from a remote objective perspective, however, one can see that the greater the divergence between these two sets of preferences the higher must be our evaluation of the success of Soviet central planning and management systems.

Evolution and Reform

Perhaps the single most dramatic change that has taken place since Stalin's death in 1953 has been the gradual but steady upward revision in the relative priority of the consumer sector. Personal consumption has more than doubled, for example, over the last twenty-five years, and even casual visitors to the Soviet Union cannot fail to note dramatic changes in the apparent well being of the population over periods as short as five years. As we shall see, an increased priority for the household sector has entailed revisions in priorities all along the line. The production of consumer goods and services poses tasks that are new for Soviet industry, and that production has depended heavily upon improvements in agricultural production, which has always been a realm in which traditional Soviet planning methods have tended to go askew.

Soviet planning and management methods, particularly the preference for detailed planning and for administrative methods over the use of decentralized market allocation of goods and services, have been crucial to the implementation of priorities; but these methods have caused a great deal of inefficiency and waste too. Most western managers, businessmen, and even workers who have become involved in Soviet economic activity, either as consultants or participants, have been dumbstruck by the waste and the general inefficiency with which work is organized at the work site. It is reported, for example, that new records for waste and inefficiency are being set in the construction of BAM, the railway line that is being built north of the old Trans-Siberian line in eastern Siberia. The project reveals both the strengths and weaknesses of Soviet economic planning and management. Once completed, the BAM is certain to be one of the man-made wonders of the world, much as the construction of the huge dam at Bratsk on the Angara River in the same general region is today. The conditions of work are unbelievable. The line is being built in a region of permafrost, which means that the gound does not ever thaw deeper than a few feet. Construction takes place in temperatures under which steel can shatter like glass from a sharp blow. No one doubts, however, that the line will in fact be built and put into working condition, but the cost will be gigantic and will involve a large (some foreign workers say incredible) waste of materials and manpower.

The revision of priorities to upgrade the position of the Soviet consumer, recognition of the existence of inefficiency and waste, and a number of other factors have focused considerable professional and political attention in the USSR upon ways to reduce inefficiency, to increase receptivity to technological change, and to improve the quality of products of Soviet enterprises. After almost a decade of increasingly open discussion of the problems, reforms were introduced in 1965. These reforms have come to be called the Kosygin reforms in the West because Premier Kosygin, chairman of the Council of Ministers, announced them officially and because he has always been associated with economic management. They could just as well have been called the Khrushchev reforms of enterprise management, because the problems and the solutions the reforms addressed were worked out prior to Khrushchev's removal from power in 1964. They represented the most far-reaching reforms of the planning process ever to be suggested publicly since the creation of the Stalinist economic system.

Most economists in both the West and in the USSR today consider these reforms to have failed to achieve the purpose set for them, particularly by failing to provide a greater and more effective sphere for decentralized decison-making by enterprise managers. Despite this failure and the fact that no comparably significant new reforms are on the horizon, the 1965 Kosygin reforms may be seen as a signal that the political leadership knows that problems exist, and this suggests that another attempt will be made in the not-distant future to reform the traditional system of planning and central management. But we shall have to return to this topic at a later point. For the present it is fair to assume, I believe, that the description of the planning process that evolved under Stalin and that was presented above remains accurate in its essentials. We turn now to more detailed consideration of the main regulatory and central management institutions of the Soviet economy.

The Main Money-Circuit of the Soviet Economy

The emphasis of Soviet planning is upon physical quantities, physical ratios (such as measures of labor or capital productivity), and the allocation of physical units of scarce commodities. It is easy, therefore, to slight flows of money and the pecuniary aspects of the Soviet economy. It would be a great mistake to do so, however, for the result would misrepresent the nature of the Soviet system substantially and lead to an exaggeration of the difference between the Soviet economy and the economies of western capitalist countries. That there are differences in the way certain pecuniary institutions work in the Soviet economy is true, but the position many observers hold — that a difference of kind exists — is quite wrong.

The various payments that are made in a modern industrial economy such as the Soviet Union form a system, the principal elements of which compose what is sometimes called the main money-circuit of the economy. One may conceive of an economy as a special kind of game, like poker, in which there are rules for participation. To gain access to the products and services of the economy, the individual must find a source of money, because the goods and services available in the economy are, with some exceptions, obtainable only in exchange for money. There are several different ways for a potential participant to obtain money, both legal and illegal; but the main way in an economy like that of either the Soviet Union or the United States is to assume a risk or to contribute something to production. Enterprises and administrative units in such an economy are also subject to a budget constraint — that is, they must find a way to increase the funds at their disposal or to limit their expenses to what they have. The expectation is that they too must contribute a desired good or a service in order to receive money payments.

The fact that individuals, enterprises, and other agencies must have money to obtain goods and services, and that they can spend only what they have or what someone else will advance them either as a tax, gift, or loan, means that each transactor in the economy needs to have some sort of cash balance all, or most, of the time. Unlike a barter system, one cannot hold on to one's product or service until he is ready to spend (trade) it. Since the Soviet economy is a money economy, individual transactors, private as well as governmental, must manage their accounts, remain within their budgets, and hold cash balances most of the time; and this is the basis for the role of a banking system and for conscious fiscal policy in the Soviet economy. For similar reasons, a financial plan is developed on the basis of the physical plan for each enterprise, for each administrative level, and for the economy as a whole. Besides there are lots of flows of money that do not involve a flow of goods or services, as when individuals or enterprises pay taxes or receive subsidies, and these cash flows must be monitored to avoid misappropriation of funds or the unwarranted exercise of discretion.

Moreover the fact that these moneyflows form a system, the main money-circuit, affords planning and management agencies with still another avenue of potential central control over economic activities and with additional means to monitor the economic activities and performance of subordinate units. The Soviet banking system provides an important supervisory role in this respect.

There are three kinds of banks in the Soviet Union. The least important for domestic economic activity is *Vneshtorgbank*, the Foreign Trade Bank, which is responsible for keeping track of international transactions and for the receipt and disbursement of foreign exchange. This bank also controls the country's gold stock and manages reserves of foreign currencies and gold so as to maximize the purchasing power of the USSR in world markets and to maintain its reputation for financial probity. The ruble is not a convertible currency, which means that it cannot be used to purchase anything outside the USSR. The Soviet government, therefore, does not attempt to maintain the external value of the ruble and uses the dollar, other hard convertible currencies, and gold in settlements with foreign transactors. Thus foreign firms that operate within the Soviet Union and private individuals who come as tourists, newspaper reporters, diplomats, and so forth must accept the exchange rate the Soviet government sets or stay away. The nonconvertibility of the ruble also means that the bank deposits and other cash balances of state enterprises and of private Soviet citizens have absolutely no external purchasing power. If they wish to purchase foreign goods, they must buy them through a Soviet import enterprise at an exchange rate determined by the state, or obtain permission to exchange rubles for foreign currency at an outlet of Vneshtorgbank, which is almost impossible unless one is on an official mission abroad, or exchange rubles for hard currencies with foreign visitors to the USSR, which is, of course, illegal. The nonconvertibility of the ruble is, therefore, an important element in the isolation of the Soviet consumer within the confines of the Soviet economy, and it helps the Soviet government to conserve on the use of foreign exchange by preventing individuals or enterprises from satisfying consumer needs with it. The restrictions on access to hard currency tend to encourage the illegal exchange of rubles against hard currencies in Soviet cities where large numbers of foreigners reside and visit. The difference between the official exchange rate and the unofficial "street" rate is ordinarily substantial. In 1979 the official rate was $1.50 to the ruble, whereas the street rate was three rubles for one dollar or better.

Stroibank is the only other specialized bank in the USSR today. Stroibank supervises the distribution of investment funds from the state budget (Gosbiudzhet) to the enterprises that are slated for expansion or construction during the plan period. The bulk of investment by state enterprises, including state farms, is financed by direct interest-free grants from the state budget; and Stroibank is responsible for monitoring the uses to which these funds are put. The Kosygin reforms called for an interest charge on the existing capital stock of all state enterprises, and they enlarged the role of long-term borrowing at the expense of interest-free grants of investment funds from the budget. The aim of these changes was to impress upon enterprise managers the social cost of these investment allocations in the expectation that this would improve the efficiency with which managers use them. Thus far, however, charges have been too low and costs too insignificant to effect any substantial change in managers' attitudes.

The only true bank in the Soviet Union today is Gosbank, which combines the functions of a central bank with those of commercial banking. It is a monopoly, and all other banks (other than the two already mentioned) are branches of Gosbank. The most recent census indicates that there were over 3500 branches throughout the USSR employing more than 150,000 people. Prior to 1963 a separate bank was responsible for personal savings accounts, but since that time it has been consolidated with Gosbank. Gosbank was also made independent of the Ministry of Finance in 1954, and its powers and duties have increased substantially both through the consolidation of the functions of previously existing specialized banks and by means of its independent position.

Gosbank is located in a strategic position with respect to moneyflows and the Soviet income- and money-circuit. Apart from international transactions, which remain relatively insignificant despite an increase in total foreign-trade turnover in recent years, and the flow of capital investment funds through Stroibank, the main money-circuit flows through Gosbank, which gives it the most comprehensive and up-to-date picture of the Soviet economy in action. Gosbank is a bank of issue, and state enterprises may borrow on a short-term basis only from its offices. Enterprises and agencies obtain the hand-to-hand currency to pay Soviet workers and salaried officials directly from the local branch of Gosbank, and these payments are closely scrutinized to ensure against misappropriation, excessive wage payments, or the failure of actual payments to conform to plan targets. Moreover all transactions among Soviet firms are made through Gosbank by "offset" accounting. That is, the shipper of a product, enterprise A, has its account credited with the value of the shipment when and only if the receiving firm, B, declares itself satisfied that the shipment meets contract specifications. Gosbank records an accounting transfer between the two firms. The failure of B to accept a shipment from A would immediately call for investigation by Gosbank. Thus Gosbank is in a position to monitor outlays by enterprise and receipts on a day-to-day basis. As the sole source of short-term finance, Gosbank is in a strategic position to be alerted to enterprises that are having difficulties in meeting planned obligations. For example, enterprises borrow funds on a short-term basis — that is, for thirty to ninety days — because receipts from sales to other enterprises or to individuals do not come in at the same rate that expenses are incurred for wages, materials, fuel, and the like. Short-term borrowing helps to smooth out these discrepancies between the "time shapes" of receipts and disbursements. It also affords Gosbank an index of enterprise performance, because a slower rate of inflow of sales receipts than called for in the plan may reflect subpar performance. Excessive wage payments would also tend to violate limits set for short-term borrowing in the firm's plan.

As a result of its strategic position with respect to Soviet moneyflows, Gosbank is to day-to-day operations of Soviet enterprises and collective farms what Gosplan is to annual, quarterly, and monthly budgeting. It has the power to demand explanations and even to force an enterprise into bankruptcy. Gosbank also holds the deposits of the various governmental units, which puts it into a position to register flows of tax payments and other transfers among governmental units, enterprise, and the population. Money represents power in any pecuniary economy, and Gosbank gains its power and authority from its strategic position astride the main moneyflows.

Gosbank is much more concerned with the supervision of moneyflows than it is with monetary policy. In this respect it spends most of its time performing the duties of a very conservative commercial bank in the United States. Monetary and financial policies at the aggregate level in the USSR have different objectives than in most western economies. The object of financial policy at the aggregate level is to arrive at a macroeconomic balance for the economy as a whole and for each major sector and subsector of the economy. The income of the population is estimated for the plan period and is monitored closely as the plan unfolds to make it correspond with the goods and services available for purchase during the period, plus tax and other transfers from and to households, plus the increase in savings desired by the population. The Ministry of Finance is responsible for putting together the basic balances for the state enterprise sector, for collective farms, for budgetary receipts and outlays, and so forth. Gosbank is responsible for keeping track of these flows, for identifying problems, and for correcting discrepancies.

Because there are no open financial markets and because there is no government bond market, Gosbank is not involved in attempting to influence credit through interest-rate policy. Enterprises are charged a flat low rate on short-term borrowing. Another rate of interest, somewhat higher, is paid by collective farms and enterprises on long-term borrowing. Savings deposits of individuals earn two different low rates of interest, depending upon the liquidity of the deposit. All of these rates are too low to serve as means for rationing credit. None is higher than 3 percent per annum. The flow of credit is determined elsewhere, primarily in the planning process. Monetary policy is not directed, therefore, as it is in western capitalist countries, to the manipulation of borrowing and lending behavior; nor is it directed so as to influence spending decisions or to maintain an orderly market for government securities. The rate of saving and the rate of investment are determined independently of the various rates of interest that obtain in the Soviet economy and are not important issues for monetary policy. Similarly monetary and banking authorities need not concern themselves about the impact of monetary policy upon the rate of unemployment, or the rate of inflation, or about rationing investment funds among transactors — as, for example, between residential construction and the construction of productive facilities.

Gosbank and the Ministry of Finance, which work closely on monetary policy, look at their functions from a different perspective than do comparable institutions in western capitalist countries. Their job is to manage the monetary stock so that the needs of trade are met — that is, so that enterprises and other transactors are just supplied with adequate cash to meet their spending needs, to monitor and supervise spending of all state enterprises and agencies, to enforce planned maxima and minima contained in the various plans, and, when necessary, to take action to offset adverse impacts (unplanned spending, borrowing, and so forth) on the flow of funds.

There is neither a legal nor a theoretical limit on the size of the stock of money Gosbank can permit. The size of the stock of money is governed by the expenditure rates and patterns of transactors and by the cash balances (plus savings accounts) individuals and transactors wish to hold. Transactions among enterprises are settled by special (offset) procedures, and these balances are not transferable to spendable cash. Enterprises pay cash wages and salaries, but these funds are actually disbursed by officers of the bank and never sit anywhere as a balance. The state budget receives payments into its account with the Gosbank both from enterprises, in the form of turnover-tax receipts and profit withdrawals, and from individuals; and it pays out funds to both. Individuals receive money wages and salaries from enterprise and government employments, and they pay out money to purchase goods and services from state and cooperative stores and to meet taxes; and they save the rest either in Gosbank accounts or in hand-to-hand currency. When Gosbank seeks to "offset" adverse, or other unplanned flows of funds, its concern is ordinarily with the impact of these flows upon personal income and expenditures. Consequently wage payments are closely monitored to ensure against unauthorized flows of personal income. Retail outlets are restricted to minimum "till cash" and are required to deposit receipts promptly to avoid misappropriation of funds. An increase in the cash surplus of the state budget, for example, or an increase in private savings deposits, for another, may be viewed as offsets to unanticipated increases in money wages.

The plan, therefore, governs, but cannot determine exactly, the activities of Gosbank and the size of the stock of money. The success of Gosbank in restricting expenditures of enterprises to those called for in the plan, in turn, determines the success of the plan in matching personal income with the spending and saving preferences of the household sector. Gosbank plays an important role, therefore, in trying to ensure that the economic game is played by the rules and according to plan.

Fiscal policy is also primarily restricted to the planning and monitoring of tax and other transfer flows. It is not the responsibility of the state budget (Gosbiudzhet) to concern itself about the impact of government expenditures or of tax rates upon inflation, upon the level of economic activity, or upon aggregate employment. These are matters determined in the planning process. The central government budget is, therefore, a much less active economic agency than is the case in most capitalist countries. It serves with the Gosbank, however, to keep track of moneyflows and to monitor plan performance.

Beginning in the 1930s the Soviet fiscal system was streamlined into two principal channels. The turnover tax is levied primarily on consumer goods and services and is levied as a percentage of trade turnover. It is a type of sales tax. The other principal source of funds that developed in the 1930s is profit withdrawals, which reflects the deduction into the state budget of profits earned by state enterprises. These two main sources have always been supplemented by other types of taxes. Collective-farm income is taxed, and the tax on income from private-plot sales used to be onerous. Direct taxes on the population, however, are light and are not significantly progressive. With the exception of World War II, during which direct taxes, collections, and fees on the population were increased substantially to finance the war effort, direct taxes on personal income have been used primarily to discourage certain types of income-earning activities rather than as major sources of tax revenue.

Until the 1960s the principal tax was the turnover tax on consumer goods. Since 1970, however, profit withdrawals have provided the largest source of revenue — more than 35 percent of all state-budget receipts. The shift from turnover tax to profit withdrawals as the main source of government revenue reflects a gradual elimination of the turnover tax on many food products as prices paid to farms and farmers increased while retail prices remained unchanged. In fact for many food commodities, such as meat, the state actually pays a subsidy because the retail price does not cover the full cost of producing, processing, and distributing the product. Profit withdrawals from enterprises producing industrial consumer goods have increased in the meantime, reflecting the cost savings of technical progress and of mass production.

The state budget distributes funds to finance the defense budget, the flow of investment funds through Stroibank to state enterprises, the flow of subsidies to state enterprises that operate at a loss, and the flow of various social security benefits, including medical care, pensions, child-care benefits, and so forth. These flows, as for inflows of revenues, are represented in the plan; and it is the state budget's responsibility to monitor them during the year and to investigate any unplanned developments. The state budget is also concerned with verifying the uses to which funds are put and ensuring that legal tax rates and other payments mandated to the budget are observed.

Output, Moneyflows, and Central Planning

When viewed from the top, the apex of the economic bureaucracy, the economy consists of a number of interrelated systems. The flows of actual physical products and services are related by technological and behavioral relationships that seldom change swiftly. The production and distribution of a given tonnage of high-grade steel requires quantities of iron and other ores, fuel, and man hours that are jointly determined by technology and customary patterns of work. Input-output tables have been constructed for the Soviet economy that portray the economy as a technical array of coefficients for the transformation of physical inputs of materials, fuel, and manpower into products. Central planners in the USSR have been particularly interested in the physical flows that are depicted in an input-output matrix, and the actual plan expressed in physical units may be conceived as an approximation of such a matrix.

The economy, however, is not a machine, and the relationship that exists between outputs and inputs is not adequately described by this kind of matrix. An input-output table ignores moneyflows, pecuniary incentives, labor-management conflicts, and other factors that do not lend themselves to representation as technological coefficients; but no one doubts that the coefficients are sensitive to these factors, which form other related systems of the economy. Another way of thinking about an economy is to conceive it as a collection of more or less stable stimulus-response patterns. Systems of pecuniary incentives represent such stimulus-response systems, and they may be used to guide and channel economic activity. Accounting and budgeting procedures form another stimulus-response system. These and similar systems provide a basis for manipulating or controlling behavior of the various transactors that compose the economy by modifying moneyflows, budgets, monetary payoffs, and expectations.

If an economy resembled a machine, it would be easier to plan centrally, for accurate planning requires accurate prediction of input-output relationships. The more stable these relationships, the better the plan, other things equal. Similarly the more the economy resembled a set of stable stimulus-response patterns, the easier it would be to shape economic behavior of transactors who are otherwise free to do as they please. Central planning by an agency such as Gosplan, therefore, is based upon an attempt to use both technological coefficients and stable stimulus-response patterns to prearrange economic outcomes. Because the central plan cannot be perfect, however, a certain amount of central management will be necessary as the plan unfolds; and central management will depend upon existing stimulus-response patterns for its success.

The Soviet economy is, therefore, a centrally managed as well as a centrally planned economy. Gosplan is primarily concerned with central planning. Gosbank, Gosbiudzhet, and the Council of Ministers are primarily concerned with central management of the economy. Therefore a trade-off occurs between central planning and central management. The better central planning the less central management that is required for any given degree of control, and vice versa. Because central planning cannot be perfect, some combination of management and planning is necessary.

As was indicated above, Soviet planners and high-level economic decision-makers aspire to command planning, which may be defined in this context as a preference for central planning over central management. The President's Council of Economic Advisors, the Federal Reserve Board, and the other economic agencies of the federal government in the United States represent the reverse preference — that is, a preference for central management over central planning. To a Soviet planner or economist, central management in the absence of a central plan seems a mindless exercise. Soviet central planning, however, is similarly handicapped by the weakness of, and prejudice against, instruments of central management. By and large the deficiencies of central management in the Soviet economy derive not from inadequacies in the over-all view from the top or in readily correctible errors at the top in the planning process. The problem has to do with the structure of incentives at the bottom and with the fact that central management devices do not mesh properly with existing systems of incentives. Let us turn, therefore, to the view from the bottom.

SELECTED READINGS

Bornstein, Morris, and Fusfeld, Daniel R., eds. *The Soviet Economy: A Book of Readings*. 4th ed. Homewood, Ill.: Richard D. Irwin, 1974.
Gregory, Paul R., and Stuart, Robert C. *Soviet Economic Structure and Performance*. New York: Harper & Row, 1974.
Grossman, Gregory. "An Economy at Middle Age." *Problems of Communism* 25 (March-April 1976), 18-33.

Hough, Jerry F., and Fainsod, Merle. *How the Soviet Union Is Governed.* Cambridge, Mass.: Harvard University Press, 1979.

Katsenelenboigen, Aaron. *Studies in Soviet Economic Planning.* White Plains, N.Y.: M.E. Sharpe, 1978.

Wollan, Christine N. "The Financial Policy of the Soviet State Bank, 1932-1970." Ph.D. dissertation, University of Illinois at Urbana-Champaign, 1972.

4

The Household Sector:
The View from the Bottom

Introduction: A Methodological Note

Most western economists assume that the purpose of economic activity is to satisfy individual members of society, and Soviet economists are no exception to this rule. N. Ia Petrakov, a well-known Soviet economist, defined the aim recently as "maximization of the average level of satisfaction of the needs of all members of society." Placement of the individual consumer at the center of the economic universe represents a prescriptive rather than a descriptive judgment, and I concur in the desirability of this view. From a descriptive standpoint, however, several other possible ways of construing ends and means in an economic system exist, and each approach presents certain advantages and disadvantages for analysis.

If we assume that satisfaction of the wants of the individual is the sole and proper end of all economic activity, then we shall find it difficult to justify certain kinds of government expenditures that we all take for granted, such as defense expenditures, welfare outlays, and the like, where benefits and costs are not distributed according to the individual's evaluations. Moreover our analysis cannot deal satisfactorily with a situation in which one individual's satisfaction depends upon another's fortune or misfortune. We must assume away both envy and saintliness.

Karl Marx assumed that all-round physical and intellectual fulfillment of the individual would become the goal of economic activity under socialism, at which time the creation of economic plenty would have undermined self-interest as motive to economic activity and thus the rationale for both envy and saintliness. He assumed that profit would be the goal of economic activity while capitalism prevailed, and he accordingly described the capitalist economy as based upon the exploitation of the many by the few in the quest for profits. The consumer is not, therefore, the end for capitalist economies in Marx's analysis. Similar assumptions have been, and are still, often made by non-Marxists too, particularly by certain social reformers, such as consumer advocates or environmental protectionists who see a conflict between the interests of ordinary people and those of giant corporations in quest of profits. Although this assumption often offers an interesting construction for thinking about the economy, it also presents problems from an analytic standpoint. Marx, for example, never did explain why capitalists were devoted to the maximization of profits, nor how they could remain blind to a growing conflict of their interests with those of workers and consumers that would, in his view, ultimately eject capitalists from the system. Marx also failed to explain what kinds of motives would ensure satisfactory production of goods and services for use rather than for profits in a system in which distribution would be according to need.

Thorstein Veblen drew a different distinction — between productive and pecuniary employments by which he attempted to divide economic activities into those that serve matter of fact — *real* human needs and those that serve meretricious needs derived from ignorance, gullibility, or propaganda. Hence he adopted the assumption that individual consumers *ought* to be the goal of economic activity, but tried to constrain their needs to a rational, scientifically based set of requirements. Veblen would have restricted economic activities to those that involve providing socially acceptable goods or services. In this respect he sought to combine the best features of both the neoclassical and Marxian approaches. The problem remains, of course, in distinguishing unambiguously between the good and the bad products. Veblen thought that this distinction would be resolved by a natural process of scientific enlightenment, but it is clear some sixty years later that this was too optimistic a view.

I have reviewed these various assumptions about what the goal of economic activity ought to be in order to emphasize the evaluative and thus the relative nature of any such assumption. Many western students of the Soviet economy have sought to describe it as an economy in which planners' preferences prevail. That is, they assume that the purpose of economic activity is to satisfy those who plan the economic system. The term *planner* is used here in what is ultimately a political and not at all an operational sense. The Politburo, not Gosplan, represents the planners in question. This assumption, like the others I have mentioned above, has certain advantages when it comes to describing central planning, especially where it is conceived as command planning. There are other advantages that make it attractive when describing the Soviet economy, where economic goals are at once also high political issues. Even so, as with any such assumption, it is not a purely descriptive concept. It was derived as the obverse of a system of consumer preferences, and no analyst has ever put it forward anywhere as a *desirable long-term basis* for organizing economic activity. It is a pejorative standard instead, and for good reason. Although never fully worked out, it would appear that an economy organized strictly according to the principal of planners' preferences would ultimately have to be an economy in which everyone who is not a planner would be a slave — or perhaps a mindless contributor to economic activity like a worker bee or ant.

We shall have recourse to all of the standards I have described in considering the place of the household in the Soviet economy. We shall see that there is more than a grain of truth in the claim of contemporary Soviet economists that individual satisfaction is the aim of economic activity, and it is useful in any case to assess the discrepancies between such a standard and Soviet reality. Similarly it will be informative to see to what extent the Soviet economy departs from the standard of planners' preferences and to try to understand how consumer and planner preferences are in fact mediated. We shall also find the standards erected by Veblen and by Marx useful alternative measures. As everywhere it is not always easy to distinguish "goods" from "bads" when it comes to the products of the Soviet or any other economy, and the contrast that Marx drew between capitalism and socialism is helpful because it raises two fundamental and as yet unresolved problems in the economics of distribution and the ethics of human conduct. If distribution of the products of economic activity is to be set according to need, how can this be reconciled with the demand that any incentive system, to be effective, must reward individuals according to their contributions? But if individuals are instead to be rewarded strictly according to their contributions to the economy, what do we do with the helpless? Moreover, do we not thereby also reinforce "lower" rather than "higher" forms of human conduct, thereby sacrificing saintliness and enhancing invidious comparison, envy, and unabashed self-interest? Are self-regard and greed the only workable bases of economic activity?

The View from the Bottom

By describing households as the bottom of the Soviet economy I mean to contrast the perspective of a single household with that of an agency such as the Council of Ministers or Gosplan, not to indicate the ranking of the household. Individual households look out upon the economy from narrow and highly differentiated windows. The view from the bottom is a collection of views, and we shall build up a reasonably comprehensive and representative general view from the separate standpoints of various households. Although no one household has as broad a view as members of an agency such as the Council of Ministers, there are aspects of household experience that are not visible from the top. The view from the top is not better nor more complex than the view from the bottom. It is merely different.

Over 55 percent of the Soviet population now lives in regions classified as urban, but this is a recent development and a large proportion of the urban population of the USSR is first-generation urban. Approximately 25 percent of the labor force is still directly engaged in agricultural pursuits in the Soviet Union, as opposed to less than 4 percent in the United States. The exodus from the rural community has been exceedingly rapid during the last decade, averaging about 2 million persons per year. This rapid outflow from the rural sector reflects the great differential that exists between standards of living in rural and in urban areas of the USSR, and the outflow is impoverishing the rural community, because the young, the energetic, the educated, and the ambitious are the ones who are leaving.

By comparison with the United States or the countries of Western Europe such as France, Italy, or Germany, the USSR is still highly rural in character and is experiencing rapid demographic change. Moreover the gap between living conditions and professional prospects in rural and urban areas is much greater than in the West. The USSR occupies a very large area, equal to about one-sixth of the surface of the earth. By world standards, it is still lightly populated. Population tends to be concentrated in European Russia, but even this is a large region, and population density is low by comparison with most developed economies. The transportation network is huge when measured in total kilometers. Densities remain relatively low, however, especially in the vast reaches of Siberia and Central Asia. Consequently the isolation of rural communities is far greater than in the West, and the absence of any significant number of private automobiles or trucks in rural areas is a contributing factor to their isolation. There is no equivalent in the

USSR to the pickup truck of the American farm to take the family into town on weekends. There are some regions so remote, in fact, that there is virtually no exit for months at a time during the winter. Television reaches most of these communities, but its message is the superiority of urban life, especially urban life in the choice cities of the USSR: Moscow, Leningrad, Kiev.

Not just anyone may decide to live in a city. In order to obtain an apartment or room in a Soviet city, the individual must ordinarily be employed in the city, but it is hard to find employment unless one already lives in the city. If an individual wishes to live in Moscow, for example, he could sign up with the labor exchange and take his chances on being assigned to Moscow. No one in his right mind would expect so far-fetched a hope to come true. Moscow is the most difficult city of all to move to permanently. Successful provincial administrators and party officials often are assigned to Moscow in the twilight years of their careers as a special sign of preferment and as a reward for faithful service, but ordinary folk are assigned to the regions and cities that are slated for net growth, not to Moscow. Restrictions on movement to desirable cities such as Moscow can be circumvented, but essentially only by exceptional professional success, subterfuge, or *blat*. *Blat* is probably the most important. *Blat* is used by Russians to refer to pull, connections, or string-pulling that is used to advance one's own or one's family's interests. (The polite word for *blat* is *protektsiia* [protection].)

There is a hierarchy of living conditions in the Soviet Union, with Moscow at the pinnacle and the remote villages of Siberia and Central Asia at the bottom. The upward slope measures more than access to cultural events such as the Bolshoi Ballet or the Mayakovsky Theater. Moscovites live at the center of political power, which acts as a magnet for all of the good things in Soviet life. Food supplies are more reliable and abundant in Moscow than elsewhere. Industrial commodities designed for consumers gravitate to Moscow. Housing is superior; the provision of child-care centers is more adequate; and so it goes.

Since Moscow is the political hub of a highly centralized bureaucracy, it is the best place to get things done. Moscow is the city of blat, an artificial city reflecting the best and the worst in the USSR. People who live elsewhere in the USSR must make periodic trips to this political and economic Mecca of the Soviet system to have petitions heard, to meet with superiors, to buy commodities available nowhere else, and to vacation richly. Peasants come to Moscow from the outlying regions with their bags packed with fruit, vegetables, honey, and anything else that can be sold on the rynok (private market). After selling everything, they go to see Lenin's remains in Red Square. Next they spend in Moscow everything they earned at the rynok, buying things for themselves and their friends; and they return home with their bags packed with clothing, toys, rugs, china, meat, and phonograph records. Although the details differ, a similar pattern obtains for everyone who lives outside the gates of Moscow and the other major urban centers of the USSR.

We shall begin our examination of the household sector in Moscow and work our way back along the slope down to the muddy lanes of a Siberian village. Along the way we shall need to consider differentiating factors other than urban location. National and ethnic differences, the place of women, and other factors need to be evaluated as well. Moscow is unique in many such respects, and we must bear this in mind in considering the view from the Moscovite window.

Private Enterprise and Property

The institution of private property exists in the Soviet Union, but it is circumscribed by state (public) ownership of the "means of production," which are defined to include all land, mineral wealth, and most of the reproducible capital. Private individuals may own, and are free to sell privately, or to sell through state stores that sell on commission, a wide range of items of personal property. These include not only articles of clothing, television sets, refrigerators, and other personal effects, but also certain types of capital equipment such as hand tools, typewriters, gardening supplies, and the like, plus such large items of nonproductive capital as automobiles, apartments, and houses. Moreover certain attributes of private property adhere to some forms of state property in that the right to use the property can in fact be alienated and transferred to another private party for personal gain. Families may, for example, trade state-owned apartments with each other for mutual benefit. A newly formed family, for example, where wife and husband are legally entitled to and already hold two separate one-room apartments, may trade these for a two or three-room apartment that houses two families. Similarly a state-owned apartment located in a desirable city such as Moscow may be traded for an apartment in a less desirable city, plus "considerations."

Buying, selling, and trading of personal property is a perfectly legal and open activity either through state "commission" outlets or directly. Certain locations in each city have become trading centers where advertisements are posted and meetings are arranged for purposes of direct trading. The owner of the property, or the property right, is free to charge what the market will bear, without government interference. Legal marketing, of course, shades imperceptibly into illegal trading. Certain types of transactions are proscribed, such as the exchange of rubles for foreign currency. It is also illegal to serve as a middleman in private transactions. That is, one may not legally purchase goods for the purpose of reselling them for personal gain. The deciding factor is intent, because a large number of such private transactions do in fact take place at a profit to the seller. It is also illegal to purchase an apartment or an automobile for the purpose of leasing it or otherwise using it as a source of income.

Although no private individual may own land in the Soviet Union, every citizen who is in good legal standing is provided with access through one avenue or another to land for private use. Collective-farm workers receive a plot of land on which to build a home and to maintain a kitchen garden as a function of satisfactory work on the collective farm. The legal situation for state-farm workers is different, but actual arrangements are essentially the same as for collective-farm workers. The great bulk of privately produced and privately marketed food products derives from these two types of private-plot agriculture. Rural households not engaged directly in agricultural employments, such as the local schoolteacher or a clerk in a consumer-cooperative (rural) outlet, are provided access to plots of land on which to build homes, to keep animals, and to tend gardens. Urban dwellers are also provided access to small plots of land on the outskirts of town, where they may build a dacha and keep a garden. Because the location is not ordinarily convenient, city dwellers rarely build substantial dwellings on the plots. They are used instead to build dachas as summer and/or winter retreats, and most of them are primitive and have few modern conveniences. Ownership of free-standing homes is, therefore, primarily a rural and primitive phenomenon. Similarly few urban dwellers use their plots to raise substantial gardens.

The ways in which urban dwellers gain access to plots of land are complex and varied, and the size of the plot to which individuals are entitled varies by type of access. A worker may obtain a plot of land through the enterprise for which he or she works. A military officer ordinarily receives a plot through the military bureaucracy. Individuals not otherwise covered may obtain plots of land through the city administration, or through a cooperative arrangement, and so forth. Over one-half of the privately held plots of land in the Soviet Union today are held by members of the nonagricultural population.

It has become increasingly popular for individuals to build, or purchase, apartments under cooperative arrangements. Many cooperatives are organized by a place of work, such as the Academy of Sciences, Moscow State University, and Gosplan; and employees sign up to purchase from their employer. The usual arrangements call for 20 percent down payment and the remainder in installments, frequently without interest. Apartments purchased in this way are expensive, but they offer the roomiest and most comfortable living quarters available in the major cities. A group of private individuals may also arrange to build a condominium and borrow a portion of the cost from the Gosbank. In this instance an interest charge is involved, normally 2 percent per annum. Apartment ownership affords the individual in the Soviet Union the largest and probably the most lucrative investment available for private ownership and potential gain. Individuals who purchase an apartment do not pay anything for the land on which the building sits, which is a considerable private benefit in any major city.

In addition to apartments, automobiles, and other consumer durables, individuals may purchase jewelry, paintings, rare books, and similar items as forms of private savings. Private individuals may also own financial assets, which include hand-to-hand currency, savings accounts with the state bank, and state 3 percent lottery bonds. A type of checking account is now available to certain Soviet citizens, but it is of little domestic use in an economy in which almost all payments are made in cash. Apart from interest receipts on savings accounts and winnings on state-lottery bonds, income from property is illegal in the Soviet Union. One may lend money to a friend, but charging interest would violate the law. Under certain circumstances one may receive something in consideration for subletting one's apartment or for renting a room (a "corner") to a student, but it is not legal to go into the business of taking in boarders or renting out apartments.

All private wealth may be legally inherited in the Soviet Union. Survivors ordinarily have first claim on the family apartment or dacha, and in this respect certain aspects of private ownership attach to such publicly owned items.

All other property, with the sole exception of collective farms, whose members are supposed to have indivisible (that is, inalienable) rights in the farms' capital stock, is publicly owned in the Soviet Union. Therefore the profits of state enterprises and rental payments of the population residing in state housing are paid into the various governmental budgets. The state claims all property income in the name of the people, and uses income from it to finance investment in state enterprises and to finance construction of new housing and other outlays.

Private enterprise is not actually prohibited, but it is severely limited by prohibitions on hiring others for personal profit, on middleman activities, and on private ownership of the means of production. What private enterprise does exist is necessarily small-scale. The line between legal and illegal private enterprise is not an easy one to draw. Individuals may sell newly produced items that they or their families have produced — for example, on private plots; and they may sell "secondhand" items too. A writer may hire a typist to type his manuscripts; families may hire housekeepers and babysitters; and anyone may hire work to be done or repairs to be made around the house, even though such hiring may contribute to personal income by making the hirer more efficient or by freeing him or her to earn more money elsewhere. True private enterprise is restricted in the Soviet Union to the sale of products of private agricultural plots and to one-man enterprises for home repairs or to such sideline activities as taking patients or clients after work. A large proportion of the latter two categories is conducted in the penumbra of the legal. Nevertheless private enterprise is ubiquitous and significant in almost everyone's economic life.

Most Soviet citizens work for the state in one way or another for wages or salaries, and most older members of Soviet society receive pensions from the state. Although at one time an attempt was made to maximize the share of earnings that the worker received in direct nonmonetary benefits, this is no longer the case. Education is free, including higher education in which success in entrance examinations assures all successful applicants free access plus a stipend. Medical care is free too. Prescription drugs are highly subsidized, as are public transport and even the apartments that most urban dwellers rent from the state. Meals are served very cheaply both in schools and at places of work, and child-care facilities (when available) are provided essentially free. Even so the bulk of the typical Soviet household's income is received in money, which necessarily implies the existence of retail outlets in which households may choose the ways that their incomes are distributed among the various goods, services, and financial assets that are available. Hence we see the importance of urban retail markets in the USSR.

Urban Retail Markets

Urban consumers are served by four different types of retail markets. All urban areas are served by state retail outlets. The great bulk of urban household income is expended in these shops. Soviet marketing follows the general European pattern, and most state retail outlets specialize in particular types of products, such as fish, meat and dairy products, bread and confectionary items, clothing, drugs, paper supplies, and so forth. The supermarket and the discount house are found rarely in Moscow and a few other large cities. Most families shop everyday in the assortment of stores in their neighborhoods, purchasing bread in one, milk and dairy products in another, meat in a third, and beer in a fourth. Before American-style retail marketing could become widespread even in Moscow, the average household would have to buy a larger refrigerator, and automobile ownership would have to quadruple. What supermarkets do exist in Moscow work poorly because crowds are too great. One must queue to enter various departments of the store, which defeats a main function of supermarketing. Household members would also have to become accustomed to eating food that is several days old, which would require both a revolution in Soviet packaging and a deterioration in the average citizen's tastes.

Prices are fixed for state retail outlets and are not subject to bargaining. Restaurants and hotels are all state retail enterprises in the Soviet Union too, and uniform pricing frequently causes anomalies. For example, most meat markets do not grade the meat that they sell by cut. Butchers (who work only with meat axes) divide the meat into portions that are equally composed of good and poor sections of the animal. The flat two-ruble charge per kilo is "justified" in this way. If one knows the butcher, the effective price for "good" cuts may be very low. Similarly, prices on similar dishes are exactly the same in good restaurants as well as bad. Consequently a meal in a good restaurant is a great bargain, and the same meal in a poor restaurant may be indigestible.

Two kinds of subsidies obtain for many state retail outlets, therefore. Many food products are substantially underpriced and are directly subsidized by the state budget. Most meat products, especially beef, are instances. Underpricing tends to cause queuing for the products affected, not because people go hungry or do without adequate protein, but because at state-quoted prices, which retail outlets cannot vary, these goods are a great bargain. Uniform pricing and the restricted mobility of the typical Soviet customer causes customers of poorly run shops and restaurants to subsidize the well run. Because the better managed shops cannot expand and compete with the poorly run, these differences tend to be self-perpetuating.

An experienced and energetic Soviet shopper learns where to shop for particular items in order to take advantage of peculiarities caused by uniform prices and variations in quality. The system rewards specialized knowledge, friendship, and reciprocity. Goods do not get distributed evenly, and as we have seen, the farther one lives from a major city the less likely that any desirable commodities will ever appear. Meat, including beef, is usually relatively plentiful in Moscow; but 200 kilometers away probably none is to be found most of the time. Moreover goods are not distributed evenly within the confines of a city such as Moscow. For complex and little understood reasons, certain shops tend to get better and more reliable supplies than others. A certain buffet in a dormitory, for example, may almost always have beer in stock, while regular retail outlets run dry for days at a time. State retail outlets also operate "casual" stands and kiosks for "surplus" items at irregular intervals as well as their regular outlets. An alert shopper learns that certain corners frequently have temporary outlets where particularly desirable goods (such as oranges and apples in winter) are sold when available. By keeping an eye on these locations, remembering which stores nearly always have milk or beer or better meat, and by staying alert to the formation of a queue anywhere, a smart shopper can maximize his opportunities to procure what Soviets call "deficit commodities." The term is used to refer to goods or services that are in short supply all or most of the time. Although there are exceptions, deficit commodities are underpriced items in the state retail network, which causes excess demand to exist for them most of the time.

It pays to make friends with sellers in the USSR, for nearly all the desirable goods that are sold in Soviet state retail outlets are in deficit supply and require the exercise of purchasemanship, the technical equivalent of salesmanship in an economy such as that of the United States. A judicious gift may get deficit commodities set aside for you. Tickets to the Bolshoi Theater ballet performances, for example, ordinarily are impossible to obtain in any normal way from a ticket window in Moscow. They are all either specially ordered for tourists, high officials, and special purposes, or they are distributed under the counter. Soviet shoppers worth their salt develop networks of contacts among those who sell or distribute state retail products and services which allow them to jump the queue for deficit commodities. Frequently the recipient of such a favor is not required to pay extra for it, but he or she incurs a reciprocal obligation for the future.

Most deficit commodities and services are goods and services provided through state retail outlets, and the individuals who market them can collect what economists call the monopoly rents on these scarce and underpriced items. That is, the employee is in a position to capture a part, or all, of the difference between the actual price established by the state committee on retail prices and the (higher) price that would be required to clear the market (that is, exactly match the number of buyers with the number of items available). For all intents and purposes this is a property right individuals acquire by default from the state and are able to exchange for the other deficit commodities they desire.

The second type of retail outlet is the rynok (also called the collective farm market). About one-third of the value of all retail food sales in the USSR flows through the rynok, which is a completely unfettered market where farmers and others who have grown or produced their own products may hire a stall (and refrigeration if necessary) to sell them. Collective farms may ship their surplus produce to the rynok too. Every city has one or more such markets. Many are enclosed for operation during the winter. Typical products available are carrots, potatoes, pickled cucumbers, tomatoes, peppers and apples, pickled cabbage, honey, cheese and fermented dairy products, dried mushrooms, flowers, spices, seed, and fresh meat in winter time; and the list includes more fruits and vegetables in summer. Prices are generally much higher on the rynok than in state retail stores, and one is free to haggle about price. Many Soviet shoppers visit the rynok at least once a week, even though it is more expensive than state outlets. Quality tends to be higher, and some items sold there are unavailable in other retail outlets. Anyone planning a dinner party would be certain to visit the rynok to buy a delicacy or two. The role of the rynok is probably less significant in Moscow than it is elsewhere as a source of staples such as potatoes, milk products, meat, and vegetables because these items are more readily available in state outlets in Moscow. Even so, Moscovites are relatively wealthy and able to afford the higher prices charged on the rynok. As a general proposition, it is fair to say that the rynok plays a pervasive role in the supply of food products to the Soviet household, and all would be poorer without it. Thus, strange as it seems, most Soviet households deal regularly in a perfectly legal free market for day-to-day needs.

The third type of retail market available to urban dwellers is a private, informal, and legal market in homemade and in secondhand commodities, in apartments and in certain personal services, such as television repair and hairdressing. The state operates secondhand stores on a commission basis. In addition certain corners have become customary trading sites, and individuals meet there at customary times privately to trade apartments and to sell used automobiles, clothing, records, and the like. Much of this trade is barter, and some of the items that are traded, such as state-owned apartments, are not in fact the property of those trading them. Newspapers take advertisements for certain types of goods, and both formal and informal bulletin boards are used to place advertisements. In addition, certain individuals sell their labor services informally. Any person with a skill, such as repairing electrical equipment, may work on the side on his own time. Whether or not the activity is legal depends upon the nature of the service, the source of spare parts used, and the social implications. Unskilled women frequently do laundry for busy single men, and they may help in shopping, child care, and cooking on a strictly private basis.

This third category of legal informal marketing is difficult to identify uniquely, for it shades off into illegal economic activities on the one side and into legal state-organized secondhand markets on the other. It is worth attempting to isolate this category because of the private and legal character of these transactions. It is important to grasp the volume and diversity of private economic transactions that take place in the USSR on a perfectly legal basis. These transactions are also absolutely unavoidable if the institution of private property in personal possessions is to have operational significance. Open exchange of private property is also important as a means for redistributing durable property from those who no longer require it to those who need it. As with garage sales in the United States, in the process everyone is made better off without anyone being harmed.

Illegal market transactions comprise the fourth and final type of retail market in the Soviet Union. This market is very complex and ranges from misdemeanors to very sinister economic dealings. Because these transactions are illegal, the outside observer can obtain only a very sketchy impression of them. The evidence suggests, however, that illegal trading at the level of misdemeanor is widespread. A large proportion of the Soviet urban population is implicated — at least on a petty level. Illegal transactions are described variously by Soviet citizens. Soviets talk of obtaining goods *nalevo* (on the left), *po znakomstvu* (through a contact), *na chernom rynke* (on the black market), and *po blatu* (through pull). Each describes an important aspect of this market. Buying po znakomstvu is perhaps the most common and least criminal of all. In many circumstances it is more improper than illegal. Normally in this type of purchase no direct pecuniary gain is involved for the friend, who instead merely earns a reciprocal claim upon the purchaser. Purchases on the black market are ordinarily from private entrepreneurs who operate for a profit. Blat, on the other hand, can be accrued either by bribing someone or by being someone important with whom others seek to curry favor. The most colorful phrase, buying nalevo, is the most general: its meaning encompasses the entire range of illegal and semilegal activities, both in markets and outside of them, that are encouraged by the institutional and legal structure of the Soviet economy. (Although it may offend the ears of native speakers of Russian, for convenience I shall henceforward use nalevo as an adjective as well as an adverb.)

The most desirable consumer goods and services are in deficit supply most of the time in the Soviet economy, and yet prices on these deficit commodities are kept constant. Consequently queues always develop when these commodities become available, and those who deal in them for the state cannot but be tempted to take advantage of their strategic monopolistic positions to increase their own incomes, to curry favor with superiors, or to benefit their friends. Oddly enough, then, the institutional structure of the Soviet economy actually fosters a large volume of petty trading, petty middleman activities, and petty private enterprise. Today the Soviet Union is an acquisitive society, a nation of marketeers; and an enormous amount of time is absorbed in shopping, selling, trading, scouting, and queuing for deficit commodities.

Consumption and Living Standards

By the most careful western estimates, consumption per capita has almost doubled since Stalin's death in 1953. The fact that deficit commodities remain numerous reflects both the incredibly low standard of living at the end of postwar reconstruction and the continuation of official policies that tend to perpetuate such deficits. In planning the volume of consumer goods and services to be made available, Gosplan must consider two aspects. First it is obvious that the total value of consumer goods and services provided by the state must have *some* relationship to the quantity of labor the state intends to employ and the average earnings of these workers. Second, and more important, the more developed the society is, the proportions in which the different consumer goods are produced (that is, how many automobiles, refrigerators, and sewing machines, and how much meat, milk, and wool cloth to produce) must bear a definite relationship to the way in which consumers wish to distribute their incomes among them. The output of consumer goods has increased very sharply in the USSR over the last twenty-five years, but changes in the composition of output have not kept pace, perpetuating the existence of deficit commodities.

Prices in state retail outlets are set by a state committee of the Council of Ministers, and they reflect many factors other than supply and demand. Prices on many items of food, such as bread, meat, and milk, have been set below cost, whereas prices on certain scarce luxury goods are set relatively high, approximating supply-demand conditions. Therefore willingness to stand in line becomes a factor in the distribution of many goods, and the final result is a distribution of goods and services that is probably more equal than the distribution of money income. To some extent, this is deliberate policy, but it also reflects a policy of stability in retail prices that Soviet leaders have promised the population ever since Stalin died. Accordingly, apart from surreptitious price changes, mainly on nonessentials, retail prices have increased only marginally in more than two decades. The Soviet population clearly appreciates this policy, for it prevents the erosion of their savings by inflation; and this is particularly important in an economy in which installment payments and other forms of credit buying are not available to consumers.

The policy of price stability has had adverse effects, however. For many food products, notably meats and products of animal husbandry, retail price stability has led to massive subsidies by the state, for the real cost of producing agricultural products has been rising rapidly since 1953. Relative prices for industrial commodities and for agricultural products are completely unrealistic, therefore, and an adjustment is long overdue. Thus far, however, the political leaders have apparently felt that trading nalevo (that is, under the counter) and all that it implies is more acceptable than the adverse reaction they expect to increased prices. Eventually, however, an adjustment will have to be made between agricultural products and industrial products, and among individual food products as well.

In addition to a policy that fosters the persistence of deficit commodities, the system of state retail sales outlets is inadequate to the task of supplying the Soviet consumer. Space for retail sales is inadequate. Poor service has no effect upon the incomes of retail service workers, and inventories that cannot be sold do not have a serious impact upon incomes or incentives of those who work in retail outlets. There is little incentive to provide good service, therefore; and that many commodities remain in deficit supply makes service workers surly more often than not. Retail outlets cannot respond to their customers' preferences in any case, but must retail what they receive. The only room for maneuver they have is on an individual basis, which means nalevo.

The scarcity of the more desirable consumer goods and services has become institutionalized officially as well as privately. Whereas the private response has been to expand activities nalevo, the official response has been to create special shops which permit selected people to avoid queuing for deficit commodities. These special groups include foreign tourists, correspondents, and diplomats, which is understandable in a country anxious to earn foreign exchange. But these groups include individuals in Soviet society who are rewarded through special access to stores that are well stocked and do not have queues. The temptation posed by the existence of deficit commodities, which produces trading nalevo privately, yields special stores, with curtained windows to screen out unwelcome eyes, for high-placed party and government officials and for other successful people as well. The right to purchase deficit commodities in special stores or by special order is clearly a powerful incentive in the Soviet economy, and it certainly makes sense to exempt hard-working highly placed officials from queuing with the population. Yet the persistence of deficit commodities is having a negative effect upon the fabric of Soviet life.

The closest analogy in American history is perhaps Prohibition, when keeping the right hand from knowing what the left hand was doing became a national pastime, encouraged general contempt for the law, and facilitated the widespread development of organized crime. The great expansion of trading nalevo and of special stores in the Soviet Union during the last decade or so is undoubtedly not only contributing to similar developments but to widespread cynicism regarding the idealistic goals the regime so often and loudly proclaims.

As I already indicated, Moscow is an artificial city in many respects, particularly when it comes to retail trade. Moscow's retail network is larger and better supplied than elsewhere in the USSR. The state also operates a large number of special stores, most of them known as *berëozki*, where foreigners, and Soviets who somehow acquire foreign currency, or are given special privileges for some official reason, may purchase goods not available elsewhere or may jump the queue on generally scarce items. Naturally there is a good deal of leakage from these special stores into private markets, and foreign visitors and dwellers offer many additional opportunities to purchase foreign-made items, such as blue jeans, Persian coats, and the like, as well as for exchanging currency. Nalevo markets in Moscow are, therefore, also better stocked than elsewhere.

Because of these exceptional opportunities and because of the relative wealth of the city's population, Moscovites are better dressed, better housed, better fed, better entertained, and more sophisticated than Russians in other cities, although Leningraders would be reluctant to agree on all points. Moscovites are also probably more alienated than any comparable population in the USSR too. Certainly it is a hotbed of dissidence. Nonetheless what is true of Moscow is true in one degree or another for other parts of the USSR. The Soviet retail distribution system is sluggish and works only in fits and starts. The farther one gets from Moscow, the less effective it is, and the smaller the community to be served, the worse the service.

Even in Moscow, for example, oranges will suddenly flood the city in the middle of winter. Oranges will be seen being vended everywhere: in regular retail outlets, in dining halls, and on street corners by state retail clerks; and for two weeks there will be an orgy of orange sales and consumption. Just as suddenly as the sale began, it will end because the entire boatload from Egypt or Sicily will have been exhausted. Wise customers, knowing that sales will soon end, will have bought as many oranges as possible. A few weeks later a similar scene will involve lemons, which will have been unavailable for a month or so previously.

Moscow and other large Soviet cities are "black holes" in the Soviet system of retail distribution, which is why smaller communities rarely see deficit commodities in their stores or on their streets. That such commodities appear first in the major cities encourages villagers to visit periodically to exploit their availability, and city folks always buy extra for their relations in less favored retailing regions. In this sense Moscow is the supermarket of the USSR, for the Soviet retail distribution system relies heavily upon private cash-and-carry distribution of deficit commodities beyond the confines of Moscow. An examination of the personal cargoes of individuals returning to Novosibirsk, Omsk, Tomsk, or Irkutsk will provide astounding confirmation of the actual volume of private distribution of deficit commodities. All major cities serve similar roles.

Rural areas are officially served by what is known as consumer cooperatives, but this network only had a true separate existence years ago. Today these outlets are indistinguishable from state retail stores (except, perhaps, in being more poorly stocked), and its employees are state workers. The consumer cooperative network is, if anything, less efficient and effective than the state network, primarily for the reasons given above. In 1974 the total turnover in trade carried on in this system was less than one-half that of state retail outlets, despite the fact that it serves almost as large a population. Consequently those people who live in the thousands and thousands of villages that compose the state and collective farms of the USSR must rely much more heavily than urban dwellers upon their own productive efforts and upon the rural rynok, which is a more informal market than its urban counterpart. Rural dwellers in warm agricultural regions fare quite well when it comes to certain kinds of food products, such as tomatoes, cucumbers, and fruits, which are deficit items in northern cities. Opportunities to trade these products in urban markets can offer substantial profits too. Even so, a drawback for all who live in places distant from major cities is the need both to transport their own products to market and to carry back industrial products at their own expense. Having a relative or two in a major city is an essential condition for reasonable living in most rural regions. In a similar way, although cultural oportunities are provided by state agencies in remote cities and even in villages of the USSR, such appearances are sporadic and rarely include leading performers.

The difference between retail distribution systems in most western capitalist countries and that of the USSR resembles the difference between a gravity-flow and a forced-air central heating system for a building. The latter tends to distribute heat more or less uniformly throughout the building, with only minor losses of efficiency in extreme wings. A gravity system must be properly designed to avoid uneven heating problems. The Soviet retail distribution system resembles a malfunctioning gravity-flow system, with Moscow located in such a way that deficit commodities gravitate to it at the expense of all other regions. Leningrad, Kiev, and Novosibirsk, for example, do better than Novgorod, Alma-Ata, or Irkutsk; and a hierarchy exists in the supply system that stretches all the way to the village. Moreover the state retail system operates primarily on the basis of the tastes and cultural preferences of the great majority of the population that lives in European Russia. There are villages in Siberia and in Central Asia, for example, that are so remote culturally as well as geographically that the state retail system does not penetrate at all. The weakness of the state retail distribution system is, therefore, a powerful contributor to maintenance of the already large discrepancies that exist in the USSR today between urban and rural standards of living.

According to western estimates, the Soviet over-all standard of living has almost doubled since 1953; but this seems difficult to believe when one examines Soviet life firsthand today. It seems unreasonable, in the first place, that the standard of living in 1953 could have been as low as is implied. Our evidence indicates that the standard of living in 1953 was not materially different, over-all, than it had been in 1928; and 1928 was probably not much better than 1913. For forty years, then, Soviet living standards remained at, or below, the prerevolutionary level. In the second place it is not immediately apparent to a contemporary observer what the improvements have been.

The most striking advances in living conditions for anyone who has watched these improvements over the years are in clothing, including shoes; the supply of food, particularly in animal husbandry products, fruits, and vegetables; housing; and in ownership of consumer durables and automobiles. Ten or fifteen years ago, any foreigner in Moscow stood out like a sore thumb because of the quality and cut of his clothing, and his shoes were a dead giveaway too. When women dressed their best in those years they looked inferior to women in ordinary street clothing in Moscow today, and the same holds for men's suits, overcoats, and shoes. Vegetables and fruits were simply never available in the wintertime, and the amount of meat regularly available today is striking by comparison. Housing construction has continued at a high rate for two decades now, and renovation of older dwellings has also been carried out on a large scale. The number of square feet per urban dweller has increased despite a rapid increase in the size of the urban population, and the quality of new apartments has improved because they are self-contained, not communal. Actual construction quality has probably declined, however. Some consumer durables that are commonplace today were rarities only fifteen years ago. Even the peasants have refrigerators today, although many complain that they stay empty most of the time. Sewing machines are widely owned, as are, or course, radios, television sets, and stereo systems. Finally anyone who visited the Soviet Union in the early 1960s and returned for the first time today would be amazed by the number of private automobiles on the streets of Moscow. In the 1960s even Moscow looked like a huge construction site or a giant factory, for the streets carried mainly trucks and buses. The few automobiles were official cars or taxis.

I believe that it is possible to credit a large increase in the Soviet standard of living over the last twenty-five years, but this increase has not been evenly distributed geographically. A visit even to a large city in Siberia, for example, takes one back to the way Moscow looked ten or so years ago. Queues have diminished everywhere, and they exist in the major cities mainly for luxuries — for the best meat, for premium butter, for cucumbers or lemons in March, and so forth. The population has money, and it has the habit of queuing, and it will be a long time before queuing is eliminated from Soviet shopping habits. Scarcity-mindedness causes individuals to buy large quantities of scarce items when they appear. They buy for the future, for their relatives, and for their friends. Thus, as a hedge against doing without, individuals provide the storage space for many items that are not actually scarce. Psychologically the Soviet shopper has been traumatized by shortages, and has organized her or his life in such a way that queuing, taking advantage of unexpected appearances of deficit commodities, and sharing with friends are integral aspects of everyday life. The long years of sacrifice will take an even longer time to be compensated and forgotten. Meanwhile everyone shops with determination, a pocketful of rubles, and surprising generosity.

Labor Markets and Private Entrepreneurship

Gosplan and the various ministries plan the allocation of labor in the same way that they do other resources. Labor balances are worked out for each region and republic and compared with enterprise requirements. The allocation of labor involves markedly different problems and methods. Marxist theory, of course, distinguishes sharply between labor and commodities under socialism, for labor represents a very special kind of resource and one for which economic activity is largely intended, according to Marxian assumptions. In addition the labor market is open. That is, although it is a regulated market in the sense that a state committee of the Council of Ministers sets wage rates, safety standards, and other conditions of work for all public employment, individual workers exercise primary discretion concerning their own participation in the economy.

Labor markets may be separated into five different categories: state, collective-farm, private-plot, and legal and illegal private labor service. This division emphasizes the significance of private markets. I am not suggesting that these markets operate separately. On the contrary these various markets are intertwined in complex ways, and to an unknown degree private markets actually help to explain why the Soviet economy functions as well as it does concerning the satisfaction of consumer preferences. Products and services that would not otherwise be available are produced privately in the USSR, and private trade helps to distribute and redistribute commodities and services that would otherwise never reach those who want them most. In addition, and of particular importance, private markets tend to convert public property into private property for private gain. One result is a different distribution of final consumer goods and services than would take place in the absence of private enterprise and trade, and this means in all likelihood a distribution of goods and services that benefits higher income classes more than the state intends. Another result is to convert what are intended as investment and government expenditures into private consumption, which tends to benefit all current consumers taken together at the expense of state nonconsumption projects. In other words private markets, particularly illegal private markets in this instance, tend to undermine the percentage shares given in the plan for investment and for government outlays. It may, of course, be argued that current consumers are gaining at the expense of future consumption or the future military safety of the population, rather than at the expense of the state; but few citizens would be deterred by such an argument after long years of sacrificing for a future that never seems to arrive.

Immediately prior to, during, and for some years following World War II, strict controls were applied in the allocation of labor and to minimize labor shirking; and civilian labor was even at times conscripted along with military. Soviet citizens today, however, exercise considerable freedom of calling in that they may decide whether or not to work, allocate themselves among jobs, and, to a lesser extent, among locations of work; and they may determine the intensity with which they will work as well. Freedom of calling is further bolstered by the availability of employments in occupations not controlled by the state, both legal and illegal.

Most Soviet ablebodied citizens work for the state in one capacity or another. Most work for a state industrial or agricultural enterprise, but no small number is employed in the various state bureaucracies. The largest exception to state employment is the collective farm, but employment on collective farms today is not significantly different in terms and conditions than employment on state farms. For the present we therefore shall lump together collective- and state-farm workers. Both in the countryside and in urban areas the rate of female participation is very high in the Soviet Union, higher than anywhere else in the world. The high rate of female participation reflects at least two factors: liberation of women by the Bolshevik philosophy and the necessity of two incomes for maintaining a satisfactory standard of living.

All ablebodied citizens are under considerable social pressure to contribute gainfully to the economy. Legal measures are also possible, and have been invoked, against those persons who are designated *social parasites*. The charge of social parasitism is more common these days, however, as a weapon against political dissidents than it is as a source of labor. Recently ablebodied individuals, including those who are alienated from Soviet society, have been allowed to remain outside of regular gainful employment so long as some family member is prepared to guarantee support. If the person in question is an ablebodied woman with young children she may withdraw from employment voluntarily to care for them and her husband with little notice. The wives and children of well-to-do successful members of Soviet society are not troubled by antiparasite laws either. There are many other Soviets, most of whom are beyond the age for retirement (sixty for males and fifty-five for females), who have the choice of supplementing their incomes by working as cloakroom clerks, doormen, watchmen, and so forth. A large proportion of the existing Soviet labor force is completely free to work or to withdraw from employment as it sees fit. As a result, the Soviet labor force must be regarded as a function of individual evaluation of real wages, as it is in labor markets in capitalist countries. Thus we shall describe the labor market as open, and this has an essential bearing, as we shall see, upon the central planning and management of the Soviet economy.

The labor market comprises a complex collection of markets — some public, others private; and it is a huge market because it touches the life of every Soviet household and every enterprise and organization. Because it is an open market in which individuals exercise freedom of vocation within broad limits, it is more accurate to conceive of labor as being centrally managed rather than planned, for planning under such circumstances can mean little more than extrapolation of current trends. Direct central allocation applies only to the military service, to the penal system, and to available educational slots in the USSR today. The remainder of the labor force is self-allocated by incentives provided in public and private employments, and the intensity with which individuals work in any given employment is also self-determined.

The largest and most important single labor market is employment in state and industrial enterprises. Most ablebodied men and women in the Soviet Union work with one of these economic enterprises or with the administrative, military, or police bureaucracies of the state. A large number of retired persons are also employed by state enterprises and agencies on a full- or part-time basis. Pensions are low, and not everyone of pensionable age today is entitled to a pension. Thus many old persons work to make ends meet. A pensioner is entitled to earn up to a fixed amount per month before his pension is docked, which is a powerful incentive to work because the upper limit is relatively high.

Employment with state enterprises and agencies is, superficially at least, not noticeably different from employment in similar occupations elsewhere in the developed world. Although there was some disagreement during the 1920s about adopting the factory system that the Bolsheviks inherited from Tsarist Russia and Europe, the system was adopted in all important respects. State employees work a fixed time now averaging close to forty hours per week, are expected to appear regularly and punctually, and to work under the supervision of foremen, who are themselves directed by a single manager and his staff. In general a casual observer from the West would see nothing peculiar about the way work goes forward on the shop floor in a Soviet enterprise.

There are, however, some distinctive features of this labor market. No Soviet enterprise or official endeavor lacks a corresponding branch of the Soviet trade-union system, known as the *profsoiuz*. But, as was pointed out earlier, trade unions have no say in the management of state enterprises or agencies. Neither do they have the legal right to strike or to order any organized withdrawal of efficiency or to protest about wages, hours of work, and so forth. Agreements are worked out periodically between the profsoiuz and enterprise, trust, or other administrative level, which spell out conditions of work, safety provisions, welfare benefits and so forth, but they do not specify wage benefits. Local profsoiuz representatives serve as grievance boards to settle petty disputes among workers and between workers and management, and they also serve as "cheerleaders" in support of fulfilling plan targets. The Soviet profsoiuz is little more than an in-effectual company union, with all that implies in the way of serving the interests primarily of the bosses. Recent efforts to create independent, worker-controlled, nationally affiliated unions in Poland have no visible counterparts in the USSR, but success in Poland might very well set a powerful example for Soviet workers. Hence the Soviet government's watchful concern.

Salary and wage scales are determined for all state enterprises, including state farms and organizations, according to schedules that are developed and maintained by the State Committee on Labor and Wages. Wage differentials are determined by considering a number of factors — such as unpleasant or dangerous conditions at work, remoteness of the region in which employment is offered, the degree of skill or educational preparation required, and seniority. Many of these factors reflect, of course, the evaluations that many individuals would make concerning the desirability of these various jobs, and to this extent centralized wage-setting reflects supply conditions indirectly. The ultimate test of a wage rate is whether too few or too many workers apply for the jobs that it governs, and in this respect the State Committee on Labor and Wages is ultimately influenced by general conditions of supply and demand as well as by the formal criteria elaborated for wage determination. The government has been trying to persuade workers to move permanently to Siberia, for example, to take part in the exploitation of the vast, almost untouched resources of the region, and wage differentials are set to make working in Siberia attractive. The differential has attracted workers, but it has not been sufficient to induce them to bring their families. Consequently workers return home to warmer, more hospitable climes after several years of concentrated saving. Given the priority that development of Siberia has had for more than two decades, this example illustrates the limits that freedom of calling places on the State Committee on Labor and Wages.

Moreover enterprise managers compete with each other for skilled reliable workers, which has reinforced the impact of specific shortages upon effective wages. Although managers cannot change wage-rates, they can promote desirable individuals into higher pay-categories in order to retain them. Or the managers can let their employees hold more than one position--so that they earn two, three, or even four salaries. In general, then, supply and demand do influence the allocation of labor in the Soviet Union both between state employment and employment in the private sector (or leisure) and among employments in the socialized sector of the Soviet economy. Wage differentials in the state sector have, however, been diminished substantially in recent years by relatively high minimum wages and by the difficulty that managers face in attempting to eliminate redundant labor. Incompetent, or otherwise unsatisfactory, workers are almost impossible to fire; and wage differentials are often too weak to prevent the oversupply of some kinds of labor at the cost of undersupply for others.

Collective farms employ a large but diminishing number of individuals in the Soviet economy, and the conditions under which collective-farm workers (kolkhozniks) work are not substantially different today from those under which state-farm workers (sovkhozniks) work. Kolkhozniks are eligible for pensions; they receive the bulk of their pay in money wages rather than in kind; and they receive regular wages based upon a minimum guaranteed annual wage. Kolkhoz workers normally are given access to a larger private plot than the state-farm worker, and children of kolkhozniks have a right to become a member of the kolkhoz, a right the children of sovkhozniks do not have. More important today is the fact that members of wealthy collective farms, which usually means those that specialize in the production of certain labor-intensive and highly valuable commodities such as tea leaves, silk, or tobacco, do better on the average than state-farm workers. Most collective-farm workers do worse, however, although the difference has narrowed recently as a result of converting poor collectives into state farms.

The income that peasants earn from both state and collective farms has increased substantially over the last twenty-five years. Although the rate of increase has reduced the gap between industrial-urban occupations and rural employments, it has not prevented the continued migration of the most ambitious and highly skilled young people from rural occupations. Cultivation of private plots by kolkhozniks, sovkhozniks, and other rural dwellers is the third largest source of employment in the Soviet Union today, and it is the largest single private sector. At one time Soviet economists believed that private-plot agriculture competed with collective-farm agriculture for workers, and it may once have been so. Today, however, Soviet economists are persuaded that few ablebodied workers are engaged in private-plot agriculture, and the few who are ablebodied are nearly always women with young children to care for, who would not offer extensive employment to the collective in any case. Even so, the presence of the private plot serves as a powerful incentive to have one member of any rural family qualify as a full-time worker on a state or collective farm. Earnings from the plot provide an important source of consumption and of additional money income for rural families, and labor is utilized that would not otherwise be available to the farm, particularly that of the very young and the old. Private-plot agriculture supplies most of the products that flow through the urban rynok, and plays an important supplemental role in both the income of farm workers and the diets of urban dwellers.

There is a fourth legal labor market in the USSR of indeterminant size. It is not possible to distinguish unambiguously between the legal market in private labor services and the illegal, but the distinction is important. Many individuals participate in both legal and illegal aspects of private employment, and some activities take place in the penumbra between the legal and illegal where the distinction is one for the courts to resolve. Among the legal occupations are those which involve a direct personal service for someone, such as caring for children, housekeeping, typing manuscripts, doing laundry, and gardening. In addition anyone may sell the products of his own (or of his family's) labor in the rynok or personally. It is also legal for a group of individuals, such as carpenters, bricklayers, or other craftsmen to band together in a collective to build homes, do repairs and the like on a private, but cooperative, basis. Just how important such collectives are is not an available statistic, but they have always been more important in rural areas than in urban because there are many more private homes and dachas in the countryside. In general an individual may exercise a skill that he has acquired in order to earn, or to supplement, his income; but here we move into an obscure territory. A person who knows how to repair electrical equipment may freely repair his own or his friend's television set. He might also repair a set belonging to a "friend of a friend" without charge, but with the clear intention of collecting a reciprocal favor at a future time from the friend or the set's owner. It may even be legal for the repairer to receive a cash payment for his service, although this is not patently clear. The situation, however, is rarely so neatly defined. Any of these instances would be illegal if the repairman used spare parts taken from his official place of work, used stolen tools, or did the repairs on working time in the state shop without billing the customer for it.

Plumbers, carpenters, repairmen of all sorts, handymen, individuals who own private cars or who chauffeur for the state, and so forth can periodically earn a personal profit on the basis of their skills or their access to state property. Although it is technically illegal to do so, chauffeurs for state officials frequently use time that they know will otherwise be spent sitting in wait to taxi individuals for private gain, and the state pays for the gasoline. Some individuals specialize in approaching foreign tourists in hopes of buying or begging some prize item for subsequent (illegal) resale or in the expectation of obtaining foreign currency in exchange for rubles. Many individuals manufacture *samogon* (illegal drinking alcohol) in their kitchens, and those who make it well and in large quantity can exchange or sell it as a sideline. Drivers of state-owned taxis frequently take advantage of late-night fares to earn something over and above the standard fare, to sell liquor after hours, and to refer clients to ladies of the night.

In a similar vein blat can get one out of a difficult spot, it can help one jump a queue, and it can be used for personal advancement. For deficit commodities or services, rubles are frequently useless unless mixed with blat, friendship, or a contact in the black market. Where legality ends and illegality begins in these instances is hard to determine, and anyone who is involved in these kinds of transactions takes a certain risk in doing so. Interestingly enough, this implicates almost every household in the major cities of the USSR and no small number of rural folk, where producing samogon is the most frequently cited crime. The exceptions are likely to be officials so highly placed that blat works silently and unbidden for them anyway. There was a time when it was said that "blat is higher than Stalin." Today it is accurate to say that blat is the only hard Soviet currency.

To exaggerate the volume of illegal and quasi-legal economic transactions in the USSR today would be wrong. No figures and no official estimates are available about them, as there are for the collective-farm markets and private-plot agriculture, but no one doubts that private trading, both legal and illegal, is extremely pervasive. Whether total turnover on this market is 10 or 15 percent of total real Soviet national product, no one can say with confidence; but that it touches every household on at least a weekly basis no one could doubt. The apparent sharp increase in nalevo markets in recent years may serve as a measure of a growing disparity between planners' and consumers' preferences in the USSR. The lesson seems to be that planners cannot enforce their own preferences in the face of an open labor market. This would require, in all likelihood, a return to strict labor controls, a resumption of forced labor, and much more extensive policing of economic activities. No current leader has indicated willingness to pursue so drastic a solution, although one does hear nostalgic references to the public "order" that Stalin maintained. We shall return to these issues in Chapter 6.

Labor-Force Participation, Mobility, and Productivity

Given existing legal restraints on working age, existing wages, and work conditions, and the social and legal pressures on the individual to contribute to economic activity, the available labor force in the USSR is determined essentially by the rate at which the over-all population grows and by the way this increase is distributed geographically. The Soviet population as a whole has been growing relatively slowly over the past two decades. The rate for both the USSR and the USA has been in the neighborhood of 1.4 percent per annum, and it is declining. Like the United States the USSR experienced a postwar baby boom. Now that this bulge in the population has been absorbed into the labor force, available labor will increase at a much slower pace than previously, and the miniscule growth of the labor force in the 1980s will adversely effect the growth of Soviet national income. Because labor-participation rates of both men and women are high, little additional labor can be obtained by trying to increase participation rates. The Soviet labor-participation rate for women is so high that it is much more likely to fall than to rise, and the same may be true for males too, unless purchasing power increases steadily.

The main source of possible growth of the labor force for the industrial sectors of the economy would be by the diminishing of the labor force required by the agricultural sector. As we have seen, the proportion of labor that is currently devoted to agricultural production is large by comparison with other developed countries — about 25 percent of total employment. It is doubtful, however, that this potential pool of industrial labor can be realized in the near future because productivity is increasing very slowly and because of the priority that expansion of agricultural output occupies at present.

The distribution of the rural population poses an additional problem for Soviet planners. Population-growth rates are generally lower in the cities than in rural regions; and, more important, growth rates are highest in both urban and rural regions where certain minority ethnic groups live. The populations of Central Asia, for example, are growing rapidly, especially in rural areas. Growth of the Soviet industrial-labor force will require the absorption of the net increase in these populations. There are two ways to go about it. One is to encourage non-Russian nationals to move to the industrial cities outside their traditional cultural regions by creating appropriate wage differentials. Thus far Soviet planners have been reluctant to encourage members of minority groups such as those of Central Asia to move to the cities of European Russia, and it would appear also that the campaign to induce workers to move permanently to Siberia has been conducted mainly among the various European populations of the USSR. In any event Soviet planners have not looked with favor upon the creation of ethnic outposts in the main industrial centers of the USSR. Great Russians go out to the various non-Russian republics to fill high administrative posts and skilled occupations, but no significant reverse flow of the unskilled to European Russia has taken place. Many Soviet and western students of Soviet ethnic groups claim that these ethnic groups do not wish to move and cannot be induced to move in any case, but the argument is undermined by the presence of similar cultural and ethnic minorities — that is, Turks, Pakistanis, Indians, and Persians, in the cities of Western Europe and England, which are further removed from the centers of their native cultures than are the cities of European Russia or Central Siberia.

The alternative is to distribute investment preferentially to these minority republics and regions in order to utilize the relatively rapid natural increase in their populations; but this procedure tends to reinforce "undesirable" centrifugal ethnic and national forces already under way in the USSR. Soviet planners, therefore, face a difficult dilemma, neither horn of which can be completely evaded. This is just one component of the problem that the Soviet Union's restless national minorities pose for Soviet planners and political leaders in the near future, and the underlying economic problem of labor scarcity cannot be resolved independently of official nationality policy. It is useless for Soviet leadership to proclaim, as Brezhnev has said repeatedly, that the nationality problem has been solved. The problem is yet to be addressed as a living fact, but labor scarcity and rising ethnic-consciousness ensure that it will be posed, probably in dramatic fashion, in the near future.

If little industrial labor is likely to result from a diminution in the agricultural labor force during the next five years, the main source of growth must lie in the productivity of labor already in the industrial sector. When measured on an average annual basis, Soviet industry has a good record regarding increases in labor productivity since the early 1950s. The increase has, however, been erratic; and a more serious problem is an apparent downward trend over the last decade. This trend may be spurious, of course; but the evidence for stagnation in the rate of growth of labor productivity seems firm. The decline that has taken place probably reflects the fact that the largest gains from borrowing new technology from the West and from training the illiterate have already been assimilated. The decline no doubt also reflects the shift of a much larger share of investment resources to the agricultural sector in the last decade or two, for agriculture has not yielded the kind of gains in productivity that were registered in the industrial sector earlier. There is another problem that may be more fundamental — the intensity with which Soviet labor works. Increased productivity in industry, and in agriculture as well, will require the elimination of redundant labor and a renewed willingness of Soviet workers to work harder and to learn new skills.

A good deal of evidence suggests that Soviet workers could readily increase the efficiency and intensity with which they work. The problem for central planners, however, is overcoming the institutional barriers that encourage and protect redundancy and low productivity. Even casual observation reveals several different types of redundancy in the Soviet economy. In the first place a large number of jobs exists that appears to signify little economically. For example every public building has a doorman or woman, several coatchecks, a number of janitors, and various repairmen. Moreover every separate institute or administrative division within the building has a watchman or woman who controls access to the floor or wing that the office or institute occupies. University dormitories and many apartment buildings have similar persons who ensure against unauthorized entry and therefore against theft or encroachment. Similarly almost every office, institute, factory, and store has a fleet of automobiles and vans that are used to transport authorized people on business; and many people have chauffeured cars assigned for their exclusive use. These drivers sit idle much of the time, waiting to take someone to or from an assignment. Many of these functions are either necessary or useful such as the ubiquitous coatchecks in a country where one wears heavy clothing over half the year, and many are sinecures that provide small incomes to retired or invalided persons. Other positions, however, such as personally assigned chauffeurs and KGB guards, are held by the ablebodied and afford good incomes.

The second type of redundancy that casual observation reveals in the USSR is in staffing services, particularly in certain types of retail sales and in offices. Oddly this may not be true redundancy on a global basis because retail sales, for example, are understaffed in aggregate. Existing workers are badly distributed among outlets. Some hardly have enough people to serve all the customers, while others have few products to sell and nothing for half the staff to do most of the time. Judging by comments in Soviet professional magazines and newspapers, this kind of maldistribution of the existing labor force is characteristic of industrial and agricultural enterprises as well. The institutional basis for the persistence of an inefficient allocation of the labor force lies, first, in the legal difficulties that managers face in removing individuals from the work force and, second, in the fact that there is little incentive for managers to trim redundant labor. On the contrary it is often convenient to have a certain amount of redundancy (the Soviet terminology is *reserves*) to handle peak demand, for managerial bonuses result primarily from fulfilling annual output-targets, not in minimizing costs.

A third source of the inefficiency that characterizes the Soviet labor force taken as a whole is the ineffectiveness of the material incentive system. Much emphasis has always been placed in Soviet industry upon moral incentives. Moral incentives refer to nonmaterial kinds of gratification workers and managers may obtain from doing good work. They include the receiving of medals, winning competitions, having one's name or factory written up in the newspaper, and the like. Moral incentives were important sources of productivity gains in the 1930s, during World War II, and afterward; but they have apparently lost much of their effectiveness today. Unfortunately the system of material incentives has never been thoroughly overhauled to reflect its increased significance as the prime mover in inducing efficiency and conscientiousness. Moreover persistent shortages in retail outlets tend to undermine the effectiveness of material incentives, particularly where the individual cannot be fired for laziness or have his salary docked for lacking ambition. Obviously a society in which acquisition of the most desirable commodities requires either queuing or nalevo involvement in the economy is one in which a clever worker may find advancement to a more responsible or otherwise demanding position no advantage whatever. The move up may reduce the time that he or she has available for queuing, or it may remove the individual from the strategic position he or she occupies with respect to deficit commodities or blat.

Increased productivity is an inviting path toward increased output in the Soviet economy, but it can only be attained in the long run by changing the institutional structure within which Soviet workers and managers operate. That the great bulk of all Soviet employed persons work for the state in one capacity or another makes the problem of eliminating redundancy and increasing productivity a political issue in the same way that the pricing of products in state retail outlets is a political problem. As an economic problem neither issue presents any conceptual or behavioral difficulties. Socialization of the means of production has politicized economic decision-making in the USSR, as it has elsewhere following widespread nationalization. Some important problems are solved, of course, by taking them out of the economic realm; but others that are very intractable for political decision-making are often created at the same time. Although the balance depends upon one's objectives, wholesale nationalization has become less attractive to many contemporary socialists owing to this realization.

One problem that wholesale nationalization did solve in the USSR, however, involved periodic layoffs resulting from business fluctuations.

The fact that Soviet enterprises do not lay off workers when sales or profits lag is, of course, the obverse side of the job-security problem that managers face in trying to use labor forces efficiently. Soviet national income and industrial and agricultural output do fluctuate, but for reasons distinct from those that bring about business cycles in capitalist countries. Employment does not fluctuate systematically with output because the two are severed by job security and by the commitment of the government to provide jobs for all who seek to work. Redundancy in Soviet economic enterprises reflects these factors.

The Soviet Union has unemployment, however; but it tends to be one of three noncyclical types. Individuals who are in the process of voluntarily seeking different or better-located employment as well as those who have just joined the labor force through graduation from school contribute to frictional unemployment. Structural unemployment also presents problems in the Soviet Union. That is, as the economy changes under the impact of new technology and changing tastes of the population or the government (military demand for example), certain jobs are eliminated, causing skills of established workers to become obsolete. Because the USSR does not pay unemployment benefits, individuals who suffer from structural or frictional unemployment may be obliged to take much inferior jobs — or to do without work until something suitable opens up. The third type of unemployment that individuals suffer in the USSR is seasonal, which affects primarily the rural population.

Education has always been an important means for upward mobility in the USSR, and the Soviet Union adopted the American open-enrollment educational system at its inception to maximize opportunities for individuals to become educated and to learn skills. Education remains today a very important basis for successful advancement on the job, but the USSR is running into the problem of overqualified workers that afflicts many advanced countries today. Individuals who find that they must accept employment in positions which are inferior to the positions for which they prepared themselves are likely to become alienated, and they are *underemployed* members of society. This should perhaps be listed as a fourth type of unemployment in the Soviet Union.

In the USSR women are heavily represented in the category *overqualified workers*. Over one-half of the total Soviet labor force is female. Official doctrine calls for equal educational opportunities, equal pay for equal work, the provision of child-care services, and support for the desirability of female participation in the labor force on a full-time basis. Even so several factors militate against the attainment of true equality with men when it comes to economic opportunities and achievements. Soviet data reveal, for example, that occupations in which women form the majority of employees, regardless of the status of these occupations outside the USSR, tend to be low-prestige, poorly paid occupations. The most flagrant example is medicine, in which women dominate the ranks of MDs. Yet, even in occupations such as medicine or primary education, men dominate both the higher administrative and most specialized categories and thus the higher-paid employments. Most enterprise managers and collective-farm chairmen are men, and most high officials in the party are male.

There are many reasons why women have not been able to take full advantage of the Bolsheviks' ideological commitment to equal opportunity for women. Soviet statistics make it clear that women do take advantage of early educational opportunities, but they are less likely than men to continue education to the highest levels. Accordingly few women are surgeons, although many earn MDs. Second, although child-care centers exist, the spaces available are inadequate to provide care for the children of all women who wish to work, and the deficiency increases the farther one moves away from major urban areas. Third, although it seems very unlikely that there is any official support for a secondary role for women in the Soviet system, the state conducts no affirmative-action programs to reverse longstanding patriarchal attitudes. These attitudes are particularly strong in certain ethnic regions, such as Central Asia, where they take the form of social prohibitions on participation by women in factory employment or the appearance of women in certain public situations. Even in European Russia familial expectations and cultural patterns seriously handicap women. Most women do work full-time throughout the USSR, but fewer put their careers ahead of other considerations than do men.

A woman who desires to compete with men for success in a career can probably do so in the USSR more easily and with less criticism than in Europe or in the United States, but she still runs counter to cultural expectations, and this takes its toll. Women in European Russia, for example, are expected to work full-time and yet do the shopping, prepare meals, keep house, and care for the children. According to reports, husbands are more willing today than in the past to assist in all of these activities, but primary responsibility remains with the woman. Should a child be ill, for example, it would almost certainly be the mother rather than the father who would stay home. Job advancement involving a change of cities would be more likely to follow the husband's opportunities than the wife's. Many women do not object, of course, to the pattern in which they, like their husbands and parents, have been inculcated. But for those women who do object the situation is no less fraught with contraditions and emotional tensions than in the West. Women comprise, therefore, the largest proportion of those who are overskilled for the positions they occupy in the Soviet labor force.

No discussion of labor in the Soviet Union would be complete that failed to take forced labor into account. Although forced labor is apparently no longer a significant source of labor in the USSR, at one time forced labor contributed significantly to national income. The total number of individuals so impressed remains secret and is thus disputed among western scholars, and the matter will not be resolved in the near future. Everyone agrees, however, that the total was great, that it reached a peak in the years immediately following World War II, and that it began to be reduced systematically under Khrushchev, especially following his secret anti-Stalin speech in 1956. Economists generally believe that forced labor is inferior to paid labor in efficiency, and maintaining large forced-labor camps is expensive. In any event, forced labor was used in the Soviet Union to perform very dangerous or particularly arduous tasks, such as construction and mining in the Arctic Circle.

The Household Sector

The typical Soviet urban household contributes labor to the economic process and receives pecuniary and nonpecuniary benefits in return primarily for its contributions. Nonpecuniary benefits have been declining as a share of total family income, and thus most of the family's time is spent earning and spending money income. From the family's standpoint it does not matter whether its transactions involve the private or the public sector, but when things go wrong in the public sector the state is blamed. Most households in the USSR have more than one primary wage-earner, and most also receive some direct payment from a state agency. A grandparent may live with the family and draw a pension. He or she may also work at a part-time job, and in any event the grandparent would be fully occupied helping in queuing for deficit commodities, walking the baby, sitting with the children, gardening, and helping with the housework. The family may have a child in the university or in a technical school, in which case he or she would receive a stipend that would be contributed to the family's weekly income.

Spending the family income is also a collective affair, involving state retail markets, the rynok, private trading, and nalevo markets, without anyone paying much attention to the breakdown among them. Family members old enough to be responsible would normally carry a substantial sum of cash with them at all times against finding unexpected deficit commodities. Everyone in the family knows what these are and what a reasonable price would be for them. What the family does not spend is set aside for purchasing large durable goods such as automobiles, stereo sets, and so forth. Some western observers claim that Soviet families are unable to spend as much as they like in Soviet markets and that they are therefore accumulating savings unwillingly. This is a most unlikely conclusion for the simple reason that households do not have to earn more income than they wish. The amount of income that a family earns is not determined by the state, but by collective decision of the members of the household. Because queuing is so important a function in the acquisition of deficit commodities in the Soviet Union, it will always pay for one member of the family to increase his or her free time for queuing rather than to work at a job from which the income would be of little or no use.

So long as individuals are free to make their own purchases in the market and so long as individual households may elect the total number of hours that they wish to be employed, planners are not able to determine unilaterally either the total volume of labor forthcoming in the economy or the total amount and composition of consumer goods and services that it will make available, and this constraint is enhanced by the presence of private employment and private retail markets. It is further enhanced by the opportunities that individuals have to convert public property into private means to personal gain.

If the state wishes households to contribute more to economic activity, it must provide something in exchange, and that has increasingly come to mean commodities and services rather than promises of a better future or assurance against an aggressive external force. In this respect the member of a Soviet household does not experience a different economic world than does his counterpart in the West. A Soviet who is suddenly transposed into a capitalist economic environment is not disoriented by the difference, although the plethora of goods and of choices available might be overwhelming at first.

Neither is a western shopper disoriented in Soviet markets. The difficulties involved are irritating, but not completely strange, for there are still queues in the West for certain kinds of sporting and cultural events, and queues for gasoline have reeducated an entire generation. The Soviet system of central planning and management has not yet, however, learned to accommodate independent-minded workers and equally independent-minded consumers.

The term *second economy* has become popular among certain western specialists on the Soviet economy to describe various aspects of what I have called open markets and trading nalevo. The term *second economy* is potentially misleading because it may be taken to imply a greater degree of distinctness between the "first" economy and the "second" than exists. The concept of a dual economy was first developed in the study of developing economies to describe the difference between the advanced sector of the economy and the traditional predevelopment economy. Since the advanced sector in a primitive economy may be an exclave of western or Soviet technology, the notion of a dual economic system is not remote for many countries, but the concept has proved troublesome even in the development literature because there are usually connections and therefore interactions between the two parts of the dual economy that are important to the functioning of each. Such is the case regarding economic transactions that take place nalevo in the USSR. As a matter of fact, neither the "first" nor the "second" economy would work as well in the absence of the other, although there are, of course, contradictions between them too.

The second drawback with the notion of a "second" economy is the fact that no investigator has yet advanced a definition that everyone finds satisfactory. Every adult Soviet citizen knows the difference between the nalevo economy, the legal private markets, and the public economy; and it seems preferable to stick with common usage. Some western scholars define the second economy to consist of all free-market transactions, legal and illegal. Others define the concept as comprising all illegal economic transactions, but this bunches general criminal activities with market transactions and loses altogether the distinction between private- and public-sector transactions. Enterprise managers, for example, know how to use the nalevo economy to achieve state enterprise targets as well as their own creature comforts. Finally still other western specialists define the second economy to include only private economic activity and use it to contrast private enterprise with state planning and management. Each aspect involved in the various definitions is as important as the other in gaining an understanding of the way that Soviet planning and management of the economy interacts with the interests and behavior of the private individuals and households that compose the system. Soviet households are involved simultaneously in planned and unplanned economic transactions, in market and nonmarket economic relationships, and in private and public economic institutions. They form an undifferentiated whole in the experience of a household member, and each is an essential component of the way the Soviet economy functions for the people who live and work in the system.

SELECTED READINGS

Dodge, Norton T. *Women in the Soviet Economy: Their Role in Economic, Scientific, and Technical Development.* Baltimore: Johns Hopkins University Press, 1966.

Grossman, Gregory. 'The "Second Economy" of the USSR.' *Problems of Communism* 26 (September-October 1977), 25-40.

Katsenelenboigen, Aaron. "Coloured Markets in the Soviet Union." *Soviet Studies* 29, no. 1 (January 1977), 62-85.

Kirsch, Leonard. *Soviet Wages: Changes in Structure and Administration since 1956.* Cambridge, Mass.: MIT Press, 1972.

Lapidus, Gail Warshofsky. *Women in Soviet Society: Equality, Development, and Social Change.* Berkeley: University of California Press, 1978.

Matthews, Mervyn. *Privilege in the Soviet Union.* London: George Allen & Unwin, 1978.

McAuley, Alastair. "The Distribution of Earnings and Incomes in the Soviet Union." *Soviet Studies* 29, no. 2 (April 1977), 214-37.

Ofer, Gur. *The Service Sector in Soviet Economic Growth: A Comparative Study.* Cambridge, Mass.: Harvard University Press, 1973.

Schroeder, Gertrude E., and Severin, Barbara S. "Soviet Consumption and Income Policies in Perspective." In U.S. Congress, Joint Economic Committee, *Soviet Economy in a New Perspective.* Washington, D.C.: U.S. Government Printing Office, 1976.

Smith, Hedrick. *The Russians.* New York: Quadrangle Books, 1976.

Weitzman, Phillip. "Soviet Long-Term Consumption Planning: Distribution According to Rational Need." *Soviet Studies* 26, no 3. (July 1974), 305-21.

5

Industry, Agriculture, and Natural Resources: The Intermediate Sectors

The Context of Soviet Industry

As we have seen, the private sector of the Soviet economy is an important source of goods and services and a means by which certain aims of Soviet central planning are sometimes subverted, allowing private parties to use goods and services planned for government sectors — such as investment in state enterprises or the military — for personal gain. For the most part, however, the private sector of the Soviet economy serves as a supplement to the activities of state economic enterprise, either by offering additional goods derived from resources that would not otherwise be exploited or by redistributing the existing output of the society to those who can pay or who have blat. These private activities, both legal and illegal, are pervasive today, and they touch the lives and welfare of nearly all Russians, but there is no evidence to suggest that the volume of these goods and services is great. The core of the Soviet economy is the state-enterprise sector plus collective farms. The general welfare of Soviet citizens taken together depends primarily upon the sensitivity of the state economy to their needs and the efficiency and foresight with which it functions.

Since World War II the Soviet Union has maintained its position as the second-largest economy in the world and the second-ranked military power as well. Maintaining the military position has competed sharply with providing consumer goods, and the USSR's ranking with respect to per-capita consumption is much lower than the size of the economy would suggest.

The decision was made in the late 1920s to accelerate the rate of growth beyond what most economists and politicians believed was possible voluntarily, and the adverse impact of collectivization on food and fiber production produced a highly unbalanced pattern of growth, one that favored heavy industry at the expense of light industry. This emphasis reflected in large part the realization of planners' preference for growth in economic capacity over immediate consumer satisfaction. World War II and its aftermath increased the priority of military spending permanently, and the damage the economy suffered during the war led Soviet planners to give heavy industry high priority once again.

Specific historical factors, plus fortunate geographical location, are responsible also for the extreme self-sufficiency of the Soviet economy since the revolution. The vast extent of the territorial limits of the USSR provides almost unlimited potential surface and subsurface resources, but much of this potential is located in regions where conditions for human existence, not to mention settlements, are extremely unpromising. The long period of political and economic isolation of the USSR during its first two decades, plus the adverse impact upon imports and exports of all countries during the great depression of the 1930s, encouraged Soviet leaders to seek self-sufficiency at almost any cost. Military considerations during and following World War II reinforced the autarkic tendencies of Soviet economic planning.

International trade has not, therefore, played a large role in Soviet development, and it is not a strong factor in planning Soviet output today, despite growing interest in trade. Total trade turnover, which is measured as the sum of imports and exports, represents a small fraction of gross national product in the USSR. Soviet development has taken place mainly on the basis of the country's own resources and with benefit of little foreign investment. Consequently few Soviet products have been developed primarily for export, and the absence of such competition has had an adverse effect on certain products, particularly consumer goods, which have also been protected against competition domestically by the state monopoly of foreign trade. Some products, particularly products with military applications or implications, such as weapons systems, aircraft, and space technology, have proven competitive in world markets. The difference in the salability of these products in world markets reflects Soviet priorities, not those of the international marketplace.

Soviet Industry

Administration of the Soviet economic bureaucracy is currently organized according to the principle of branch rather than territorial management. That is, the primary basis for grouping or aggregating specific plants and industries is by type of product or service they provide. Product groups and service complexes are broken down into territorial components only for management convenience. The controlling factor remains hierarchal, running from central ministries in Moscow down to peripheral units scattered throughout the country. Although some functions are directed primarily at the republic rather than the national level, the principle of organization remains the branch of production and not location within republic or autonomous region.

The principle of branch management produces characteristic types of problems anywhere it is applied. One of the most troublesome is a high degree of centralization and the obstacles that this presents in local coordination of activities of two or more different branches of industry. Managers and administrators at the various levels below the central ministry are frequently reluctant to, or perhaps even constrained from, making decisions on their own. Thus, even trivial decisions, such as adjustments in delivery schedules, often must travel all the way to Moscow for resolution. Branch management tends to encourage the various branches to become conglomerates that actually produce a range of products in order to protect themselves against supply shortages. Ministries tend, therefore, to become minor empires, with highly centralized, sometimes quite arbitrary, decision-making. This is one of the most important reasons why location in Moscow is essential. It is the only place where decisions can be expedited because it is the location of all important and a great deal of unimportant decision-making.

Nikita Khrushchev experimented with several different approaches to industrial organization. The most thoroughgoing was a switch to the territorial principle of industrial organization in 1957. The country was divided into 105 regions *(sovnarkhozes)*, each of which was supposed to organize production and distribution of the goods and services produced primarily within the region. While this system did assist in shunting decisions out of Moscow, it created new problems, the most undesirable being the tendency for territorial regions to become autarkic miniature economies. Rather than being ordered across the border from a neighboring sovnarkhoz, supplies were shipped from an extreme corner of the region instead. It became necessary to restore centralization to some degree to prevent parochialization of decision-making. In the end Khrushchev's successors abandoned the territorial principle and reestablished the old ministerial principle of branch management.

Continuing experimentation with different organizational schemes indicates continuing dissatisfaction with the organizational principles that inform Soviet central planning and management. Basically the problem is to ensure that decision-makers at the enterprise and regional levels of the economy operate according to priorities that reflect the preferences of the political and economic leadership. Top management can be assured of this, of course, by making the decision itself; but it does not have the kind of detailed information on production possibilities that local and regional economic management have. On the other hand local decision-makers have the information, but do not necessarily have the same priorities as do central planners and politicians. A coincidence of priorities is inclined to occur in wartime, when the populace supports the war effort, or in a system in which there is widespread support for a clear set of ideological principles. Under such circumstances local commanders, ideologues, or party leaders can be relied upon to put the interest of the country or the movement above their own parochial interests. Stalinism also provided heavy penalties for those inclined to follow their own interests irrespective of those of the center.

Although Soviet leaders still call upon moral incentives, no one takes this call as more than pure nostalgia. The Soviet economy is based today as much upon the principle of self-interest as are all other highly developed economies: monetary and other material incentives afford the only workable levers for the central manipulation of the economy. Since the central plan as promulgated by Gosplan cannot be perfect, managers of state enterprises and managers of various regional offices must make decisions as the plan year unfolds. These managers cannot simply be given orders to fulfill or exceed the plan if productivity and efficiency are to be achieved at the enterprise or regional level.

A solution to the problem of achieving a coincidence of interests between planners and managers in the USSR superficially appears quite simple to any western economist, but it is in fact a problem for the

Soviet economy of the order that the business cycle is for the American economy. Analytically the problem presented by periodic unemployment and periodic cycles of inflation under capitalism is not difficult to understand. There are two obvious solutions. First, if all private economic decision-makers would act on the assumption that aggregate demand will not fall, no one would be laid off and no decline in production would occur. Similarly, if all private individuals, private unions, and private business-managers were to behave as though prices would remain constant, it would be so. Of course private decision-makers cannot afford to act according to an expectation they know to be false — or according to an implicit contract that they have no means to enforce. Conversely both unemployment and inflation resulting from cyclical fluctuations in the American economy could be cured by the use of production and price controls; but most Americans, including most economists, consider such a cure worse than the disease.

An analogous dilemma confronts Soviet planners. Central planning is as much an article of faith among Soviet planners and economists as it is a means to satisfactory economic performance. Serious dilution of central control is as undesirable to those who run the Soviet economy as is dilution of private enterprise in the United States to American leaders. Merely telling Soviet enterprise-managers that all would be better off if they would all make decisions uninfluenced by their own private interests is as unrealistic as expecting American business to eliminate involuntary unemployment and inflation by disregarding its own criteria of performance and success. Designing a workable managerial incentive system is, therefore, a chronic, but not fatal, challenge for Soviet planners.

Three characteristics of the Soviet economy have made it impossible for Soviet economists and reformers to design a fully satisfactory system of criteria for evaluating successful managerial performance, and most contemporary Soviet economists recognize these character-istics as fully as western critics. Soviet planning is overcentralized, overly ambitious, and short-sighted.

We have already discussed the overcentralized character of both central planning and central management of the Soviet economy. Final word concerning targets rests with the center, and the detail of Soviet plans is not justified by equally detailed central intelligence and knowledge. Similarly, changes that must be made in the plan as it unfolds must climb the hierarchal pyramid to Moscow for confirmation. Overly ambitious planning was established early in the development of Soviet planning, and it may be impossible to eradicate so long as the degree of central control sought by planners is as high as it is. Resources tend to be overcommitted in Soviet planning because central authorities are unsure of their knowledge and do not trust lower levels to comply wholeheartedly. In anticipating a divergence of interests between the center and the enterprise, they try to compensate by guessing how much slack has been deliberately introduced by local managers. Moreover plans are conceived as motivational devices. High-plan targets, it is believed, will stimulate managers and workers to high-performance levels. Planners seek to compensate for their own lack of precise knowledge about production possibilities and about individual motivation by erring on the high side. The pressure placed on managers and upon workers by management to fulfill targets of the current annual plan tends also to obscure and undermine the five-year horizon of Soviet planning. Rewards are tied to current performance much more than to long-run performance variables, and managers of enterprises adopt an appropriately short-run outlook. Accordingly Soviet enterprises are reluctant to experiment with new forms of management, new products, or new production methods, for these experiments have the immediate effect of reducing current premiums without offering a counterbalancing long-run reward.

Overcommitment planning of outputs makes all managers anxious about securing inputs, and it leads them to seek good plans — that is, plans that can be readily fulfilled or overfulfilled. The fact that managers pad input requirements and understate output possibilities, that they seek safety factors to protect themselves against the inevitable supply insecurity of such an economy, and that they can be careless about meeting specifications of those they supply — all tend to enhance recourse to centralized measures, which in turn enhances supply insecurity and short time horizons for managers. The Soviet system of central planning and management is ordered in such a way, therefore, that centralization, overcommitment of resources, and low time horizons are mutually reinforcing. These three characteristics generate the conditions Soviet households face as well, for they guarantee persistence of deficit commodities in consumer markets, a lack of interest in consumer tastes and convenience, and poor quality where quality depends upon special care or handling or upon time-consuming innovation.

To contrast an economy such as that of the United States with the Soviet economy is useful. Enterprises operate in the United States in an economic environment of relative excess supply. In one degree or another, most industries must worry about finding and maintaining their customers, and businesses as well as households are presented with wide latitude of choice in most products and confronted with substantial salesmanship efforts from producers who fear unsold inventories or excess capacity more than any other problem. Enterprises and individuals in the Soviet economy live in an environment of scarcity. What possible motivation can enterprises have to innovate, to bring out a better consumer product or to make technical progress when almost all are faced with demand that will absorb traditionally low-quality products without effort or cost? The effort of marketing in the USSR is almost all on the side of the prospective purchaser. Moreover this is so common that even enterprises that build up unsold inventories manage to treat potential customers with indifference. The exceptions follow the rule: the producer is king. Unsold or slow-moving inventories are, when necessary, reduced by tying sales of unwanted goods to those that are in high demand. Each economy, therefore, faces certain chronic problems that result from this fundamental difference in supply-and-demand conditions. Most enterprises in the United States face demand insecurity most of the time, and those that do not face such insecurity often do not behave any differently than those which do. Witness the advertising of certain monopolies. Most enterprises in the USSR face supply insecurity and benefit from sellers' markets most of the time, and those that do not nevertheless generally follow suit in behavior.

Reforms in Planning

After Khrushchev was deposed in 1964, his successors introduced an important reform in planning and management. Because Kosygin announced them, they have come to be called Kosygin reforms. The factors that led to the reforms were examined extensively in public discussions of the deficiencies of Soviet central planning and management that began in earnest when a series of articles in 1962 by Professor E. Liberman of Khar'kov University was published. The Liberman proposals opened a discussion among economists, planners, and managers regarding the proper design of managerial incentives.

The main elements of the system Liberman proposed were: 1) introduction of a charge on capital to encourage managers to use capital efficiently, 2) enhanced prominence for profits as a general index of enterprise performance, and 3) decentralization of managerial decision-making. Many economists proposed similar reforms, some of them quite sophisticated; but all agreed with Liberman about these three characteristics. As the discussion continued it became clear that the primary purpose of the reform was not to decentralize decision-making further, but to improve central control over enterprise decision-making, thereby increasing central control over-all. That is, what Liberman and others pointed out was not the undesirability of central control, but the fact that the center did not control many decisions at the enterprise level. Effective central control was being frustrated by a lack of information at the center about enterprise capabilities and by a lack of consistency in enterprise plans, both of which forced managers to make decisions without adequate guidance.

The Kosygin reforms developed under the influence of this public discussion and were consistent with the aim of improving central control by means of permitting an increase in formal decentralization. These reforms sought to replace de facto exercise of discretion with formal discretion at the enterprise and to provide criteria that would permit the center to evaluate enterprise decision-making more effectively — thereby actually increasing central control. This attempt to substitute *central management* for *central planning* was founded on the hope that the degree of central direction of the economy would increase. The Kosygin reforms were not as thoroughgoing as many economists and managers had proposed, and they have proven even less effective. The charge on capital that they provide is too low to serve as a serious constraint on managers. Profits matter more than previously, but not sufficiently to change managerial attitudes. Premiums are still awarded for plan fulfillment, not for high profitability. Finally central planners have been reluctant to give up even the facade of central control, and the extent of decentralization has been minimal. Many of the economists who were avid contributors to the reform discussion and who were sanguine about the prospects for resolving the persistent problems of Soviet central planning and management have become quite pessimistic today about the prospect for substantially reforming the Soviet system of central planning.

Reform of planning and of enterprise management continues to be a popular topic in Soviet professional economic, management, and planning journals, for everyone concedes that improving the efficiency of Soviet enterprises and their receptiveness to innovation and consumer preferences will require significant changes. Moreover, given the manpower shortage that is anticipated in the economy, increases in productivity represent the main sources of satisfactory growth of Soviet output through the 1980s. Although everyone agrees about the need to improve the system of planning, there is little agreement about what better planning entails today.

One common view of better central planning is planning that is better organized. Historically this has been a typical Bolshevik reaction to any problem: to attempt to increase the extent of organization. In practice this would mean even less discretion at the enterprise level than currently exists, for its objective would be to eliminate insofar as possible uncertainties arising from spontaneity. This kind of response was typified by Stalin's reaction to the grain crisis of 1928 and by the repeated reaction of the party to major crises. It represents the response of an *apparatchik*, of a bureaucrat, to a problem, which is to reorganize, to lengthen the table of organization, and to make someone personally responsible for a better outcome. The school of thought advocating better organization has, then, a very conservative approach, one that appeals primarily to members of the planning bureaucracy and to older party organizers.

A second school of thought seeks better planning through more sophisticated planning methods such as much more extensive uses of computer and other high-speed data-processing facilities. If successful, this approach would also reduce the total amount of discretion enterprise managers exercise de facto today. This is, then, also a conservative approach to the problem of ensuring a coincidence of interests between planners and enterprise managers in that it increases the surveillance range of the center. At one time this was a particularly influential viewpoint, especially among academic economists, for it was believed that input-output and linear-programming methods of analysis could be developed to the point that it would be possible to program the entire economy according to an optimal plan. The problems of constructing very large systems for tracking economic relationships and realization of the limitations of optimal programming methods have dimmed the hopes of those who dreamed of a centrally determined and (almost) perfect plan.

The third principal school of thought has sought to establish a division of labor between central planners and enterprise managers that reflects the actual division of expertise and operational capabilities that obtains in the economy. This is regarded as a radical view in that it would increase the realm of decision-making power which is formally allocated to managers of enterprises and because it implies a decrease in the extent of direct control over details exercised by the center. Soviet leaders today frequently talk about reducing the amount of petty tutelage that is exercised by higher administrative levels over lower eschelons, but few leaders apparently are prepared to do more than loosen the leash a bit. This third view is attractive both to managers and to certain academic economists who have studied systems, especially cybernetic systems, which involve self-correcting subsystems. It is not surprising that this view would be regarded suspiciously by a regime in which even the organization of student revolutionary councils in universities is centrally controlled. Even this is a conservative view since the aim is not to decrease centralization in the economy as a whole, but instead to increase the degree of central control by relying more on indirect influence via centrally managed incentives rather than on centrally planned directives that empirically are poorly based.

Many people in the West interpreted the Kosygin reforms of 1965 as far more radical than they proved to be. Some even saw in these reforms the possibility for a departure from Stalinist methods as radical as the introduction of a variant of Yugoslavia's workers councils or of creeping capitalism. Today no one has high hopes for the Kosygin reforms. Everyone pays them lip service, but no one expects any new departures while the current leadership remains in control. No major new initiatives have been forthcoming in economic policy since 1965 and none are likely until the next generation of leaders. When that generation comes to power, achieving a coincidence of interests between planners and managers will doubtless be one of the first items on the agenda. In the meantime change will be incremental and will partake of all three approaches to some degree. Minor organizational changes, applications of computer technology and of various optimal programming methods, and lip service to decentralized exercise of enterprise-level discretion are the most that can be expected. As elsewhere in the economy and in politics, the Brezhnev-Kosygin leadership has sought merely to temporize with structural problems.

Now that Kosygin has died, reform is even more unlikely under Brezhnev alone.

Transport and Industrial Resources

The USSR is extremely well endowed with natural resources, both renewable and nonrenewable. It occupies one-sixth of the land surface of the earth and yet contains only about one-fourteenth of the world's population. Measuring physical resources solely by volume of proven and estimated deposits, by cubic meters of water flow, and so forth reveals that the USSR is doubly blessed by sheer territorial size and by the quality of deposits and renewable resources. Moreover the ratio of natural resources per citizen is unusually high for nearly all important minerals and sources of energy. Whether or not a given natural resource becomes a viable economic resource depends, however, upon the cost of developing and delivering these resources to locations where they can be put to economic use. The severe climatic conditions of the greater part of Soviet territory tend to restrict the availability of these vast reserves by raising the cost of extracting and delivering them to industrial and population centers. About three-fourths of the land area of the USSR is found above the 49th parallel of latitude; and almost the whole of Siberia, which contains the greatest and richest deposits and energy sources, lies above this latitude.

High continentality, that is, the remoteness of the land mass occupied by the USSR from the moderating influences of the major world oceans, together with the northerly latitude of the entire territory, yields extremely cold temperatures over the greater part of the country. The extreme cold requires the use of special materials and lubricants and the adaptation of technology to cold-weather conditions. Even the provision of water for mining and industrial use, for example, poses difficult technological problems in much of Siberia. More than a third of the USSR is located in permafrost zones, where the soil thaws only a few feet during the warm months, which greatly hampers mining activities, construction, and transportation facilities. Moreover poor weather and the remoteness of the regions in which rich sources of energy and rich deposits have been found discourage the development of population centers near them. Siberia has long been used as a place of exile for the simple reason that daily life most of the year is extraordinarily demanding and because contact with cultural and metropolitan centers is exceedingly difficult.

The key to the development of Russia as an industrial nation in the nineteenth century was construction of the railway, and long-distance transportation remains the key to Soviet development, especially the exploitation of energy and mineral resources in Siberia. These resources will little benefit the Soviet economy unless the transportation system can be developed sufficiently to permit a steady low-cost flow of energy and minerals to European Russia. Hopes of moving substantial population to these resources instead have been greatly disappointed, as the latest census shows.

The Ural Mountains pose a barrier to direct east-west ground transport. Consequently the rail and road networks appear schematically as an elongated J resting on its back. The tip of the base begins at Leningrad and curves through Moscow and Kuibyshev and then below the Urals to Omsk, after which it traces out a straight line through Irkutsk eastward. Consequently west of the Urals the transportation system is oriented north-south, with latticelike branches running east and west. On the other side of the Urals the system is oriented east-west and has a diminishing latticelike extension running north and south. The system narrows as it moves eastward because of the severe climatic conditions one encounters to the north and the difficulties encountered in constructing railway rights-of-way on the permafrost.

The river systems accentuate the general north-south flow of the transportation network in European Russian and east-west flow beyond, for rivers in the European section run generally southerly, while those to the east of the Urals flow northerly into the Arctic Circle and are more useful when frozen as highways for ground transport than when flowing freely. The construction of BAM (the Baikal-Amur spur) will widen the area in Siberia with direct rail contact, but it too runs east-west. Most north-south transport is motor transport. Although Soviet rail and road systems total many miles in absolute figures, the density of all transportation networks is low because of the huge territory of the USSR. Rail and road networks in Siberia and in Central Asia are low even by standards of most underdeveloped economies, and European Russia also has relatively low-density networks when compared to more developed economies. Low densities in underdeveloped regions such as Siberia reflect the vast extent of the region and the fact that exploitation of its resources was previously unnecessary. The low transportation densities of European and of more developed regions of the Soviet Union reflect the generally low priority that transport holds for planners, for it was one of the more highly developed sectors prior to the revolution.

High-capacity usage of rail and road systems helps to keep cost per-ton mile and per-passenger low, but it causes bottlenecks when the systems come under stress, as at harvest time. The low priority of transport systems also was probably responsible for the belated development of pipeline transport, and the deliberate neglect of private automobile transport also slowed the development of all-weather highway systems. The growth of automobile and truck output in recent years suggests that major highway construction will soon become prominent.

Meanwhile railways still carry the bulk of the traffic in both goods and passengers, although the share carried has declined over the last twenty-five years. Between 1950 and 1977, for example, the share of railways declined from 90 percent of passenger miles and 85 percent of transport tonnage to 38 percent and 59 percent respectively. Highways have absorbed most of the loss of rail transport, and Aeroflot, the Soviet domestic and international carrier, has absorbed most of the relative loss in passenger miles on railroads. But the most spectacular growth has taken place in pipeline transport, which had been neglected for many years. Given the great distances in the Soviet Union, extensive use of airline transport makes good economic sense, and pipeline haulage, primarily of oil and gas, is also reasonable given the climatic constraints on road and rail transport.

After years of relative neglect, the transportation network of the USSR is being revamped to reflect new needs and to expand total capacity. The increased importance of new sources of energy, particularly petroleum and natural-gas deposits in Siberia and in other regions remote from traditional population and industrial centers, has put new demands on the transportation system, for the cost of developing resources close to population and industrial centers, particularly in European Russia, is rising sharply as the better deposits are worked out. Passenger transportation is being improved because of the importance of reducing the distance between the remote areas of the USSR in which mineral and agricultural resources are located and the developed cultural centers where people prefer to live or visit.

Industrial Resources

The territory of the USSR is stocked with more than adequate physical supplies of all minerals. Soviet policy, based upon a sense of ideological isolation and upon military considerations, has followed an autarkic policy with regard to minerals and energy sources. As a result, the USSR mines and refines all necessary minerals regardless of cost. The most important minerals for industrialization, coal and iron ore, exist in vast quantities throughout the country. Some deposits are of very high quality as well. One unchallenged estimate puts coal reserves at 99 percent of all stocks of Soviet nonrenewable energy. Since other energy sources are also very considerable in size, this is an astonishing total. Over one-half of these coal reserves are located in the harsh regions of Siberia, and they will not become economically meaningful until other potential sources of energy have been consumed.

High-grade iron-ore deposits, as well as deposits of other ferrous metals, lie near populated regions. The relative abundance of high-grade coking coal in the same regions has minimized the need for eastward movement or for extensive transportation thus far. For the immediate future it would appear to be more promising to move minerals and energy sources than to coax the population to move permanently to the eastern regions of the USSR. The old Donbass-Dnepr industrial belt is founded upon the Donbass coalfield, which still produces almost one-third of all Soviet coal. Krivoi Rog, the largest single producing iron-ore mine in the USSR today, is linked with the Donbass; and they have formed the single most important source of iron, coal, and related products since the 1917 revolution. Nearby a new iron-ore deposit, the Kursk Magnetic Anomaly, is being developed and is probably the largest deposit in the USSR today. Thus European Russia and nearby population centers should retain their dominance in mining and related industries for the foreseeable future.

An extraordinary variety and quality of metallic minerals are deposited on the eastern slopes of the Urals, and new iron deposits have been discovered in Bakal and Kachkanar to replace Magnitnaia Gora and Nizhnyi Tagil, which are being worked out. Some nonferrous metals are also located in the slopes of the Urals, and this location is therefore certain to remain a very important center of mining, smelting, and manufacturing for years to come. In the long run, however, Siberia will become the primary source of most minerals, and the role played by the Caucasus and Central Asia will grow as well. Many of the scarcest minerals are found even today only in Siberia, and the relative significance of Siberia as a treasure chest is bound to grow. The vast reaches of Siberia contain sufficient resources to ensure that the USSR will be among the last, if not the very last, to suffer from the complete exhaustion of important nonrenewable resources. But development of these resources will be very costly, and the dream of Soviet planners to increase the population of Siberia to exploit these vast resources is now fading. The net growth of population in Siberia and equally remote regions has hovered close to zero for many years despite substantial incentives to move permanently to these regions. The prospect is for small settlements of hardy souls, most of them working temporarily to build up a nest egg to return with to European Russia. They will produce the fuels and minerals a European-oriented Soviet industry and population require, shipping them via pipeline and rail.

The prospects for producing energy in the Soviet Union are, if anything, even more favorable than the situation for other types of resources. It has been estimated that the territorial limits of the USSR contain nearly one-quarter of the world's reserves of energy. Total coal reserves, for example, are estimated today at 6.8 trillion tons. Proven reserves of petroleum, natural gas, and hydroelectric potential are large also when compared to total world potentials. A measure of Soviet energy potential is the fact that it is the only major industrial power in the world today that is self-sufficient in energy production, and the total potential has hardly been touched. The problem, as with other resources, is not whether stocks exist somewhere in the territorial limits of the USSR: it is the cost of producing them and delivering them to using regions. Some 70 percent of all energy consumption takes place in European Russia, for example; but well over 80 percent of all known energy reserves are located in Asiatic regions.

Pollution and Environmental Quality

Socialist theorists have frequently argued that socialist systems are less likely than capitalist systems to destroy the environment, waste natural resources, or pollute the atmosphere because socialist enterprises are not guided by short-term profit maximization. Production for use rather than for profits would allow consideration of adverse external effects of industrial and agricultural production ("externalities") as well as for decision-making with a long lead time.

Socialist enterprises would, it is claimed, be able to take into account the costs that any economic decision imposes upon *all* affected parties — whether or not those costs appear on the enterprise's income statement and therefore affect actual profits.

Whatever the theoretical merits of this view, two factors have worked against practical realization in the USSR of economic decision-making based on so global an evaluation of costs and benefits. The first is the structure of planning that developed in the Soviet economy, which, as we have seen, tends to operate with short lead time and which bases material incentives upon current output targets, not global cost-benefit analyses. Second, like the United States, the Soviet Union is rich in natural resources relative to the rest of the world. By comparison, therefore, both the U.S. and the USSR tend to waste resources. The drive for rapid industrialization and the continued drive for high rates of economic growth have tended to make questions of environmental preservation secondary and to create resistance to pollution controls that have adverse effects upon growth rates.

The worldwide movement to improve the quality of the environment has, therefore, met obstacles in the USSR that appear to be as tough to surmount as those we find in western capitalist countries. Even so, serious, and in many cases comprehensive, steps have been taken in the USSR to reduce pollution, waste, and careless destruction of the environment. Soviet specialists on this subject claim that new legislation ensures adequate emission-standards and other controls for all newly constructed factories and operations. They also point to the protection of certain regions as recreational preserves that industrialization will never touch. The beautiful littoral of Lake Baikal in south-central Siberia is a case in point. Even the use of pesticides has been greatly restricted in or near the lake, as any recent visitor can attest.

The main problem, according to Soviet experts on these matters, rests with older industrial and other establishments, where controls on pollution and waste run counter to other objectives. Many older plants are now located in what have become urbanized regions. Shutting them down would inhibit growth, and it would create pockets of labor redundancy too. Thus pollution continues to trouble many Soviet cities (especially Moscow) despite strict legal limits on emissions. Similarly, Soviet techniques of construction as well as habitual practices tend to result in high negligence of environmental concerns, as anyone who has ever visited a construction site in Moscow can attest.

Although no over-all evaluation is now available, or possible, concerning the effectiveness of Soviet environmental protection laws, some progress is being made; and public concern is reasonably strong on the issue. Incentives to conserve resources, to reduce pollution, and to improve the quality of everyday life are, however, weak and uncertain. Thus, much remains to be done.

Agriculture

Although the total land devoted to agricultural production is quite large in absolute terms in the USSR, the continental and northerly location of the land mass of the country limits its agricultural potential far more than it does other natural resources. Some 225 million hectares is regarded as arable, which is only 10 percent of the total land mass. By comparison the United States has 186 million hectares that are regarded as arable, and this represents 20 percent of the continental land mass. Moreover only about 27 percent of the area of the USSR is used for all agricultural purposes, including pastures, meadows, orchards, and so forth, as opposed to 43 percent for the United States. Hence a much larger proportion of the Soviet Union is not suitable for agricultural production, and what is in production is qualitatively inferior to agricultural land in the United States.

The better land in the USSR is contained within an elongated equilateral triangle, the base of which runs from Leningrad in the north to Odessa in the southwest. The sides taper southeasterly to the foothills of the Altai Mountains, just beyond Semipalatinsk. A spur of relatively productive agricultural land runs down the western side of the Caspian Sea too, and there are several relatively limited regions in western and central Siberia and in Central Asia that are important for land cultures, but the remainder is only useful for pasture at best.

Cultivation expanded by 36 million hectares under the virgin lands program of the middle 1950s, mostly in northern Kazakhstan and southwestern Siberia. But a part of these lands have been and still more are likely to be withdrawn from production because they cannot support sustained cultivation. The practical significance of this huge expansion of cultivated lands was to buy time for intensification of agricultural production in traditional growing areas. The campaign marked the end, however, of the centuries-old process of expanding the area under cultivation in Russia; and, from 1958 onward, progress in increasing output in the Soviet Union has depended almost exclusively upon increasing the productivity of land. As in the United States, the amount of land under cultivation will contract gradually in the USSR.

Agricultural output did increase sharply in the 1950s thanks to the virgin lands program. It also allowed grain production to migrate to interior, more lightly populated regions of the USSR, and it permitted the development of alternative, more labor-intensive, and more difficult-to-transport products in traditional agricultural regions. On the other hand the development of these marginal new lands increased the already high inherent instability in Soviet grain yields. The output of Soviet grain is so large today that its instability is sufficient to destabilize world grain markets, the most dramatic instance being the shortfall of 80 million metric tons, or 40 percent of normal grain output, in 1975.

Soviet agriculture starts off, therefore, with a serious handicap when it comes to agricultural production. Only about 25 percent of the arable land is classified as one of the three best soil types: black, chestnut, and gray-brown forest. Climatic conditions are also relatively poor. The continental position of the USSR causes rainfall to be erratic and unreliable, increasing the risk of drought. Mean temperatures and the length of the growing season vary significantly from year to year, and the differential between temperatures in the north and in the south is not very great. These factors enhance the risk of losses and restrict year-round cultivation to relatively small regions. Consequently the better agricultural regions, as in the Ukraine, approximate conditions of production no better than in western Nebraska; and large regions, such as South Siberia, have conditions that approximate those of Saskatchewan and Manitoba in Canada. A combination of soil and climate comparable to Iowa, Illinois, or Florida is not to be found anywhere in the USSR. It would be pointless, therefore, to expect Soviet yields to compare favorably with those of these regions in the United States.

Agricultural experts, including many experts in the Soviet Union too, do not believe that the large difference between the over-all productivity of American and Soviet agriculture can be explained entirely by climatic, soil, and other natural causes. The very fact that the agricultural sector has undergone almost continuous reform since 1953, when Stalin died, indicates continuing Soviet dissatisfaction with the performance of agriculture, and it shows an attempt to remedy the fundamental organizational and institutional causes for low productivity. The most fundamental changes in the structure of agricultural production, as in many other areas, took place while Khrushchev was in power, and the current leadership has continued or accelerated most of his policies.

Khrushchev initially attempted to make the Stalinist model of Soviet agriculture work by providing increased incentives and eliminating arbitrary administrative interference. The most dramatic program of these early years was developing virgin lands. Because these new lands were developed primarily by creating new sovkhozes, the economic significance of the state farm increased significantly, and conversion of weak kolkhozes into sovkhozes has continued since that time. As a result, state farms work approximately the same areas that collective farms do today, whereas in 1953 the output of state agriculture was negligible. State farms have always been quite large, and they average six thousand hectares per farm at this time. The consolidation of collective farms has increased their average size too — to about three thousand hectares per farm. Thus another structural impact of reform during the last three decades has been to increase the size of agricultural production units.

Disappointment with the performance of collective-farm agriculture led Khrushchev to abandon the Stalinist model and to restructure production in kolkhozes along lines more nearly like those of state farms. These reforms abolished the MTS system, the old four-channel procurement system that had developed in the 1930s, and the in-kind orientation of collective farm organization. In addition, renewed efforts were made to calculate costs of production, to provide adequate incentives, particularly pecuniary incentives, and to create the basis for modern agricultural practices. Heavy investments were made in the chemical industries to facilitate the production of fertilizers and pesticides, and steps were taken to provide more desirable conditions for life and work in the countryside. A minimum annual wage is now guaranteed to collective-farm workers, and they are eligible for state-supported pensions as well. Prices paid to kolkhozes and sovkhozes have been increased manyfold to finance the increased real earnings of their workers, and the state has both financed and encouraged capital investment. The Brezhnev-Kosygin leadership continued and in some ways accelerated these developments. One structural consequence is that no longer any substantial difference exists between a state farm and a collective farm. Earnings, working conditions, and techniques of production have converged. Historically speaking, these developments in Soviet agriculture have largely abolished both the structure and the low priority of agriculture under Stalin. A much more pragmatic and a much less ideological approach has been adopted, and the organizational structure is far more conducive to growth in output and productivity than at any time in Soviet history since the NEP.

If one considers output alone, the results of heavy investment by the state in the virgin lands program and in intensifying production in traditional growing regions are quite impressive. The output of socialized agriculture has exceeded the growth of agricultural production elsewhere in the world over the last twenty-five years. The average annual rate of growth of agricultural production in the USSR exceeded 3.4 percent per year, as compared, for example, to growth of 1.6 percent per year in the United States. As population grew at comparable rates in both countries (about 1.4 percent per year), the gap between per-capita production of agricultural products in the U.S. and USSR was significantly reduced. Consequently the diet of the typical Russian has improved greatly. Increases in specific products have been impressive too. Grain output has increased from an average of less than 90 million metric tons during 1951-55 to an average of over 200 million metric tons during the first three years of the tenth five-year plan (1976-78). The output of meat and of vegetables also more than doubled over the same period. Total output and output per capita of agricultural products have increased at very high rates in the USSR since 1951, and the increase per capita is particularly striking when compared to the extremely poor performance of Soviet agriculture between 1928 and 1951.

The problem that specialists see in Soviet agricultural performance is not, therefore, with the rate of increase of output. The problem instead becomes obvious when one compares the rate of increase in inputs into the agricultural sector with the rate of increase in outputs, for it becomes painfully obvious that the increase in agricultural production has been bought at a very high price in additional real resources. The increase in output has been achieved largely through the application of additional inputs of resources rather than by means of aggregate productivity increases. According to western estimates, for example, about two-thirds of the 3.4 percent per-annum growth in agricultural production between 1951 and 1975 was attributable directly to increases in the physical resources devoted to agriculture. Hence gains in productivity for all inputs taken together, which measures the result of improvements in technology, organization, and scientific know-how, explain only about one-third. This is a slower rate than U.S. agriculture has achieved over the same period, which means that the already large gap in productivity that existed in 1951 between U.S. and USSR agriculture has apparently not been reduced by the massive expenditures of the state budget on Soviet agriculture during the last twenty-five years.

Intensification of state- and collective-farm production since 1953 has absorbed large amounts of capital. Since the late 1960s, for example, the share of total Soviet investment in agriculture has been in the neighborhood of 25 percent of total investment as compared to roughly 5 percent for the United States. If one counts investment in related industries and in nonproductive establishments such as rural housing, schools, roads, and cultural facilities, then the share of investment in this sector was about one-third of all investment in the Soviet economy in the late 1970s, a figure that overshadows comparable figures for other countries of the world and is an extraordinary number under any circumstances.

Unfortunately this enormous investment has not yet led to any significant release of labor from agricultural employments in the USSR. Comparison of manpower requirements of Soviet and American agriculture reveals that the production, processing, and distribution of food and fiber products in the United States absorbed approximately 12 million worker years (i.e., standardized man years) in 1972 as opposed to 43 million worker years in the USSR, and the number of man hours appears to have been approximately constant in the USSR since at least 1966, despite the great investments. Thus the production of food and fiber in the Soviet Union is becoming increasingly capital intensive without becoming significantly less labor intensive. And Soviet agriculture remains relatively land intensive as well. Meanwhile the populace is still not satisfied with the volume or the composition of agricultural output. Since the amount of land in production cannot increase and will almost certainly decrease through exhaustion of marginal land and since the labor force is diminishing too, increased investment in fixed capital and in research and extension services must not only replace the lost inputs of land and labor but bring about productivity increases that permit continued increases in output and improvements in the range of products made available to Soviet consumers.

The principal and thus far intractable problem of Soviet agriculture is, then, the high cost of production. Agricultural production continues to absorb very large quantities of scarce manpower and an unusually large share of total productive investment, and these resources are going to become increasingly scarce in the near future in the USSR. The manpower pool is growing much more slowly than in the past, and Soviet consumers do not appear to be willing to suffer further increases in the rate of investment. They want to enjoy the fruits of previous saving. Meanwhile the military is making large demands upon Soviet output. Unless productivity begins to grow sharply in agriculture, the conflict of interests between consumers, planners, and the military is bound to worsen.

Private-Plot Production

It is sometimes claimed that private-plot production is competitive with and more productive than socialized agricultural production, but this claim is based on two misunderstandings. Such a claim implies that the high cost of Soviet agricultural production might somehow be reduced by reverting to private cultivation entirely. The facts do not support the implication. Because private plots are very limited in size, the peasants who work them specialize in products, such as vegetables and fruits which require special care; and they frequently process them — as into pickled cucumbers, tomatoes, apples, and so forth — in order to add to the labor content and thus to their retail value. Thus yields tend to be high in private-plot agriculture *per unit of land* when compared to socialized agriculture. The catch is, however, that returns to labor expended are low when compared to the state sector, which achieves much higher labor productivity than does private agriculture. The products kolkhozes and sovkhozes produce tend to be land intensive but labor-saving. Each sector tends, therefore, to specialize in the products for which it has a comparative advantage.

The two sectors are not in fact independent producers but are instead intertwined in such a way that produce cannot be attributed unambiguously to one or the other. The animals that are privately owned, for example, graze on the public land; and firewood, herbs, mushrooms (and similar products) are collected on public land too. Private plots are sometimes plowed with collective- or state-farm equipment. Sovkhozes and kolkhozes fatten livestock reared on private plots, and they provide stud services for private cows. Piglets are reared privately, but sows and boars are usually socialized-sector animals. The fact is, then, that the two sectors are interdependent; and nalevo transactions, which of course extend to rural USSR, enhance the de facto extent of interdependence. No one knows the extent to which public fertilizer, seed, pesticides, technology, and expertise are expended on private plots; but it cannot be a negligible factor in private-plot production.

Neither private nor public agriculture is very productive in the USSR when compared to the United States. In any event, reversion to private agriculture at this point in time is unthinkable politically and economically. The capital stock of agricultural production has been built up on the presumption of large-scale factory-type production. Conversion to private agriculture would entail enormous losses in effectiveness, even if we assume that a way could be found to divide up the existing capital among individuals. Moreover the peasants do not possess the skills required to produce and market the quantities the Soviet economy routinely produces and delivers today. The current structure of the capital stock and the institutional structure that has been developed since the 1930s, when private farming was last permitted as more than a sideline, militate against any return to private farming; and Bolshevik ideology sees large-scale factory farming as a social end quite as much as an economic means.

The Prospects of Soviet Agriculture

It is easy to exaggerate the problems of Soviet agriculture. Large recent imports of grain products in the USSR have been interpreted by some observers as a sign of agricultural failure, for example; but this misses the mark entirely. These imports are a measure instead of the high priority that the consumer sector has acquired in the USSR today, for the purpose of imports was to provide fodder to maintain a growth in livestock herds that was greater than could otherwise be maintained. Livestock targets had been set unreasonably high for the ninth five-year plan, which is not surprising given Soviet planning techniques. The fact that the regime decided to spend precious foreign exchange to attempt to meet these targets *is* surprising, though. Thus, although the Soviet Union has been converted from an exporter of grains into a net importer, this does not mean in the Soviet case a diminution in its capacity to feed its own population. It reflects instead a desire to enrich the average Soviet's diet at a rate greater than can be sustained domestically year in and year out. Population growth has been quite modest since the World War II baby boom in the USSR, and it has declined sharply in recent years. Given that the demand for food also ordinarily declines as a share of total family expenditures as real income increases, the problem of satisfying the Soviet population's demand for such products is essentially a matter of time and cost, and it is not inherently insoluble.

The Soviet Union enjoys several advantages over most developing economies of today. It is no longer characterized by the kind of political instability that frequently inhibits rational agricultural policies. Nor is it any longer primarily an agrarian economy. Less than 40 percent of the population is rural, and even this population is literate and has access to health care unparalleled in the typical developing economy. Education and good health are prerequisites for modernization of agricultural production, and the high level of industrial production in the USSR makes rural development independent of the vagaries of foreign trade and aid. The Soviet Union is, then, in a relatively favorable position when viewed in the context of the developing economies of the world today; and it does not compare unfavorably with many developed economies either, especially those that are small in extent and/or island economies. Even the European Economic Community spends over two-thirds of its budget subsidizing inefficient agricultural production against competition from North America, Australia, and Argentina. Although the problems of Soviet agriculture are real and will not be easy to solve, American agricultural performance is more important as a measure of productive possibilities than as a standard for evaluating Soviet performance. Paradoxically trade barriers in the rich, mainly European, countries of the world and poverty among the poor, hungry nations convert America's incredible efficiency and productivity into an administrative curse of unwanted surpluses or the political curse of low farm-income.

Perhaps the most disturbing aspect of Soviet agricultural performance over the last twenty-five years for Soviet political leaders and the planners who serve them is failure to achieve breakthroughs in productivity which are comparable to those they have experienced in industry. The question is why has the enormous investment of capital, organizational skill, and political careers into agriculture yielded so modest and variable a return?

Soviet investment in agricultural equipment and in structures has been carried quite far, and mechanization is probably the least of the needs at the moment. But the USSR remains far behind in agricultural research, especially in the development of hybrids suitable for Soviet conditions, in education of agricultural researchers, and in the provision of means to extend new research and methods into the field. In addition, rural roads, rural cultural facilities, and even rural retail outlets are incredibly backward and hamper efficiency and retention of skilled workers in rural areas.

The enormous investment of the last several decades has resulted in new demands for skilled workers in agriculture. Unfortunately, however, the composition of the agricultural labor force is highly disadvantageous. Rural males are more likely than women to succeed in obtaining higher education, and they frequently use it to leave and acquire urban jobs. Consequently rural areas are disproportionately populated by the very old, by women of child-bearing age, and by young children, all of whom remain relatively unskilled. Development everywhere has always involved an outmigration of population from rural areas, so this is not unusual. The problem in the Soviet case is the rate of outflow of skilled population in the face of increasing demands for high-level skills to use the new equipment and techniques being introduced. Something needs to be done to make rural life more attractive to the young and ambitious.

Apart from investing in social benefits and in rural infrastructure, rural wages need to be increased. The real income of agricultural workers has increased substantially over the last several decades, especially from the socialized sector, but so has real income in the industrial sector. The gap has been narrowed, but much more will need to be done to make work and life in rural areas competitive with urban environments. Years of neglect of rural facilities and of the retail distribution network have created a differential that will be difficult to close.

Increasing expenditures in the rural sector will exacerbate the already large discrepancy between the cost of producing agricultural products and the prices charged for them in state and cooperative retail outlets. Prices on certain agricultural products, such as beef, are so far out of line with costs of production, processing, and distribution that some adjustments are inevitable. The same goes generally for all agricultural products relative to all industrial consumer goods. A good part of the nalevo economy is based upon this discrepancy and the fact that demand greatly exceeds supply at such artificially low retail prices. The problem is highly political. The political leadership has made a point of promising not to raise retail prices across the board, or even significantly, on items of everyday consumption. It is difficult to believe, however, that the leadership can long evade a large thoroughgoing readjustment of agricultural prices.

In addition to these problems, all of which involve increasing expenditures in the rural sector and improving the living conditions of farm workers, are difficulties associated with the nature of Soviet central planning. Problems created by overambitious planning, excessive centralization, and shortsightedness plague agriculture as well as industry, and agricultural production is less homogeneous and therefore more difficult to plan and manage from the top than is industry. It is important, however, not to exaggerate failings at the expense of advantages, and various factors should affect production positively.

In the first place, the current institutional structure of agricultural production is more rational and more conducive to developing efficiency than any time previously. Soviet literature on agricultural production contains much less ideological nonsense than it did even a few years ago. Income earned in rural and agricultural occupations has increased markedly, and the technical level of production is increasing rapidly. That Soviet leaders have given agriculture such high priority is also positive, because they have historically demonstrated an ability to get results if the goals have sufficiently high priority. The high cost of achieving this end may therefore not deter them from resolving the situation as a problem of satisfying consumers. Reducing the high cost of producing agricultural products will be more difficult, but it would be foolish to rule out a solution by a system that has repeatedly shown an ability to overcome such obstacles.

Agriculture remains, therefore, a weak and troublesome sector of the Soviet economy, one that has responded least to Soviet central planning and management methods. Marx himself had little interest in agriculture, and the Bolsheviks have had little sympathy or understanding of the special character of agricultural production. Agricultural production poses special problems everywhere because of the nature of production and because everywhere it tends to be a declining sector. Factory methods have to be modified when applied in agriculture, and the continuous shrinkage in rural population and in rural occupations with development causes social and economic problems that are peculiar to the sector everywhere. The heavy-handed methods of Stalin have been abandoned, and the unrealistic expectations that Khrushchev began agricultural reforms with have also been set aside. Moreover the problem that Soviet agriculture presents today is neither strategically nor ideologically critical.

Foreign Trade

Although it has become more important recently, foreign trade has played a relatively small role in the development of the Soviet economy. Isolation from international competition helps to explain some peculiarities of Soviet economic performance. During the first several decades of Bolshevik rule, most capitalist countries sought to isolate the new regime. The great depression of the 1930s further reduced opportunities for trade at a point when the USSR was most willing to engage in it. World War II and its aftermath contributed to a postwar policy of autarky. Trade was essentially restricted to COMECON (the countries of Eastern Europe other than Albania and Yugoslavia) throughout the 1950s and early 1960s. Recently, however, Soviet interest in trade with the developed capitalist world has increased significantly. The turnover of foreign trade has been growing at 16 percent per year, and the share of trade with the developed West is close to one-third of trade volume. The aim of expanded trade has been western technology and agricultural products, particularly grains. The high degree of interest in importing industrial technology is interpreted by most western students of Soviet affairs as an attempt to compensate for the ineffectiveness of incentives to bring innovation to Soviet industry and in the economic bureaucracy as a whole. Importation of agricultural products reflects an increased priority of consumption and a way of insulating consumption levels from year-to-year variation in crops.

Expansion of Soviet trade is limited by various factors, and few economists believe that the Soviet Union intends to become heavily involved or dependent upon foreign trade. The aim instead is to take advantage of international specialization and to remedy weaknesses in Soviet economic performance. Military considerations are, of course, important in limiting the interest of Soviet leaders in expanding foreign trade very much or without considerable reflection. The non-convertibility of the Soviet ruble also tends to restrict trade, and

Soviet trade planners have preferred to seek bilateral agreements with particular trading partners in order to minimize the need to spend valuable foreign exchange. Both of these facts serve as obstacles to trade with western countries. It is not always possible to arrange barters, because countries which have products of interest to Soviet industry may not find much in the USSR worth buying, and vice versa. Nonconvertibility of the ruble does help central authorities to restrict trade to approved state agencies, of course, but it is cumbersome and adds another element of inflexibility in trading procedures.

Soviet planners, however, find bilateral trade desirable because of two features of the Soviet economy. The economy operates most of the time with very little slack. A convertible currency and freedom of enterprises to engage in trade would lead to unforeseen changes in demand, exacerbating the general problem of excess demand in the economy and complicating planning control. Since bilateral agreements must be worked out in advance between the parties, exchange commitments may be accommodated to the planning process. Multilateral trade, with convertible currency, would be much more difficult to plan and control; and it would allow enterprise managers more discretion than Soviet planners prefer to do.

Soviet foreign trade is run as a state monopoly under the Ministry of Foreign Trade and is conducted by specialized foreign-trade corporations subject to its control. Enterprises that require imported components and those that produce exportable goods must work in tandem with an appropriate foreign-trade corporation. Although these agencies provide close control and may even occasionally afford an advantage in dealing with western traders, the system is awkward. Little incentive is provided Soviet enterprises to produce exportable products, and imports from outside the USSR have little competitive effect. Because consumer goods have rarely been imported in quantity and because domestic demand precludes large-scale exportation of consumer goods, this sector of the Soviet economy has never developed the sophistication or design necessary to compete with western consumer products. Soviet exports to the developed West tend to be military hardware, or commodities closely related to military hardware (such as aircraft), or crude materials. The latter include minerals, fossil fuels, natural gas, and metals. Machine tools, trucks, and heavy equipment have been sold primarily to allies and to third-world countries.

Soviet foreign trade is expanding, and several recent reforms designed to enhance incentives for enterprises to export and to improve the links between trading corporations and producing enterprises should have favorable effects upon Soviet trade. Nonetheless, that trade expansion will be carried very far in the near future is unlikely. The limitations posed by nonconvertibility and bilateralism have not been overcome even within the COMECON bloc, and prospects are not good even in that restricted sphere. Moreover, like the USSR, the COMECON countries are seeking to expand trade with the developed West. This will tend to offer competition against Soviet products in the West and at the same time reduce COMECON demand for Soviet exports.

On the favorable side, however, recent shortages of petroleum products and of natural gas owing to OPEC policies and to political disruption have made it much easier for the energy-rich USSR to earn foreign exchange. The tremendous stocks of mineral, timber, and energy resources within the continental limits of the USSR will undoubtedly also ease the problems the USSR has had in financing substantial imports on a sustained basis. Two problems remain. Leaders of noncommunist European countries will be reluctant to become heavily dependent upon the USSR for energy. Soviet leaders will similarly be wary of developing a dependency upon foreign sources for any strategic materials or supplies. Moreover Soviet planners will undoubtedly be cautious in depleting Soviet energy and other valuable resources unnecessarily. From a purely selfish standpoint, there is much to be said for using other countries' resources up before you use your own.

Another and very troublesome disadvantage to greatly expanded Soviet trade with the developed West exists. The greater the USSR's dependency upon international trade, and thus upon the world economy, the more difficult it will be to insulate the Soviet economy from the vagaries of international business fluctuations and inflation. Soviet planners can be expected to resist the loss of control that such dependency implies, for this has been one of the enduring positive aspects of the Soviet experiment with central planning. The possibility of deliberate trade disruption for political reasons, as in the recent grain embargo by the United States, offers another serious concern. Over-all, therefore, I believe that planners and leaders will find the net balance for expanded world-trade negative once the current surge has helped them to diminish the technological gap between the developed West and Soviet industry. The successful expansion of agricultural output, combined with the marked decrease in population growth of the last several decades, will eventually reduce (or level off) food and fiber imports. I expect, therefore, for the turnover of Soviet trade to stabilize in the near future.

Tourism has provided considerable foreign exchange to the USSR in recent years also, and efforts are being made to expand tourist attractions in the major cities of the USSR. Increased tourism in the USSR presents a problem, however, because it affords a point of contact, permitting private importing and exporting of consumer goods. The unreasonableness of the stated exchange rate between dollars and rubles, for example, invites private and illegal exchange of currency, and the creation of numerous special foreign-currency stores in which tourists may shop without queues and at relatively advantageous exchange rates invites private middleman activities by Soviet citizens.

Interest in acquiring foreign exchange has become an obsession not only of the state, but of the population of major tourist cities as well. Access to cultural events, such as the Bolshoi Ballet, and to good restaurants and hotels is scarce in every Soviet city. Tourists are given special advantages with respect to tickets, reservations, and accommodations in such facilities, much to the disadvantage of Soviet citizens. The special privileges accorded tourists, foreign visitors, and diplomats provide a particularly rich tributary into nalevo markets, and foreign tastes quickly affect Soviet attire and practices.

The impact of the official quest for foreign exchange upon domestic consumption was revealed to me by an old Russian, who told me not long ago: "No matter what, in the old days we always had three things: vodka, caviar, and natural fur. Now these are sold only abroad or in special-currency stores." World demand, especially for premium vodka, caviar, and fur, has in fact priced them out of Soviet retail markets. They are available domestically only through blat.

SELECTED READINGS

Berliner, Joseph S. *The Innovation Decision in Soviet Industry.* Cambridge, Mass.: MIT Press, 1976.
Feshbach, Murray. "Prospects for Outmigration from Central Asia and

Kazakhstan in the Next Decade." In U.S. Congress, Joint Economic Committee, *Soviet Economy in a Time of Change*. Washington, D.C.: U.S. Government Printing Office, 1979, I:312-40.

Goldman, Marshall I. *Detente and Dollars: Doing Business with the Soviets.* New York: Basic Books, 1975.

Gruzinov, J. P. *The USSR's Management of Foreign Trade,* translation ed. and with an introduction by Edward A. Hewett. White Plains, N.Y.: M. E. Sharpe, 1979.

Hewett, Edward A. "Most-Favored Nation Treatment in Trade under Central Planning." *Slavic Review* 37, no. 1 (March 1978), 25-39.

Holzman, Franklyn D. *International Trade under Communism: Politics and Economics.* New York: Basic Books, 1976.

Millar, James R. "Soviet Agriculture since Stalin." In *The Soviet Union since Stalin,* ed. Stephen F. Cohen, Alexander Rabinowitch, and Robert Sharlet. Bloomington: Indiana University Press, 1980, 135-54.

Millar, James R., ed. *The Soviet Rural Community: A Symposium* Urbana: University of Illinois Press, 1971.

Millar, James R. "Union of Soviet Socialist Republics: 8. The Economy." *Encyclopedia Americana* (1979), 428-428m.

Schroeder, Gertrude E. "The Soviet Economy on a Treadmill of 'Reforms.' " In U.S. Congress, Joint Economic Committee, *Soviet Economy in a Time of Change.* Washington, D.C.: U.S. Government Printing Office, 1979, I: 312-40.

Swianiewicz, S. *Forced Labour and Economic Development: An Enquiry into Experience of Soviet Industrialisation.* London: Oxford University Press, 1965.

Symons, Leslie, and White, Colin, eds. *Russian Transport: An Historical and Geographical Survey.* London: Bell, 1975.

Wädekin, Karl Eugen. *The Private Sector in Soviet Agriculture.* 2nd ed. Trans. Keith Bush. Berkeley: University of California Press, 1973.

III
The Soviet Economy
as a System

6

Macroeconomic
Performance and Policy

A Methodological Note

The conception of an economy as a system is based upon empirical observation. Individual transactors and groups of transactors are linked by a number of subsystems which cause their behavior to be interdependent. For example one transactor's expenditure is, simultaneously, another's income. Because economic activity is finely divided into many different specialties, each transactor is dependent upon a network of others for its income, and each transactor's expenditures affect a large network of other transactors. Consequently a decision by some to reduce expenditure levels is simultaneously a reduction in total income of the community — and vice versa. This is a social-accounting fact of economic life with wide ramifications. A second fact is that income is an important *determinant* of expenditure for many transactors. This is a fact about behavior, and it is not true for all transactors or for all sectors of the economy. This is important because it means that a decision by one sector to change its rate of spending is likely to be amplified by others following suit. The income-and-money circuit, therefore, links government to consumers and links both to enterprises and so on — as accounting entities and behaviorally.

Changes in prices charged in state retail outlets, in tax rates, in the distribution of investment funds, or in welfare-support payments produce a series of repercussions that ramify throughout the economy and rebound in some economic way to the initiator of the change. The repercussion may also be political, because such changes ordinarily affect the distribution of income to the benefit of some at the expense of others. The enormous increase that has taken place in prices paid to collective and state farms for their products, for example, has been absorbed almost entirely by the Soviet state budget. The turnover tax on most agricultural products has thus been eliminated and even converted into a subsidy to keep retail prices essentially constant on important food products. Thus increased supplies of food products have been available at highly subsidized constant prices, which has benefited those able and willing to queue for them. But this situation invites speculation and nalevo dealings because there are others who have blat or are willing to pay a price well above the state retail-market price to avoid queuing. Raising official prices on meat, for example, would reduce nalevo dealings in meat, but it would also redistribute income significantly from those who have blat or the time and patience to queue to those with the ability to pay. Political repercussions are feared as a result.

The Soviet economy forms a system because it consists of a seamless web of interrelated transactions. Prices, wages, tax payments, welfare benefits, investment allocations, lending and borrowing, bonuses and plan documents tie the various transactors together; and the system is sufficiently complex to make the outcome of any particular economic policy uncertain to some degree. Freedom of calling in labor markets, open consumer-goods markets, private property and freedom to buy and sell these property rights privately, and private enterprise, even though severely limited, provide room for households to maneuver, to respond with discretion to government economic activities and to central plans. Similarly the expertise of enterprise managers and the complexity of the economy affords managers considerable room to maneuver as well. It is possible, therefore, for any given economic policy to fail its object, and that failure might make matters worse too. Economic interdependency in the USSR is compounded by the fact that Communist ideology links political and economic phenomena very closely, and Bolshevik policy and promises have reinforced the link. Thus economic policy is highly loaded politically, and this includes even a number of quite minor economic matters.

The economic (and political) interdependence of the various sectors of the Soviet economy is a fact. Ever since the time of Adam Smith, economists have been impressed by the orderliness economic systems exhibit most of the time. Even primitive economic systems evidence complex patterned relationships among individuals. Consequently as a matter of intellectual curiosity economists ordinarily have been fascinated by the task of understanding how economic activity is coordinated among the different individuals and specialists. Interest in how the economy works, however, leads naturally to a desire to evaluate the performance of the economic system, for the description of how it works implies making distinctions regarding how well certain subsystems work and comparisons with the way various subsystems function in other economies.

Part of an animal physiologist's job is to explain how the healthy animal, or healthy organ of the animal, works; and this involves identifying pathological symptoms. A scientific description of the physiology of a species must not be based solely upon observation of a pathological specimen. The economist has similar concerns. When it comes to describing the way an economy functions, however, evaluation is much more difficult, because one cannot so readily set up a standard of what normal physiology or behavior is on the basis of a statistical sample or in some similar objective fashion. Good performance of an economy is a prescriptive and not a descriptive matter, and it depends therefore upon the standard of performance adopted by the observer. Because Soviet and western economists do not accept identical ends for economic activity, our evaluations of Soviet economic performance must also differ if each insists upon his own as the only standard. Unlike our characterization of the Soviet economy as a system, the purpose or end of economic activity is not a question that can be determined empirically as a general proposition. We ought, therefore, to temper our evaluation of the performance of the Soviet economy with consideration of evaluations that flow from standards held by members of the Soviet economy — consumers, managers, the military, the party, and so forth.

Our concern in what follows is, then, with presenting a more abstract picture of the important subsystems and institutions of the Soviet economy and with providing an evaluation of how well these subsystems, institutions and the economy as a whole function.

A Macroeconomic Model of the Soviet Economy

It is an interesting exercise to begin with the kind of capitalist economic model that is presented in elementary and intermediate economics textbooks in the United States and to revise and tailor it to fit Soviet conditions. The fundamental model, as tailored to Soviet institutional arrangements, has been specified more fully elsewhere for the benefit of those who find mathematical formulation congenial. (See Millar and Pickersgill, *ACES*, Spring 1977). Here I shall suppress the mathematical aspects as much as possible and focus primarily upon the essential features of and main inferences that can be drawn from the model. Those who find algebraic and functional notation inhibiting or disconcerting should still be able to follow the argument presented in the text, for I have made an effort to explain in words the content of each equation.

The standard macroeconomic demand submodel of a western capitalist economy contains two statements. First the various sectors of the economy are identified and put into a social-accounting equation that expresses the fact that one sector's expenditures represent (simultaneously) the income of the other sector(s). Thus the incomer (or product) of all sectors taken together (Y) is equal to their joint (deflated) expenditures:

$$Y = C + I + G. \tag{1}$$

We assume here that foreign trade can be neglected and exclude that sector from consideration. Our equation states, therefore, that the sum of real consumption outlays (C) by the household sector, of investment expenditures (I) of state and collective-farm enterprises, and of government expenditures (G) on military and nonmilitary goods and services equals the real income of the economy (Y).

The second statement of the basic macroeconomic submodel expresses consumption (C) of the household sector as a positive function of disposable income (Y_d), which is the income that remains in the hands of members of the household sector after they have paid their taxes and/or received welfare or social-security payments and other transfers from the government sector:

$$C = f(Y_d). \tag{2}$$

This basic two-equation model contains, therefore, a social-accounting equation and a behavioral expression. (Technically we have another equation which defines Y_d in terms of Y — e.g., $Y_d = Y + [$Social security benefits minus personal taxes$]$.)

For any western mixed economy we would go on from this basic model to attempt to explain investment expenditures (I) behaviorally, perhaps as a function of expected profits and the current rate of utilization of industrial capacity. The next step would be to attempt to explain government outlays by another behavioral equation. In the USSR, however, investment expenditure (I) is determined by Gosplan and the Council of Ministers in the planning process, and no one has yet proposed an explanation of the process that permits simple formulation, as for C in the consumption function. Government expenditure is determined similarly, although with the participation of Gosbiudzhet and certain political and military establishments. Because it is not clear just what the behavioral determinants might be, we are forced to treat these two components of the domestic products as fixed *exogenously.* which is a useful word behind which to screen our ignorance of the way they are in fact settled upon. Thus we may rewrite our equation (1) to reflect this fact:

$$Y = C + I^* + G^*, \qquad (1^*)$$

in which the asterisk indicates determination outside the model.

Once we begin to reflect upon this equation in the light of central planning, however, we find ourselves in an awkward situation. The comprehensiveness and detailed character of Soviet planning means in this context that Gosplan is attempting to fix Y as well as I^* and G^* in advance of the start of the plan year. If Y is fixed as Y^*, however, then every variable in equation (1^*) is determined, for consumption (C) must be equal to the difference: $Y^* - (I^* + G^*)$. That is, if consumption $(\hat{C})$ is determined as a residual, we have no need for equation (2) above which explains C as a positive function of disposable personal income. We know that equation (1) is a true equation as a logical proposition, and empirical measurement bears it out as well.

There is no way out. If three of the variables in equation (1^*) are determined by central planners, the fourth follows as a residual, and there is no need for an independent behavioral explanation of consumption expenditures.

For this reason western scholars believed for many years that western-type macromodels could be of no real analytic value in examining the Soviet economy. We know now, however, that this was a hasty opinion. It ought to be clear at this point that residual determination of the goods and services that are made available to households in the Soviet Union is unlikely as a general proposition. Household members in today's Soviet economy are not without direct means for influencing the division of product between investment and government expenditures, on the one hand, and personal consumption expenditures on the other. A Politburo that is fearful of raising consumer-goods prices and that is expending precious foreign exchange on fodder and meat for domestic consumption would have every reason to shun residual determination of consumption in practice, for it could only exacerbate the problem of deficit commodities.

The first obstacle that we confront in attempting to construct a basic macromodel for the Soviet economy is the possibility that the two most fundamental propositions of any macromodel, our equations (1) and (2) may contradict each other. That is:

$$Y = \hat{C} + I^* + G^*, \tag{1*}$$

$$C = f(Y_d) \tag{2}$$

where Y_d, disposable income of households, is defined as above; the prefix f means it is dependent upon Y_d. $\hat{C}$ is residually determined consumption goods (that is, actual or planned). What happens if $\hat{C} \neq C$? Suppose, in other words, that households decide on the basis of disposable income (Y_d) to spend more than $\hat{C}$? Demand would exceed supply, and there is no obvious mechanism to assure us of equality or that would set forces in motion to restore equality when demand exceeds (or is less than) supply. It would be inappropriate to introduce flexible prices to allow aggregate supply and demand for consumer goods to move toward equilibrium, because the price level is controlled and is inflexible in the USSR.

It has frequently been argued that most of the time demand does indeed exceed the supply of consumption goods in the USSR. Some analysts have argued, for example, that households taken as a group cannot spend all of their income and find themselves saving more of their disposable income than they want to save. If we let S_p represent real personal saving in any period, it is defined as $Y_d - \hat{C}$. That is, the increase in saving of households in savings accounts, bonds, and in cash during the period equals the difference between disposable income and actual consumption. Unwanted, or "forced," saving (S_f) is defined by our equations, therefore, as:

$$S_f = C - \hat{C}.$$

The notion that households can be forced to save more than they want to save implies a premise of doubtful validity: that there is no way for households to evade the compulsion to save. Open labor markets and, to a limited extent only, the existence of certain nalevo markets and channels both represent possible avenues through which households may avoid the compulsion to save.

In order to examine the question of forced saving more closely, let us look more closely at the aggregate labor market. As indicated in our discussion above of the Soviet labor market, pressure is put on individuals, particularly upon ablebodied men and women of working age, to participate in the labor force. Labor is not conscripted, however, and there are many individuals currently engaged in economic employments who are free to withdraw from the labor market, or to withdraw efficiency from their employments, if they wish. Consequently we may reasonably assume that the supply of labor (N_S) in the Soviet economy is, at least in large part, a positive function of the real wage (W/P), in which W is money wages and P is a price index which reduces W to real purchasing power. In order to make the possible influence of forced savings explicit, let us assume that the amount of accumulated savings (M) has a negative influence on the willingness of individuals to work and/or to work intensively. That is, as unspent savings accumulate at a rate in excess of the desire of households to save, they find it convenient to reduce the family's formal work effort in order, for example, to spend more time in queues, or merely to spend time enjoying what income they have in leisure at the dacha. Our labor supply function may be expressed, therefore, by:

$$N_S = N_S(W/P, M/P), \tag{3}$$

in which we must reduce accumulated savings to its real purchasing power by means of an appropriate price index (P).

It follows from equation (3) that a persistent discrepancy between the consumption households desire (C) and the amount of consumption goods central planners made available ($\hat{C}$) will cause the total amount of labor effort available to diminish, other things equal. Labor supply curve N_S in figure 6-1 would shift to the left, say to N_S', requiring an increase in real wages (from y to z) to maintain any current volume of employment. Otherwise employment would fall, for example, to b from a.

Figure 6-1. The Labor Market

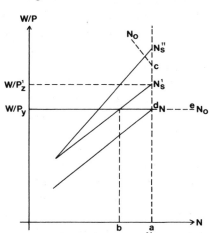

where:
W/P = real wage
N   = aggregate employment
N_F = administratively determined full employment

Representation of the aggregate demand for labor equation is complicated, but we must describe it in order to determine the volume of actual employment at any given time. Doing so brings us back to the problem we found with respect to residual determination of consumption expenditures. As far as any enterprise manager is concerned, his own demand for labor is likely to be highly inelastic. That is, little or no penalty exists for having redundant labor. There are always times of the year, such as just before the plan period ends, when extra personnel are useful to have around. Moreover managers cannot readily fire employees. Consequently managers are not likely to be concerned about the real wages they must pay so long as funds are provided in the plan. But it is clear in any case that managers as a group are not in a position to determine the real wage of the aggregate labor force. If the central plan determines $\hat{C}$, then the most that any manager can do is to increase the real wages of particular employees by advancing them in rank or through bonuses. If other managers follow suit, the result will be a general advance in money wages unaccompanied by any increase in $\hat{C}$. This is why wage payments are closely monitored by Gosbank. Competition among managers for labor is regarded as primarily inflationary. (Of course, if raising wages leads to higher productivity or is taxed away elsewhere in the system, then the whole increase is not necessarily inflationary.)

Central planners face a dilemma, therefore. If they determine $\hat{C}$ as a residual, this, in turn, determines the real wage and thus employment too. If this level of the real wage is too low to maintain total employment, total output (Y) must fall, for it is clearly a direct positive function of employment N:

$$Y = Y(N, \overline{K}), \qquad (4)$$

in which N is total employment and $\overline{K}$ is the capital stock (which is fixed in the short run). If Y falls, $\hat{C}$ will fall still further, unless Gosplan is prepared to reduce I and/or G in compensation.

The model shows that, given I* and G*, central planners can set *either Y or C, but not both.* The model reveals that "forced saving" ultimately requires "forced labor." It is obvious from figure 6-1, for example, that planners could set W/P, the real wage, at will if, and only if, they have first fixed employment. So long as workers are free to withdraw labor or efficiency from the market, it is not possible for the central plan to determine arbitrarily the consumer goods and services to be made available, because workers are in a position to retaliate by reducing total income Y. It follows that the determination of I and/or of G must involve an adjustment to the real wages that workers demand to produce any given level of income Y.

The open-labor market is only one avenue by which workers can influence the actual amount of consumer goods and services that they receive. In the first place, demand for additional commodities and services may call forth an additional labor effort outside of the state sector (we must exclude competition with it, or mere transfers of commodities and services between them in this instance) that would not otherwise be forthcoming. Individuals may produce new goods and services not accounted for in $\hat{C}$, and this is one of the ways in which private legal and illegal markets supplement state economic activity. In the second place many individuals can convert goods destined for I or G into de facto consumer goods. A hunting lodge built for the Soviet general staff with military funds may be used extensively by civilian relatives. Government cars may be used to taxi private individuals and gasoline may be siphoned from public vehicles into private. Materials may be pilfered from construction sites for private construction, and so on. The actual distribution of final goods and services between government (G), enterprise capital accounts (I) and private consumers (C) may, therefore, differ significantly from official records. A discrepancy between desired consumption (C) and planned consumption ($\hat{C}$) invites this kind of illegal conversion of public property into private consumption for private gain in the USSR.

Because households do have ways to influence their own real wages, it seems reasonable to conceive of the determination of total employment as a supply and demand adjustment, but we need to add one more proposition to illustrate how this might occur. As we have seen, managers are in a position to influence only relative wages of their employees. The real wage for all workers taken together is determined elsewhere. The labor-demand function must reflect the following influences. Since it has ordinarily been the primary goal of planners to maximize output (subject to certain constraints we shall here neglect), let us assume that overcommitment planning is based upon an attempt to pick an employment level that matches or overcommits full employment (N_F). Presumably central planners are also conscious of the tradeoff we have just specified between the real wage and the other components of national income. Let us write the labor-demand equation as

$$N_d = N_d(W/P, N_F). \tag{5}$$

where N_F is full employment and is defined as the point at which the supply of labor becomes completely inelastic (insensitive) to further increases in the real wage (figure 6-1, c). We assume therefore, that, within a reasonably wide range (say, below point c in figure 6-1), Gosplan sets the real wage to correspond to full employment (N_F). At some point, of course, as W/P increases for a given definition of N_F, state demand for labor would presumably become elastic. This point is given by c, beyond which demand is elastic and one would expect the usual type of supply and demand intersection.

Equation 4, which is a production function relating the input requirements to each level of output, and equations 3 and 5, the aggregate supply and demand for labor functions, form the aggregate supply submodel. Between them they determine the real wage, W/P; employment, N; and the level of real output, Y. Equations (1) and (2) above compose a demand submodel, but, as we have seen, we need to treat either investment, or government expenditures, or both as residually determined. Let's assume that investment has priority and is fixed by Gosplan, which gives us the equation:

$$I = I^*. \tag{6}$$

The model now determines the following variables: C, I, G, Y, N and W/P. (We have another equation, of course, which determines disposable income, Y_d.)

The model also incorporates M, the sum of cash balances and savings deposits held by households at the beginning of the year. The capital stock, $\overline{K}$, in equation (4) is determined exogenously as a carryover variable determined at the beginning of the year; and full employment, N_F, is determined administratively. One more exogeneous variable, the price index P, needs to be specified, and, for simplicity of analysis, we shall assume that it is a policy variable set by the various state committees on retail and wholesale prices. We shall return to discuss the reasonableness of this assumption subsequently.

Although complex, the model yields an insight that was not previously obvious. Consumption goods and services made available by Gosplan cannot be set at just any level above subsistence. Quite apart from any political or other noneconomic retaliation that might follow from arbitrary determination of $\hat{C}$, the open-labor market provides an avenue for direct economic response. It is nonsense, for example, to speak as though Soviet households cannot find enough goods and services to spend their incomes on — at least as long as any significant fraction of the labor force is free to withdraw time or efficiency from state employments. The notion of a command economy implies, ultimately, conscription of labor. This military analogy is misleading for the contemporary Soviet economy precisely because most military systems have been founded on the principle of conscription. Although the labor market is only one market, it is a large market that ramifies into all branches of the Soviet economy. Gosplan must come to terms with it or return to some brand of Stalinism.

Macroeconomic Policy in the USSR

Before the basic model can be used to analyze macroeconomic policy and to compare Soviet and western macroeconomic tactics, one more modification is necessary. The amount of private consumption was originally made dependent solely upon real disposable income: in which $Y_d = Y - \frac{X}{P} + \frac{(U-T)}{P}$. In this equation, X is the proportion of total income deducted as profits and taxes from state enterprises, and U-T is the net flow of transfers to and from the household sector in the way of welfare payments, pensions, and personal taxes. Exogenous variables X, U, and T are policy variables, like P, in that the Gosbiudzhet, the Council of Ministers, and Gosplan may set them to effect specific policy objectives. Given P, increases in U work to increase Y_d, and conversely for increases in T and X. Even with this specified we are missing an important element from our model: the role of monetary policy. The easiest way to add it is in the consumption function, so let us revise equation (2) to read:

$$C = f(Y_d, r), \qquad (2^*)$$

in which r is the rate of interest paid by Gosbank on private savings accounts. The question addressed by the addition is whether the rate of private saving is affected positively by the rate of interest. If so a shortfall in the amount of consumer goods made available could be compensated by a rise in the rate of interest paid on the (extra) savings, thereby circumventing adverse effects of forced saving upon the volume of employment and the level of total output. We assume that the rate of interest, r, is set exogenously and that it is adjusted for inflation.

With this modification of the model we can now examine macroeconomic policy in the Soviet Union.

Overly ambitious planning in the Soviet Union leads to the overcommitment of all resources and to chronic supply shortages in all sectors. Excess aggregate demand appears to be as chronic a feature of the Soviet economy as is insufficient aggregate demand for most western capitalist economies. One obvious remedy would be for Gosplan to decrease the demand of the sectors it controls directly. Investment and government expenditures could be reallocated with the aim of apportioning the potential full-employment national product in such a way that aggregate demand and supply reach equilibrium at the given aggregate supply price (P). This would be the equivalent of fiscal policy in which variations in government expenditures are used in a country like the United States to stimulate or to retard aggregate demand. Thus far, however, the Soviet government has been reluctant to reduce investment expenditures. Until quite recently the share of investment in Soviet national income has been increasing, and the declining rate of growth in national income of the last decade or so makes Gosplan understandably reluctant to reduce the share of I in GNP.

Military outlays present another kind of problem, mainly because they depend as much upon the evaluation of external factors as upon domestic and because, in any case, Gosplan has no expertise to evaluate them. Some western observers have read into the Soviet Union's recent interest in détente a desire to reduce the relative significance of military expenditures and therefore the conflict with direct consumer purchases of final goods and services. Others have pointed out, on the contrary, that military expenditures are also increasing rapidly. Let us assume that reduction in the share of I + G is the least desirable alternative for planners and those they serve, and let us examine the alternatives for bringing aggregate supply and demand into line with one another.

Price Policy

As we have seen, the overriding objective of state retail-price policy has been to stabilize the aggregate price level. Incorrect relative prices would be sufficient to explain the widespread queuing in the Soviet Union. It does not necessarily indicate that the *aggregate* price level (the weighted average of all prices) is too low. That political leaders are reluctant to change relative prices, however, is sufficient to militate against the kind of price flexibility required in a changing world to adjust aggregate supply to aggregate demand. Official price policy is not used to equate aggregate supply and demand. Unofficially, however, an excess of demand, whether originating in retail or in wholesale markets, should be reflected in an index of prices in the black market or in other nalevo markets. Unfortunately we have insufficient data to construct a reliable price index of this sort. The best substitute we have is an index for the private rynok, which indicates relative aggregate price stability. This market carries such a small and selected volume of commodities, however, that it probably cannot be used to measure discrepancies in aggregate supply and demand.

Soviet planners are not able, or willing, to use prices to adjust aggregate supply and demand for consumer goods. Were they to do so, however, there is no reason to suppose that it could satisfactorily adjust a discrepancy between supply and demand for consumer goods. Raising all prices on consumer goods would only make apparent what most workers would already know: that the current real wage is less than the money wage. Unless they fail to think in terms of the real purchasing power of their incomes, income earners would see a general rise in prices as a decrease in unspent cash balances, but no change in what can actually be bought. There would, of course, be a redistribution of income favoring some at the expense of others as a result of the elimination of certain black market and nalevo transactions, but this would only occur if relative prices are changed appropriately, and it has little to do with the aggregate price level. There is no reason to suppose that relative price adjustments would cause the labor supply function to shift one way or another, but they might cause considerable political opposition from those who lose real income in the process.

Besides the political problem of readjusting real income to a new situation of relative prices, there is another good reason why Soviet planners and politicians might be reluctant to use retail prices as a means to bring aggregate demand and supply for consumer goods into equilibrium. An increase in the general price level, P, which occasioned an expectation of further increases might very well aggravate the situation in the current period by inducing households to spend now rather than later. The general expectation of shortages is likely to be a self-fulfilling and self-perpetuating expectation, for there is no point in accumulating cash and savings accounts if inflation is expected to erode their purchasing power significantly. In the long run, therefore, it may very well be preferable policy from the standpoint of Gosplan and the Politburo to promote popular expectation of aggregate price-level stability rather than the reverse in order to validate and thus encourage private, voluntary saving. (Price increases do occur in the USSR, but surreptitiously, through, for example, the introduction of new labels and or slightly modified products at higher prices and the subsequent disappearance, or substantial reduction in output, of older lower-priced varieties and brands.)

Thus, although price policy leaves much to criticize from the vantage point of the relative prices of consumer (and other) goods and services, it is not necessarily unreasonable for policy-makers to shun price-level changes when a gap in consumption (C-Ĉ) is expected to persist for any considerable period. A sudden general rise in prices sufficient to equate aggregate supply and demand might well prove politically hazardous. A slow gradual rise might well prove economically counterproductive through its impact on expectations. Aggregates of markets do not ordinarily work the same way that individual markets do. The experience of simultaneously rising prices and rates of unemployment in most western capitalist countries over the last decade offers scant ground for criticism of Soviet reluctance to use general rises in prices as an instrument of policy.

Interest Rate and Monetary Policy

Interest rates paid on private savings accounts are very low and stable in the USSR. Most accounts receive 2 to 2.67 percent per annum simple interest. This rate clearly has no bearing on investment decisions. The low and constant level of interest rates paid on household savings are good indications that they are not used to influence consumption and saving. The interest rate, r, is included in equation (2*) because western economists believe that it may have some influence on the decision to save. Confirmatory evidence is scant, even in the West, and Soviet policy certainly operates on the assumption that higher rates would not encourage additional saving. Even if we assume that Gosplan can in fact determine $\hat{C}$ as a residual, independently of the labor market, neglect of the rate of interest would be unreasonable if some higher rate would help to provide an outlet for disposable income. Similarly, if employment and the real wage are really determined in the labor market, then an experiment with higher interest rates on private savings would seem well worthwhile. Failure to try out higher and more flexible rates of interest can only be interpreted as irrational.

Here, as in other ways, Soviet financial policy appears backward and excessively conservative to any western economist. Interest charges on short- and long-term borrowing by state and collective enterprises are too low to encourage managers to conserve scarce capital. These charges are instead intended to defray the cost of providing and servicing loan accounts. The main function of enterprise borrowing from the standpoint of Gosbank is to provide a means of controlling their expenditures and for monitoring plan performance. Interest-paying private accounts appear to have significance only as a way to monitor private saving.

Until 1957 households could buy state bonds, but over the years the purchase of state bonds had become as compulsory as personal taxes, and they were abolished for this reason. Thus there are few instruments available for personal saving today. Consequently interest-rate policy is a particularly neglected aspect of Soviet economic policy generally, and it is therefore an area in which one should expect changes if reforms of economic policy continue. It is senseless to allow an otherwise effective instrument of policy to fall into desuetude, especially when existing instruments are inadequate to the tasks set for them. The constraint on more rational use of interest rates is doubtless ideological in origin, but inertia probably has more to do with its neglect today than ideology.

Monetary policy, in the usual western sense of the term, simply does not exist at the aggregate level in the USSR. Monetary policy is inextricably linked to interest-rate policy in western economies, but these interest rates are not used in the USSR to influence changes in the stock of money or to allocate investment funds. Monetary policy is directed primarily to the needs of trade, and investment decisions are made without regard to raising funds. All consequential policies regarding the flow of money and other funds are microeconomic in character rather than macroeconomic. There is no reason to attempt to influence the level of output or employment through monetary policy. This is not to say that monetary policy is unimportant. On the contrary banks directly supervise enterprise expenditures, especially outlays on wages and salaries; and this plays an essential role in preventing competition among enterprise managers for scarce skilled labor from causing an unplanned upward drift in money wages. These controls were weak during the 1930s, and wage inflation led to considerable inflation in retail prices. Gosbank also plays an important role by monitoring short-term borrowing by enterprises and thereby constraining their deficit spending to planned totals or to proportional increases (where plans are overfulfilled).

Fiscal Policy

We have already considered the spending side of fiscal policy. Thus far the state budget, which finances most investment as well as all government expenditures, has not been called upon to manipulate expenditures or transfer payments (to enterprises) as a means of achieving equilibrium between aggregate supply and demand. Our simple model does not contain the state budget explicitly. We can readily add it, however, as a budget equation

$$G + I = \frac{X + (T-U) + Z}{P} \tag{7}$$

in which X represents tax and profit receipts, (T-U) is net receipts (or payments) to the household sector, and Z is the surplus or deficit for the Gosbiudzhet as a whole. The budget normally runs a surplus at the present time. Deficits were common during the 1930s and 1940s, however. The main thrust of fiscal policy in recent years, therefore, has been to ensure that the various state agencies do not add unplanned demand, thereby exacerbating the chronic condition of excess demand existing in the economy.

Our macroeconomic model suggests that excess aggregate demand could be reduced by increasing personal income taxes (thereby reducing Y_d, disposable income, in equation (2*)). Western economic theory holds that any kind of personal income tax, expecially a progressive income tax, is bound to affect adversely incentives and thus efficiency. An increase in personal taxes, plus the application of a progressive principle, could be expected to have a negative effect on incentives to work which would be analogous to the effect produced by the accumulation of unwanted real-cash balances (M/P) in equation (2*). Thus what is gained by reducing M/P would be lost by the decrease in employment. The conclusion is inescapable formally, but empirical experience in western economies suggests that tax rates can be much higher than they are in the USSR and much more progressive before significant negative incentive effects come to into play. Direct personal taxes are, therefore, underutilized by comparison with the West. Instead indirect taxation and retained profits of state enterprises are relied upon for government revenue.

Examination of macroeconomic issues and policy under chronic excess-demand conditions reveals several insights. The Soviet economy suffers from chronic excess of aggregate demand. In many respects the symptoms are reciprocal images of the symptoms many western capitalist countries display as a result of a tendency to chronic deficiency of aggregate demand. Faced with persistent supply insecurity, enterprises and individuals alike seek to ensure a steady supply of deficit commodities by concentrating attention and resources on purchasing or otherwise acquiring goods. The sales effort of enterprises or individuals is of no real consequence. Persistent excess demand of this sort would generate relatively rapid and serious price-and-wage inflation in the absence of price-and-wage controls, but continuous application of such controls leads to undesirable side-effects in the form of black market operations, barter exchange, or privileges and special opportunities, and a general erosion in popular respect for legal restrictions on trading, prices, and individual enterprise.

Because the central plan seeks to specify all macroeconomic, as well as microeconomic flows of goods, services, and money in the economy, macroeconomic instruments that are commonly used in western capitalist economies are neglected in the Soviet Union. Tax rates are not systematically adjusted to constrain or to increase consumer demand in the short run. Monetary policy is not used to influence employment, investment, or the price level in any usual sense. Bank policy is important as a means of controlling enterprise expenditures and pegging them to plan targets, and it is important as a means of keeping track of household savings. These two policies have significant antiinflationary implications. Gosbank, however, is not free to change the tightness of bank loan policy generally in order to effect any particular macroeconomic end. Interest rates play an insignificant role in determining the rate of investment or the level of economic activity.

There seems to be no reason why interest rates paid to Soviet households ought not be increased substantially to test the possibility of a favorable effect upon saving rates. Progressive taxes on personal income might also be used experimentally to ascertain the response of the public. As increases in the general level of prices are ruled out on political as well as on *reasonable* economic grounds as a way to equate aggregate supply and demand, it would appear to be irrational to neglect these other macroeconomic instruments. The alternative is to reduce the share of $(I + G)$ and/or to increase net imports to reduce the gap between desired consumption (C) at current real wage rates and available supplies $(\hat{C})$. The alternative must be persistent conflict between households and planners than can be resolved in one of two ways. Either Gosplan and the decision-makers it represents will lose and be obliged to reduce the share of $(G + I)$ in order to maintain a reasonable rate of growth of factor productivity and thus of national income and product, or controls and restrictions on labor will have to be introduced that will necessitate a return to a form of Stalinism.

SELECTED READINGS

Ames, Edward. *Soviet Economic Processes.* Homewood, Ill.: Richard D. Irwin, 1965.

Bergson, Abram. "Socialist Economics," *Essays in Normative Economics.* Cambridge, Mass.: Harvard University Press, Belknap Press, 1966.

Copeland, Morris A. *Our Free Enterprise Economy.* New York: Macmillan, 1965.

Millar, James R., and Pickersgill, Joyce. "Aggregate Economic Problems in Soviet-Type Economies." *ACES Bulletin* 19, no. 1 (Spring 1977).

Rhee, Poong. "A Macroeconomic Model of the Soviet Union: An Analysis of Shortages of State Retail Goods." Ph.D. dissertation, University of Illinois at Urbana-Champaign, 1979.

Ward, Benjamin N. *The Socialist Economy: A Study of Organizational Alternatives.* New York: Random House, 1967.

7

Central Planning, Central Management, and Reform

Let us define the various macroeconomic policies that we discussed in the previous chapter as *central-management* instruments of control to differentiate them from central-planning devices. To these macroeconomic instruments should be added microeconomic devices as well — such as setting relative prices; establishing price ceilings or floors; setting standards of cleanliness, safety, and the like; and taking recourse to legal sanctions, such as bankruptcy proceedings, injunctions, and so forth. Central-management activities are therefore those activities of a central economic authority (or authorities) that are directed to influencing the direction and/or level of economic activity indirectly as the plan period unfolds. *Central planning* may be defined, in contrast, to include all the activities of central authorities that are directed to determining the direction and/or the level of economic activity in advance of the plan period. Central planning includes forecasting, target setting for inputs and outputs and for financial and transfer flows, and the specification of success criteria for plan fulfillment.

Given appropriate institutional frameworks, central planning and central management offer alternative methods for achieving any given degree of central control over economic activity. A perfect plan would minimize the need for central management by confining that management to monitoring and supporting target fulfillment. Enterprise managers who failed to fulfill the plan exactly as specified would obviously be guilty of either incompetence or malfeasance. Conversely perfect central management would minimize the need for central planning. Thus a trade-off may be specified between central management and planning for any given degree of central control. The aspiration of Soviet authorities for comprehensive detailed plans is reflected in a preference for central planning over central management. The United States economy presents the other extreme, a preference for central management without central planning. Because planning cannot be perfect, however, Soviet authorities are obliged to use central-management techniques. Similarly central planning takes place in the United States, but as an informal political process that informally develops acceptable goals — for example regarding the maximum tolerable rates of inflation growth and unemployment.

The popular conception of the Soviet economy as a command economy is based partly upon the notion of perfect planning. Once it is conceded that the central plan cannot be perfect, certain allocative decisions are shifted from the planning stage to the plan period itself. An imperfect plan means that enterprise managers will discover in the course of attempting to fulfill it either that it can be overfulfilled or that it cannot be fulfilled in some particulars or possibly at all. In either case the manager will be obliged to resolve the problems raised by an infeasible, inconsistent, or understated plan. If the center wishes to control these decisions it must provide rules for managers to follow in decision-making, and it must provide and manipulate incentives to reward compliance. Central planning is based upon the substitution of central calculations and priorities for individual decision-making. Central management is based upon manipulating stimuli to induce decentralized decisions that accord with the center's preferences. On a priori grounds it is impossible to pick one mode as more effective than the other. An order backed by a stick is not necessarily more effective than one backed by a reward for appropriate behavior. All modern nations use both central-planning and central-management techniques to some extent. The degree of reliance upon one or the other seems to depend upon ideology more than anything else.

The analytic model of market socialism that Oskar Lange developed in the 1930s represents a combination of central planning and management that greatly differs from the model that was then being implemented in the Soviet Union. Lange's model calls for a Central Planning Board to manipulate prices of capital goods and wholesale commodities (transactions in which state enterprises deal with each other) in such a way that equilibrium prices are established (that is, prices that clear these markets, leaving neither unwanted inventories nor queues). Labor and consumer-goods markets are left free. The only central planning involved in Lange's model involves determining the rate of investment and the final allocation of income (that is, the allocation of real income between present and future and among contemporaries), and these goals were to be achieved exclusively by means of managing the rate of interest and taxes (the social dividend).

Lange's system of central management works conceptually as well as it does mainly because he assumed that enterprise managers would follow the same procedures of profit maximization that they had followed as private capitalists prior to the revolution and nationalization of all means of production. Unfortunately he cavalierly assigned the problem of motivating these new civil servants to follow these procedures (which alone ensure efficient operation of enterprises) to sociologists. Constructing an effective managerial incentive system lies at the heart of the problem of getting managers' interests to coincide with those of planners or of society as a whole.

The Soviet Union developed a very different approach to central management. Traditional feelings of antipathy toward markets and pecuniary institutions precluded extensive use of these devices as means to regulate economic activity. Mistrust of many individuals upon whom the Bolsheviks were obliged to depend as managers in the early years and traditional mistrust of local autonomy reinforced prejudices against local exercise of economic discretion. Consequently control of the exercise of discretion by enterprise managers developed informally, by means of various sorts of priority systems, rather than formally, to counter and control the unplanned and undesired development of informal decision-making at lower levels.

Speaking generally, planning involves determining both the level and the composition of output, both in the aggregate and for each enterprise. Each aspect presents special problems. In planning the level of output Soviet planners have sought historically to maximize output. This means setting targets so that the last unit of output utilizes the last unit of some vital input — that is, planners seek to exhaust possibilities for producing goods. Elementary textbooks portray the range of maximum possible combinations of outputs as a production-possibility frontier. The first task of central planning in maximizing current period output is, then, to land on this curve (see figure 7-1). The second task is to pick a combination of investment plus government expenditures and consumption goods that satisfies the preferences of planners and their bosses — that is, to determine, by choosing ray (1), (2), or some other, the composition of national income.

Figure 7-1. Production Possibility Frontier

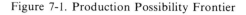
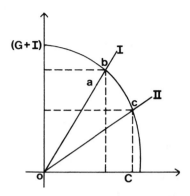

where:

C = consumption expenditures
I = investment expenditures
G = government expenditures

For the moment let us consider the first task. If planners pick a point inside the production-possibility frontier, (say, point a) the plan will clearly be feasible, but some national product will be lost by ensuring feasibility in this way. As planners push toward the frontier, however, they must become increasingly unsure about whether they have crossed beyond it into the realm of infeasibility. No one can know where the production possibility curve lies. Clearly, by picking a point well within the curve, planners can design a plan that is consistent and insist that it be carried out as planned. To avoid losing the remaining output they can instruct managers to overfulfill the plan wherever possible and reward them for doing so. Alternatively planners could pick a point known to be outside the curve and instruct managers to fulfill plan targets as nearly as possible. Either way a combination of central planning and centrally managed decentralized decision-making moves output nearer to the limit of production possibilities than central planning could do alone.

If successful either approach ought to create a taut economy, and this inevitably means supply insecurity for managers. The uncertainty that central planners face about reaching the production-possibility curve is converted therefore into uncertainty for managers about receiving premiums.

If the only goal of central planners were to ensure a taut full-employment economy, little else would be required; but planners care about the composition of national income too—that is, about the share, as indicated by rays (1) or (2) in figure 7-1, that is devoted to investment, for example, and therefore about the distribution of real income among transactors and sectors. One way to determine the composition of national income is to adjust relative prices and thus personal gains so as to encourage production of some goods relative to others. Lange's model purports to do this. The Soviets, however, elected to deal with the composition question by means of a priority system. Certain scarce inputs are allocated by direct requisition, and preferred sectors and enterprises have their supplies of these vital items guaranteed by direct rationing. An informal sense of priority mindedness also operates to protect favored sectors and transactors against the neglect of buyers' interests that sellers' markets create. Moreover it appears that enterprise plans are not set uniformly tight by central planners. Preferred enterprises tend to receive plans that are easier to fulfill as well as being protected by formal and informal priority systems. Thus, as we would expect, some enterprises regularly fulfill or overfulfill their plans and others fail frequently to do so.

Central management in the Soviet Union has been represented by various direct-rationing and other priority devices which allocate the inevitable "errors" in central plans to low-priority sectors which have no choice but to absorb them. Central-management activities of the Gosbank, Stroibank, and Gosbiudzhet are directed primarily to ensuring that excess demand created chronically by Soviet planning does not erode financial discipline, delivery priorities, and managerial integrity.

Once the plan period begins, Soviet economic activity presents itself as a free-for-all in which certain participants, both producers and consumers, are given a head start. The success of central planning in the Soviet Union has depended upon the ability of central management to enforce the priority system. Despite an aspiration to plan the economy comprehensively and minutely, central planning proper in the Soviet Union has been confined to planning high-priority sectors' inputs and outputs. Central management and the principle of the devil take the hindmost has governed the remainder of economic activity.

This analysis has an important bearing on the attempts that have been made since the early 1960s to reform the Soviet planning and management system. Some western specialists have attributed the slowdown in the rate of growth of main economic indicators such as national income and industrial production that has taken place since the end of the 1950s to an increased complexity of the Soviet economy. With more products and specialties and more sophisticated production and distribution systems, more interconnections and interdependencies must be dealt with in the central plan. A variant explanation is based on the supposition that the Soviet economy is becoming a mature economy, which presumably means more complex — and perhaps less idealistically motivated. It may also suggest an increased need to deliver the increased quantity and quality of consumer goods that have been promised the populace for many years as the ultimate reward for its efforts. Some economists have stressed the increased priority of the household sector as the primary problem, principally because, they argue, consumer goods and services face a more discriminating and varied set of tastes than do the producer goods which Soviet enterprises are more accustomed to supplying. Other economists have suggested that the obvious economic inefficiency at the enterprise level has occasioned reform, and most Soviet economists agree that Soviet enterprises are, by comparison with western enterprises, significantly inefficient.

All of these possible explanations have a certain merit. Taken together, or singly, however, they fail to provide a completely satisfying explanation. Planning methods have improved, thanks to improvements in communications, linear programming, access to computers and so forth, along with the growth in complexity of the economy. Which has increased more rapidly is an empirical question yet to be tackled. Also the concept of economic maturity remains vague and unsatisfactorily defined for empirical purposes. The primary evidence of maturity seems to be the very phenomenon that maturity is supposed to explain: a measured reduction in growth rates. Nor is it clear that consumer tastes are more difficult to satisfy than military specifications, which are based on competition with United States industry. Finally the most careful examinations that have been made into efficiency in the USSR suggest that Soviet enterprises have improved in efficiency, although they remain quite inefficient on a comparative basis.

It is possible to put these various suggestions together into a more general explanation based upon the nature of Soviet central planning and management. From the outset of planning, only a small fraction of the Soviet economy in fact has been planned and truly controlled centrally. The other sectors, which have often been described as buffer sectors, have operated in circumstances of scarcity that make their plans little more than eyewash. Similar planning systems have been used in capitalist countries in wartime, but nowhere have such systems been in operation as long as in the Soviet Union. The fundamental problem with the system is dialectical in character because it arises in part from the very success of Soviet planning in achieving relative growth of preferred sectors in the long run. Planning preferred sectors and managing priorities to guarantee them preferred access to scarce resources works, but in the long run priorities must change to avoid problems. Soviet planners were obviously quite successful in shifting priorities from investment to military expenditures when the war came and back when it ended. These two shifts in priority ranking of sectors demonstrate that the system can change gears and move in a new direction. The problem seems to be that, except when war threatens, it is difficult to revise priorities in the Soviet economy.

If the priority ranking of the various sectors becomes sticky in this way, then it is easy to explain why success would lead ultimately to a breakdown in the system. Preferred sectors would grow more rapidly than nonpreferred, and consequently central authorities would find themselves, willy-nilly, planning an increasing share of total economic activity. Moreover the various sectors of the economy are not independent of one another, and the growth of some subset of priority sectors is, sooner or later, bound to increase the priority ranking of those upon which it is dependent. Both of these factors work, therefore, to increase the job that central planners and managers must do to achieve any given degree of central control over economic activity. The importance of investment in Soviet growth and the fact that military expenditures depend upon factors completely out of the hands of economists and planners both work to make Soviet priority rankings sticky, thereby generating greater demands upon the skill and ingenuity of planners as time goes by.

After five decades, then, the slack that planners have been able to rely upon is finally exhausted. Consumers can no longer be denied, on pain of a diminution in labor force, and a concomitant of increasing the priority of consumers is an increased priority for agriculture, which supplies almost one-half of consumer demand. Meanwhile the industrial sector has increased in relative size owing to a relatively higher rate of growth over five decades. In this interpretation, planning needs reforming because it is impossible to turn the priority ranking of sectors upside-down. In this context economic maturity means a sticky and unsatisfactory priority ranking, and the task of economic planning has become more difficult because planners are attempting to plan (and manage), in the proper sense of the term, a larger share of total economic activity. Elimination of the economic inefficiency of Soviet enterprises represents, therefore, a source of additional output than can no longer be overlooked.

So long as central planners could rely upon the priority system to protect preferred sectors they could rely upon what Igor Birman calls planning from the achieved level to determine targets. As a forecasting method this technique is known in the West as riding the trend, and it is based upon the assumption that the increase (decrease) in a variable next year will be the same as this year. Targets are set this year, therefore, as last year's achieved level plus X percent. Because it can forecast nothing new, this method is useless as a way of predicting the future. As a planning method it is just as useless when innovation and experimentation with new production processes and types of products are required. Moreover its planners are completely befuddled by irregularly declining or increasing rates of change in the variables being planned. The increased complexity of the planners' task results, therefore, from the need to plan de facto more comprehensively and in a more sophisticated way and from the need to find a substitute for central management by means of priority and other direct rationing systems.

Economic Reform

Soviet planners, economists, and enterprise managers have been publically discussing and proposing economic reforms from at least 1962 onward. The various proposals that have been advanced may be divided into three schools of thought. One of them represents little more than an attempt to tighten up the old system, essentially Stalinist, of central planning and management. The adherents of this approach reject economic modeling and other control devices, such as prices, that are utilized in western capitalist countries. This approach would not be of interest were it not for the fact that active planners dominate this school and have thus far not been superseded by reform-minded economists. This most conservative approach doubtless is based upon concern that economic matters will worsen should radical experimentation be attempted. The concern also is based upon the obvious practical difficulties that the state would encounter in attempting to implement far-reaching reforms of central planning and management, particularly respecting the impact upon the distribution of real income among different classes of Soviet society. Thus far this school of thought has prevailed, mainly because of inertia and because it occupies the ranks of planners and influential political economists. They have effective control over the operational aspects of planning.

The second school of thought also represents a conservative approach to economic reform because its proposals are directed almost exclusively to improving central planning proper. It appears to have little interest in improved central-management techniques. Put simply, this school of thought seeks to counteract the increased demands for better planning by building larger and larger economic models and by using larger and larger computers to calculate plan targets and interconnections. These reformers propose no fundamental change in the way output is planned or in the way enterprise managers perform in the system. Were it possible to increase the scope of centrally controlled direct allocations of scarce commodities and to try out on very large models several plan variants, then this approach would have merit. Most specialists agree today, however, that this is an unrealistic expectation. The hopes that many western as well as Soviet economists placed in large-scale modeling through widespread applications of computers have already proven misplaced; and many, if not most, of the Soviet economists who proposed such technical reform of Soviet planning have already realized its weakness as a practical proposal. The advantage of this approach is that it offered the possibility of increasing central control without risking adverse effects upon income distribution or upon the distribution of economic power between planners and enterprise managers. Although Gosplan and other central government agencies are relying more heavily upon linear programming methods and computers and will continue to expand their use, there is no evidence that this approach offers more than marginal gains in the effectiveness of central planning and management methods.

A third school of thought includes the most radical sets of proposals that have been developed in the USSR. Reform along lines suggested by the members of this group would be quite extensive. Three aims are common to the reforms that they have proposed. First their proposals have been directed to improving and enhancing the role of central management, as opposed to central planning. Second their proposals call for increased enterprise-management discretion, subject to the indirect controls of central management. Third these proposals invariably are couched in terms of encouraging optimal economic behavior. As opposed to setting goals to be maximized or minimized, optimization involves a comparison of costs with benefits. The reforms of this third school of cost-conscious economists would involve allowing managers the latitude necessary to optimize production methods, guided mainly by general central management levers. Decentralization in turn would greatly expand the relative significance of central management, of enterprise-level decision-making, and of pecuniary instruments generally. It would also require a radical change in the structure of prices and in the way targets are specified at the present time.

Although this third school of thought has been labelled liberal or radical from the Soviet perspective, it nonetheless shares with the other two approaches a commitment to strong central control over economic activity. The way that this school proposes to establish central control is radical — through manipulating the environment in which enterprise managers make decisions. This radical Soviet school of thought on reform has yet to establish criteria for success, however, either at the enterprise level or at the level of national economic planning; and this failure has undermined the school's cause. The logical device to use at the enterprise level, given its aims, is to have managers maximize profits, subject to prices established and adjusted solely by Gosplan or some central pricing agency. Profit represents the most general index of managerial performance because it summarizes a large number of performance variables. So long as managers cannot manipulate prices or wages to increase profits without producing more or better commodities, increases in profits represent improved performance and demonstrate the satisfaction of the enterprise's customers.

The use of profits as a general index of enterprise performance faces, however, three formidable obstacles. First the notion of profit maximization runs against the grain of Marxist thought, Soviet ideology, and general feelings. Second, before profits could serve as a reasonable measure of performance, relative prices would have to be revised substantially, and that revision applies with particular force to the prices of certain staple consumer goods. Political apprehension and popular feeling both militate strongly against any such radical change. Unfortunately halfway measures would be unlikely to improve the situation even halfway in this instance. A series of gradual price increases would be likely, as we have seen, to exacerbate the situation by causing a wild immediate spending spree to avoid erosion of savings by gradual inflation. A sudden sharp rise in prices sufficiently great to preclude anticipatory spending would be certain to have serious political implications. Third, as we know from experience in western capitalist economies, profit criteria rarely suffice to ensure the performance of enterprises in the public interest in all cases; and these known examples can be used to criticize the third school of thought's approach cogently. This has particular force in the USSR since the problem of motivating managers who are civil servants remains a problem regardless of whether a profit or other criterion is used to evaluate performance. Ironically, therefore, the radical school's proposals coincide with what are considered quite conservative economic views when applied to western economies, for they call for less government interference, for an enhanced role of profits in decision-making, and for increased reliance upon market mechanisms.

At the national level resolving the problem of success criteria is no easier. What is needed are criteria for the economy as a whole. Presumably these would be criteria that reconcile the preferences of planners and consumers. To allow the composition of national income to be determined as it is in the West, without politically conscious explicit deliberation and specification, would obviously be unsatisfactory. The preferences of the population need to be ascertained and incorporated in some way into the planning of consumer-goods production. The share of investment, of consumption, and of government expenditures must, according to Soviet practices and ideology, reflect something other than blind market forces. But an alternative has yet to be developed. Some Soviet economists argue for scientific, or specialist, determination, which means that physiologists, psychologists, and other specialists in human needs and desires would decide what goods to produce. For example the number of square meters that each person needs for living space, the amount of calcium that each child needs to consume, adult tolerance for alcohol and so forth can be determined scientifically and used in formulating objectives in the production of consumer goods. Alternatively sociologists may conduct surveys to ascertain consumer tastes, and economists can calculate the elasticity of demand for certain products, and these estimates may be used as the basis of planning. The flaw in either approach, however, given the freedom of individuals to avoid purchasing certain commodities and to withdraw from the labor force, is that some kinds of goods will remain scarce, while others will accumulate as unsold inventories where consumers and specialists disagree on what is good for people. It is not clear, therefore, how the marketplace can be avoided as the ultimate basis for determining what consumers want. Intervention by specialists, moralists, and other do-gooders works better when confined to a small number of commodities or services. The idea of using markets to ascertain consumer preferences is, however, quite radical and unacceptable in the Soviet Union today for most economists as well as for most policy-makers.

Barring a major violent upheaval and a return to strong antimarket, antipecuniary sentiments, it seems reasonable to expect that Soviet planners and economists will come to rely increasingly on indirect central-management devices in seeking to improve the performance of the Soviet economy. When there is much to be done, only strong ideological commitments can prevent those who want to solve problems and to help the economy to function better from using instruments that would work but that are currently underutilized or not used. These instruments include macroeconomic policy tools, such as the income tax, interest rates, and variations in government expenditures, to achieve goals that everyone agrees upon. The same holds for price policies and for the exercise of discretion at the enterprise level. It seems improbable that a major price revision can be avoided for long for consumer goods retailed in state stores. Once a revision has taken place, central planners will be able to use prices more flexibly to allocate commodities and services in the Soviet economy. Elimination, or a great reduction, of nalevo markets and transactions, especially those that are highly illegal, will be necessary if the regime is to prevent a serious erosion in popular adherence to law and to communist goals. In order to accomplish this it will be necessary for the state to increase the priority of consumer goods still more and eventually to eliminate the permanent state of excess demand and its concomitant of supply insecurity.

The conservative nature of the current political leadership of Brezhnev and his associates militates against the possibility of radical reform of Soviet central planning and management. It is not clear that any leadership would be willing to engage in the extensive reform of prices, incomes, and decision-making that the more radical reformers imply is necessary. The fact remains, however, that pressures for reform will not diminish, and the encouragement of illegal and other *nalevo* activities that the current system provides offers another powerful force for reform. No doubt the less radical group will succeed in introducing increased sophistication in the way of data processing and high-speed computers, but it is highly doubtful that such improvements in central planning will amount to very much. Despite Soviet prejudices against pecuniary and market institutions historically, these distasteful institutions have gained ground during periods of relative quiet, and they have lost ground in major upheavals such as the civil war, mass collectivization, and World War II. The more radical elements of the reform movement represent, therefore, a recrudescence of forces and ideas that first appeared in the 1920s.

SELECTED READINGS

Birman, Igor. " 'From the Achieved Level.' " *Soviet Studies* 30, no. 2 (April 1978), 153-72.

Davies, R. W. "Planning a Mature Economy in the USSR." *Economics of Planning* 6, no. 2 (1966), 138-53.

Lewin, Moshe. *Political Undercurrents in Soviet Economic Debates: From Bukharin to the Modern Reformers*. Princeton: Princeton University Press, 1974.

Schroeder, Gertrude E. "The 'Reform' of the Supply System in Soviet Industry." *Soviet Studies* 24, no. 1 (July 1972), 97-119.

Wright, Arthur. "Soviet Economic Planning and Performance." In *The Soviet Union since Stalin*, ed. Stephen F. Cohen, Alexander Rabinowitch, and Robert Sharlet. Bloomington: Indiana University Press, 1980, 113-34.

8

Convergence, Catastrophes, and Other Speculations

Reciprocity and Rationality in Modern Industrial Economies

Throughout my description of the contemporary Soviet economy I have stressed the importance of the principle of reciprocity because this facet of everyday Soviet economic life has been neglected by western specialists, who have been more concerned with the contrast between markets and central planning. By reciprocity I refer to an exchange of goods or services which is conducted on the basis of relationships other than those of the marketplace. Market exchange, whether barter or in money terms, is conducted with an eye to equivalent exchange in the current period. Even a loan transaction, which necessarily involves an element of futurity, occurs in the marketplace as a discounted present exchange. The lender loans out only what he considers to be the equivalent today of the money sum to be repaid to him in the future. Reciprocal exchange is not based upon a direct comparison of immediate benefits. In fact those who receive value in exchange through a system of reciprocity may not be the same people who provide the initial value.

That reciprocity networks exist in the Soviet economy is not unique, but the extent and significance of these networks apparently is, given the level of Soviet economic development. From the standpoint of any particular household, the attainment of a comfortable standard of living in the Soviet Union depends as much upon reciprocity as upon markets. Both of the open markets in which individuals participate are heavily influenced by reciprocal obligations, and neither price nor wage alone suffices to determine who gets the scarce commodity or the good job. A strategically located relative or friend, however distantly connected, is as important in locating a good job in a good location as university preparation. Similarly, acquiring caviar for an important party, tickets to the Taganka Theater, access to a good restaurant, a natural fur coat, or a good brand of vodka is impossible or unlikely unless one is a member of a reciprocity network that includes individuals who have blat or some other special access to these goods and services. Even access to many important benefits — such as a university education, permission to live in Moscow, a roomy apartment, and jobs or job advancement — also frequently depends heavily upon the family's ability to capitalize on outstanding reciprocal favors.

The reciprocity system is not confined to the household sector. Smart enterprise managers know how to use reciprocity to the benefit of their enterprises and employees when supplies get tight. The general rule for families as well as enterprises and institutions is to refuse to purchase or accept nothing which might be useful either to themselves directly or to a friend or potential contact. Reciprocity is normally invoked by an individual who wishes to establish a presumptive claim upon the recipient. Obviously an individual who can distribute highly desirable favors can also collect many favors in return. It is important to note, however, that the initiator of a reciprocal relationship cannot enforce it as a legal contract, and the recipient need not reciprocate immediately — or ever. Nevertheless claims accumulate to the credit of an individual and, to an extent, may be passed on to the members of his or her family. The reciprocity system plays a very important role in the allocation of goods and services in the Soviet economy, and it works simultaneously to strengthen bonds of family and friendship. As Karl Polanyi pointed out, reciprocity systems tend to be submerged, or subordinated to, social relationships; their economic character is not necessarily the primary or most salient aspect.

As a principle for organizing economic activity, reciprocity is in no sense unique to the Soviet economy. It was first discovered by students of primitive and prehistoric societies, but reciprocity remains an important principle for organizing economic activity in even the most highly developed industrial-monetary economies. In many primitive economies reciprocity is the primary pattern, usually together with some principle of direct redistribution, for organizing the allocation of labor power, land, and capital, in which case economic organization is almost completely submerged in kinship, friendship, and ceremonial obligations. In modern developed economies certain institutions have become specialized in economic functions, and kinship systems, peer-group obligations, ceremonial exchange, and similar noneconomic institutions play a much smaller role in organizing economic life. Nonetheless the economic well-being of households and the economic success of many business enterprises still depend significantly upon reciprocal relationships. Bureaucracies generally depend heavily upon reciprocity networks also. The persistence of the family as an economic unit also ensures persistence of the principle. "Home is where you *can* go, if you have to," sums up the basis of reciprocity in the family; and it was not long ago that placing elderly parents in nursing homes was as hotly debated as rearing very young children in nursery schools is today. Both situations represent the intrusion of the market upon social and economic relationships previously determined according to noncommercial principles.

What is unique about the contemporary Soviet economy is not, therefore, that the principle of reciprocity plays a role but that the role is as extensive and significant as it is in so highly developed an economy. Persistent scarcity of luxury and sometimes even of mundane commodities, together with the state's unwillingness to set prices in retail (or even in wholesale) markets at clearing levels, creates regions in which some principle other than the market principle may flourish. Whenever there is queuing for an economic commodity, those who control sales are ipso facto in a position to allow friends, kin, or important latecomers to break the queue. Precisely because it does not operate on the basis of a current quid pro quo, reciprocity is by far safer than selling blatantly on black or gray markets. Moreover the economic conditions that make reciprocal exchange possible merely reinforce an existing set of social and familial institutions; it does not bring them into existence. The system does tend to get abused by those who mimic it in order to cover what are really black-market dealings. Such abuses may eventually bring about much stricter controls and much harsher penalties in the USSR.

A reduction in deficit commodities would reduce the role open for reciprocal arrangements, and considerable efforts are being made to reduce deficits by increasing output of high-quality commodities. Prices have been increased in some areas also, which tends to have the same effect, but radical changes are apparently deemed politically inadvisable. The thirst for consumer goods is so great, however, that eliminating deficits in high-quality commodities is unlikely in the near future. It is reasonable to expect gradually increasing inroads of market and pecuniary institutions upon reciprocal distribution of commodities in the USSR. Certainly this has been the experience of developing countries all over the world, and Soviet economic history reveals a reluctant, laggard, but sure conformity to such general patterns.

Markets have become increasingly important both to households and enterprises since the postwar reconstruction period ended, and there is every indication that the influence of market institutions will continue to expand in the foreseeable future. The most significant changes have taken place in the labor market. Freedom of calling, including the freedom to change jobs, was abrogated shortly before World War II. Since the close of hostilities, however, a gradual loosening of restrictions on freedom of calling has occurred, and this has, in turn, increased the importance of labor markets in the organization of Soviet economic activity. Because all economic activities are tied to labor markets, the influence of increased freedom of calling has been pervasive, and it has influenced consumer goods markets directly because a wage that cannot be spent will induce no one to work hard, in an unattractive location, or perhaps work at all.

By stressing the role of markets and of the principle of reciprocity I do not mean to suggest that the institution of central planning plays a minor role. To play down the institutions of the market and of reciprocity in the Soviet economy, however, would be as misleading as minimizing the central management activities of the President's Council of Economic Advisors, the federal budget, and the Federal Reserve Board in the determination of the level and direction of economic activity in the United States.

The Convergence Hypothesis

Comparison between the Soviet and American economies has frequently elicited the hypothesis that capitalist and socialist economies do not differ in kind and may be converging upon a common model. Some versions of the convergence hypothesis have bordered on hysteria. During much of the 1950s a variant labelled *creeping socialism* was widely discussed in the United States. The fear was that, by increasing the extent of government participation in economic activity, the American economic system would inevitably become like the

Soviet. During the 1960s this variant disappeared and was replaced by an equally irrational variant of *creeping capitalism* in the Soviet Union, a hypothesis that was derived from the Liberman and Kosygin discussions for reform. Few economists today, with the possible exception of certain very conservative planners and politicians in the Soviet Union, see the reform movement in the USSR in such dramatic terms.

Rejection of unilateral theories of convergence was followed in the 1970s by the hypothesis that the two types of economy are mutually converging from either end of a socialist-capitalist spectrum. Mutual convergence seems to be less threatening than unilateral convergence, and many adherents of the hypothesis have apparently believed that mutual economic convergence would have peaceful implications for international relations between communist and capitalist countries. Whether or not this would be the case is not our concern, except to note that historically it is not obvious that wars have been more likely to occur between radically different social and economic systems. More to the point here is the fact that the mutual convergence hypothesis has appeared previously. It was first advanced with particular reference to the United States and the Soviet economies during the NEP, immediately prior to mass collectivization and the industrialization drive. The hypothesis, based essentially upon the premise that people are pretty much the same the world over, was proposed again during World War II when the two countries were military allies. That it surfaced in the late 1960s and early 1970s, during a period of relative thaw in relations between the two countries, must give pause to potential adherents. A radical policy change, such as industrialization, or a catastrophe, such as World War II, could readily reverse any existing trends.

A fundamental problem with convergence theories is that they have not been based upon explicit theories of social and economic change. Indeed they have represented little more than extrapolation of observed trends. Extrapolation is a prediction based upon the assumption that nothing new will occur to deflect present trends. As such it can predict nothing new. Marx's prediction of an eventual convergence of all systems upon socialism was, on the contrary, based upon an explicit theory of the way economies and societies change over time, and it was explicit enough to have been proven demonstrably wrong in significant respects. Marx's incorrect predictions, such as the increasing immiseration of the workers under capitalism or the law of the falling rate of profits, have, of course, been explained away by adherents and emphasized by opponents, but each side has been able to persuade only those predisposed to believe Marx right or wrong in the first place.

Jan Tinbergen, who won the Nobel prize in economics, was among the first to put forward the hypothesis of mutual convergence in its most recent incarnation. His argument for eventual convergence is based upon two premises. He assumes first that there exists a single, optimal economic structure. Second he assumes that man is more or less uniform in all cultures and is dominated by rational calculation. It follows that where rational men have a common end — the provision of goods and services for consumers — they will eventually discover and implement the one optimal economic system. Students of mankind, of society, and of evolutionary history tell me that only an economist could accept the second premise, but the notion that a unique solution exists to the economic problem ought to strain the credulity even of an economist. Tinbergen is both ahistorical and nonempirical in his approach to convergence, and he cannot persuade anyone who is not inclined to a priori, putative explanations of real historical processes.

This brings us to the second fundamental problem posed by the convergence hypothesis. If one seeks to do more than merely assert the existence of converging trends in communist and capitalist countries, it is necessary to put the convergence hypothesis into a form in which the remoteness of one system from another may be measured, thereby allowing a direct empirical test. Otherwise the controversy can be little more than a matter of assertion, in which the assertions are based upon impressionistic evidence. The discussion of convergence to date has entailed three aspects of capitalist and communist economies: (1) the extent of private ownership of the means of production; (2) the pervasiveness of market transactions; (3) the proportion of decisions that are made on a decentralized basis. These three traits represent independent continuous variables. Thus an economy might display any one trait in any proportion, regardless of the other two, which means that the possible variety of economic systems that could be constructed out of these traits is indefinite in number. Although it is much more complex because three dimensions are actually involved, we can represent this conception of the distance between various economic systems as a single continuous line labelled *pure communism* at one extreme and *pure capitalism* at the other. After locating various economies on the spectrum thus created, we could ascertain, over time, whether any two are converging and, if so, whether or not the process is mutual or unilateral.

The spectrum model underlies most contemporary conceptions of the nature of economic convergence, but it suffers two grave weaknesses. First, unless one adopts Tinbergen's premises about human nature and the dominance of a single optimal economic structure, or something comparable, the spectrum model is atheoretical. A demonstration of convergence between, say, the Soviet and the United States economies could not exclude a crossover — the possibility that after converging they would continue in the same direction as before, thereby ultimately landing on the opposite poles from which they started. Tinbergen's theory rules out a crossover and would be invalidated by any such observation. A theory of social change is necessary, therefore, to prevent nonsensical outcomes such as the crossover.

The second weakness of the spectrum model is the fact that we are not told how to weigh the various differences found between two economies. Even if we limit consideration to the three traits discussed (degree of decentralization, private ownership, and market orientation), opposing trends for any two cannot be interpreted meaningfully. Moreover it is not clear how one measures each of the three variables. Thus far economists have agreed neither on the traits to be considered nor upon the way to assign them relative significance. Consequently a definitive test of the convergence hypothesis has not been conducted, and it will not be easy to obtain the kind of consensus that would be required to demonstrate convergence or nonconvergence to the satisfaction of a majority of economists (or other specialists).

The main problem with the convergence hypothesis is that it has been insufficiently grounded in theories of social and economic change to allow us to interpret just what a period of observed convergence between, say, the economies of the USSR and the USA would mean. No convergence hypothesis thus far put forward has been sufficiently well specified to allow of a definitive test, and the obstacles to a definitive test are clearly formidable. Two relatively sophisticated theories of economic change that have been put forward in the twentieth century should be noted in connection with the possibility of convergence with respect to the USSR and the western capitalist countries. One of them, proposed by Clarence Ayres, argues that technological problems do ordinarily admit of unique "best" solutions and that these solutions, such as the printing press or gunpowder, cross cultural lines more easily than do other kinds of cultural products. Common technology is, according to Ayres, a basis for common economic development. Another economist, J. R. Hicks, traces the origins of pecuniary and market institutions from prehistory to the present, arguing that the institutions of the market, money, prices, and wages, all of which antedate capitalism, have gradually spread over the face of the globe and at the same time have increasingly penetrated domestic economic relationships.

The Soviet historical experience reveals two trends that conform to Ayres's and Hicks's independent theories. For Soviet planners economic development has always meant borrowing technology from the West, and they have sought to borrow technology without importing capitalist institutions or ideological content at the same time. In respect to machine technology, therefore, borrowing has been a positive goal of Soviet planners. The development of pecuniary institutions in the Soviet economy, on the contrary, has taken place in the teeth of ideological resistance. Marx and his followers were not fond of pecuniary institutions, for these institutions were attributed to capitalism. Thus it was that early Bolshevik theorists, such as Preobrazhensky and Bukharin, were so ready to jettison them during the civil war. The initiation of the first five-year plan, collectivization, and the halcyon days of Stalin's prime coincided with a second revulsion against pecuniary institutions. The fact that money, prices, money-wages, market exchange, interest rates, borrowing, and lending continue to play prominent parts in the articulation of economic activity in the Soviet Union today testifies to the apparent indispensability of these institutions for the organization of a modern industrial economy.

The Soviet socialist economy and the American capitalist economy do share a large number of economic institutions in common. One basis for the contemporary belief in economic convergence is the overstatement of differences between the systems that occurred during periods of great conflict and hostility between them as political systems. As we have seen, Soviet households understand completely and practice a limited form of private property. They participate in labor markets and consumer-goods markets that differ in degree rather than in kind from those American households know. Soviets understand, therefore, freedom of calling and freedom of consumer choice in a market setting. Conversely Americans understand and practice reciprocity, nepotism, and blat in varying degrees. Thus, although the difference becomes quite significant on a cumulative basis along all dimensions of economic comparison, the difference between the Soviet and the American economy is apparently one of degree only (or, perhaps, degrees).

It is clear that the two economies share too many traits to be regarded as remotely connected phylogenetically. Not only did the Bolshevik economy evolve out of the Tsarist, which had earlier been deliberately attuned to western economic developments, but Marx himself represents one branch of specifically western economic ideology. It may be the better course of wisdom, therefore, to eschew the concept of convergence, which biologists confine to species that are phylogenetically remote at the time that similar structure-function systems developed, such as the development of wings in the butterfly, the bird, and the bat. Where species share considerable phylogenetic material, the development of similar structure-function systems, as the eyes of primates, is attributed to parallel evolution, which implies that similar solutions developed to similar problems from common genetic material.

As an explanation for the evolution of similarities between two economies, parallel evolution is much more modest than the convergence hypothesis, and it suggests a more prosaic outcome. The hypothesis of parallel evolution can also explain all the observations that have prompted talk about convergence. It also accords better with what we know about the evolution of other economic systems over time. If convergence is the rule for economic systems, why after all these centuries, for example, are the economics of France, Italy, and England still so distinct? The convergence hypothesis makes no provision for the appearance of completely new developments in particular economies, and novelty is, of course, the most important and at the same time the most difficult thing to predict. The concept of parallel evolution can accommodate novelty.

Catastrophes and Other Possible Outcomes

During the 1920s and 1930s many observers of the new Bolshevik regime predicted a collapse of the economy within five years. The prediction was made faithfully almost every year for over ten years before being abandoned. World War II and the continuance of Stalin's regime despite the extraordinary impact of the German invasion demonstrated a political stability and institutional viability that no one anticipated, including the invading Germans. Russian success in war brought about a radical change in western evaluations of the Soviet system. Prior to the war, most commentators in the West would have agreed with John Maynard Keynes, who argued that the USSR was unlikely ever to prove a direct military threat to the West. Instead it represented a bad example for the workers in the West. Those who considered the Soviet Union a threat to western institutions at that time saw the "red menace" in similar terms, as an ideological and not a military threat. World War II hitched a large, successful, and ruthless military machine to the red menace model, and it frightened western observers and analysts out of their wits. As a result, many were led to view the USSR as a new appearance of Genghis Khan. Hordes of ideologically saturated semi-Asiatic fanatics were pictured as poised in the east for a new sweep of destruction throughout civilization.

The evidence we have today about the state of the Soviet economy at the close of World War II belies the military threat implied by the Genghis Khan model. The military capacity and the threat posed to the West by the USSR was apparently as badly overstated following World War II as it had been understated in prewar years. Similarly many of those who had looked with favor and hope upon the Bolshevik experiment in the creation of a new society, a new culture, and a new morality during the prewar and war decades became just as blindly condemnatory and pessimistic afterward. It is clear now that these appraisals and predictions were badly distorted by the strong emotions, both pro and con, that the Soviet state and economy tend to elicit in outside observers. These wrong predictions (and there have been few correct predictions about important changes) were also caused by the difficulty of collecting reliable data on the Soviet system and the propensity of Soviet authorities to suggest false conclusions by emphasizing positive and minimizing negative aspects.

Emotional feelings still run high about the Soviet system and about its strategic objectives in the world, and there remains much that we would like to know before drawing conclusions about where the Soviet Union is headed and how. Even with the most carefully controlled objectivity and the best conceivable data, of course, prediction of social and economic change is fraught with difficulties that scientists who deal with the physical world would probably consider insurmountable. What we would most like to know about the future of the Soviet system is whether or not a radical change is in the offing. Anyone can ride the trend and predict that things will continue pretty much the same next year as this. Riding the trend is safe because a prediction based upon it will be correct most of the time — perhaps 90 percent of the time or higher. But an analyst who relies upon this method will miss every important new development. What we want to know is whether the Soviet economic system is going to change significantly over the next five to ten years and, if so, in what way. A French mathematician, René Thom, has defined trend-deflecting changes as catastrophes to emphasize precisely the fact that they do not occur in the small gradual steps which the differential calculus implies but suddenly and (perhaps) violently. Examples are the breaking of a wave on the shore, the outbreak of war, the sheering of a plane under stress, and many types of biological processes.

War with China, violent consumer (or worker) mass reaction to price increases or to commodity shortages or an ideological revulsion of the leadership and the party to the inroads of markets, pecuniary institutions, reciprocity, and corruption in the allocation of consumer goods and services represent three such conceivable catastrophes in the contemporary Soviet economy. Each represents a different source of radical change: from the outside, from below, or from above, and each would bring about different possible radical changes in the way the Soviet economy functions. We can only speculate, of course, about these and similar kinds of catastrophes because we have no reliable way to assign a probability to any of them.

War with China, while unlikely to pose a threat of foreign domination, would mean another drain of resources that might otherwise go to fill the currently insatiable appetite of pent-up Soviet consumer demand. War would presumably also provide its own justification for additional sacrifices, but it would only aggravate the problems posed by scarcities of consumer goods, inefficiency, and poor morale of workers. The leadership would have, I think, every reason to avoid military conflict and to seek to reduce the armaments race as well if, as I have argued above, satisfaction of consumer demand has become a prerequisite for improved economic performance generally. War might provide the pretext for a new antimarket, antipecuniary drive, but the evidence provided by World War II and its aftermath does not recommend it as a policy for this purpose. World War II did bring about depecuniarization and decreased reliance upon markets for allocation of labor and the distribution of real income, but these institutions were reestablished and increased in scope even during Stalin's last years, not to mention thereafter. Reimposition of terror does not appear to offer a viable long-run alternative for the allocation of labor and income. Moreover, even Brezhnev, after eighteen years of continuous rule and growing dominance, does not have the power required to do so.

Whether or not an ideologically based revulsion of the leadership to current economic arrangements and problems is likely or feasible would be very difficult to ascertain in any objective fashion, but I doubt that it would find the support among party members it would require to succeed. The references that one sees in Kremlin leaders' speeches to the exciting days of the 1930s and 1940s, when many made sacrifices willingly and uncomplainingly, have an unmistakable ring of nostalgia. So far as I can tell, virtually everyone, party devotee and careerist, as well as alienated intellectual, is inextricably implicated in market and reciprocity dealings nalevo. Besides there is not the slightest sign of any true ideological revival at present.

Although I cannot rule out catastrophes initiated either outside the USSR or from "above," these both strike me as more avoidable than one that would originate in an economic breakdown, such as great crop failures several years in a row, in clumsy implementation of economic reforms, or in an outburst of consumer-worker frustration. The Brezhnev-Kosygin leadership was unable, or unwilling, to carry the reforms of 1965 to fruition. Soviet economists who were closely identified with the 1965 reforms (and those reforms that have followed as adjustments) and who were enthusiastic about possibilities for significant improvement in the way the economy functions are pessimistic today about the near-term prospect for reform. At the macroeconomic level Brezhnev has been very conservative since 1965, and this behavior accords with his general image in other areas. On the other hand he has apparently been willing to overlook and thereby to tolerate a growth of nalevo economic activity at the microeconomic level that would certainly have shocked Nikita Khrushchev, not to mention Stalin. Some time in the next five years or so, Brezhnev will be replaced, and I expect another attempt to reform the Soviet system will take place. The direction of reform will be to introduce more realistic planning, coupled with greater reliance upon central-management instruments and upon socialist markets in the allocation of both labor and consumer goods. There is even discussion about a capital-goods market among certain Soviet economists today, and the Polish case suggests a possible increased role for trade unions. When reforms begin again, as I believe they must, they will be proposed and supported by a completely new generation of Soviet economists and planners, a generation for whom pecuniary and market institutions are neither novel nor ideologically tainted.

Reform of the Soviet economy will involve steps that may easily backfire. The population complains today when prices are increased, and it also complains that deficit commodities are allocated unfairly. The population apparently shares with the current leadership the dream of abolishing deficit commodities through increased production at reduced per-unit costs, which is economically tantamount to having one's cake and eating it too. It is possible that reform will ultimately be destabilizing politically; but failure to reform the obvious flaws in the Soviet economy is just as likely to be destabilizing. The Soviet economic structure, which involves the political leaders as trustees of national economic wealth, politicizes economic decision-making to a degree unprecedented elsewhere in recent centuries. Thus, as has been witnessed in Poland recently, any demonstration protesting economic conditions, whether in consumer markets or at the workplace, is at once a political protest and challenge. The pressure on the leadership to produce successful economic results is very great and will not diminish, barring a catastrophe, until the Soviet Union becomes a full-fledged acquisitive society. In his struggle with Malenkov to succeed Stalin in 1953, Khrushchev told the central committee: "Really, comrades, in the communist society you will not tell people to go and eat a potato without butter." Brezhnev's successors will certainly feel the same pressure.

When Soviet leaders review the parade and demonstration celebrating the great October revolution each November 7th, they stand atop the Lenin mausoleum, and the panorama must give them pause. Beneath them Lenin lies quietly and invisibly in state in perpetuity, something no one else has yet succeeded in achieving for himself. To the left of the reviewing stand is the Lenin Historical Museum, celebrating Lenin as a dedicated revolutionary, implacable enemy of conservative rule as well as first leader of the new Bolshevik state. To the right stands St. Basil's Cathedral, made famous in millions of tourists snapshots for its colorful onion-shaped domes. St. Basil's has long been famous among historians because its originality was preserved by having its designer blinded. Directly across from the reviewing stand are the windows of GUM, the largest "universal" department store in the

USSR, where armies of acquisitive Soviet shoppers clash and struggle by day. Not far beyond St. Basil's is the hotel Rossiia that Nikita Khrushchev had built to accommodate foreign tourists for the foreign currency they bring with them. Not far beyond GUM, on the other hand, is the Liubianka prison, where many unsuccessful Soviet politicians have suddenly found themselves in the terrible past. The architectural monuments surrounding Red Square are, therefore, sufficient to define both the economic aims and the political constraints under which contemporary Soviet leaders and their successors must operate.

SELECTED READINGS

Ayres, C. E. *The Theory of Economic Progress.* Chapel Hill: University of North Carolina Press, 1944.

Hicks, John. *A Theory of Economic History.* New York: Oxford University Press, 1969.

Linnemann, H., Pronk, J., and Tinbergen, J. "Convergence of Economic Systems in East and West." In *Disarmament and World Economic Interdependence,* ed. Emile Benoit. New York: Columbia University Press, 1967, 246-60.

Millar, James R. "On the Theory and Measurement of Economic Convergence." *Quarterly Review of Economics and Business* 12, no. 1 (Spring 1972), 87-97.

Polanyi, Karl. "The Economy as Instituted Process," In *Primitive, Archaic and Modern Economies,* ed. George Dalton. New York: Doubleday & Co., Inc., 1968, 139-74.

Glossary

apparatchik	a bureaucrat; member of the bureaucratic apparatus.
BAM, Baikalo-Amurskaia Magistral'	Baikal-Amur main line; a new railway spur laid 90 to 270 miles north of the Trans-Siberian railway from a juncture north of Lake Baikal to the Amur River
berëozki	special stores in the Soviet Union which sell goods to the tourists for foreign exchange only. Other kinds of berëozki have been organized for special purposes and special groups to sell scarce items to Russians who acquire foreign exchange legally.
blat, po blatu	a term used by the Soviets to refer to "pull," "connections," or "string-pulling" that is used to advance one's own family's interests
chernyi rynok	black market
CFM	collective farm market; see *rynok*
Gosbank	state bank; the Soviet central bank, including all branch banks in the USSR
Gosbiudzhet	state budget; a consolidated budget for all governmental units in the USSR
Gosplan	state planning committee
Gossnab	state committee for material and technical supply

Gosstrakh	state committee on insurance
khozraschët	a requirement that all enterprises and institutions maintain a balance sheet detailing their assets and liabilities, and determine their net income position for each accounting period; it includes the preparation of budgets for future periods on both capital and current accounts
kolkhoz	collective farm
kolkhoznik	collective farm worker
kontraktatsiia	a channel of sale of certain agricultural crops — such as sugar, beets, or flax, for example — directly to state enterprises, at prices negotiated in advance directly with the enterprises
kulak	well off, rich peasant
MTS	Machine Tractor Station, a state budget unit staffed with personnel who operated the equipment for the kolkhozes; it served for an in-kind rental charge (abolished in 1958)
na chernom rynke	on the black market
nalevo	obtaining goods or services "on the left" or "under the counter"
po znakomstvu	obtaining goods or services through a contact or a friend
profsoiuz	trade union
protektsiia, po protektsii	protection, the polite word for *blat*
rynok	any free market
samogon	illegally produced home brew
Sel'khozbank	state bank for agricultural affairs (abolished in 1959)
sovkhoz	state farm

sovkhoznik   state farm worker

sovnarkhoz   in 1957 Khrushchev divided the country into
                              105 regions, sovnarkhozes, each of which was
                              supposed to organize production and distribu-
                              tion of the goods and services produced primar-
                              ily within that region (abandoned by Brezhnev
                              and Kosygin in 1965)

Stroibank   specialized bank with responsibility for the
                              distribution of investment funds from the state
                              budget (Gosbuidzhet) to the enterprises that are
                              slated for expansion or construction during the
                              plan period

tekhpromfinplan   technical-industrial-financial plan — the opera-
                              tional annual or quarterly plan for an enterprise

trudoden'   a standardized workday unit used by kolkhozes
                              to determine the contribution of members to
                              the collective (and thus their income)

Vneshtorgbank   the foreign trade bank, which is responsible for
                              keeping track of international transactions and
                              for the receipt and disbursement of foreign
                              exchange. This bank also controls the country's
                              gold stock and manages reserves of foreign
                              currencies and gold of the USSR in world
                              markets.

zakupka   sale of the remainder of the crops by kolkhozes
                              (after "obligatory deliveries" to the state and the
                              rental payments to the MTS had been com-
                              pleted) to government procurement agencies
                              for prices considerably higher than for oblig-
                              atory deliveries. Since 1958, all sales to state
                              agencies are labeled *zakupka.*

Index

Academy of Sciences, 90
Aggregate demand: excess, 166,
171-72
Aggregate labor force: determination of real wage, 162-63
Aggregate price level: defined, 167
Aggregate sectors of Soviet economy, 59-60
Agriculture, 24-28, 98-105, 143-49;
changes in production under
Khrushchev, 138-39; climatic
conditions, 138; as declining
sector, 146-47; depecuniarization,
27; destalinization, 55; failure to
achieve breakthroughs in
performance, 144; fully
collectivized, 35; fundamental
changes in production, 138-39;
growth and foreign trade, 150;
imports, 143; labor force, 111-14,
145; labor market, 103-5;
modernization and education,
144; modernization and health
care, 144; as natural resource,
137-38; prices, 145-46; priority for
and consumer demand, 181-82;
private and peasant skills, 143;
product price, 98; quality of land,
137-38; response to planning
methods, 146; scissors crisis, 10-
11; Stalinist model, 139; and U.S.
grain embargo, 149; workers and
wages, 145; and World War II,
49. See also Collectivization
Alcohol, illegal brewing. See Samogon
Antiparasite laws, 105
Ayres, Clarence: on technological
borrowing, 195-96

Backwardness: economic, 17; industrial, 3; rural retail outlets, 145;
social, economic, political, 52;
social, educational, technical,
economical, 29
BAM, 71
Bank policy and enterprise expenditures, 172
Berëozki. See Special stores
Beria, Lavrenti, 53
Birman, Igor: on planning from
achieved level, 182
Blat: importance of, 109-10; and incentives, 114; po blatu, defined,
96; and queues, 109-10;
reciprocity network, 190; and
subsidies, 156; mentioned, 87,
121, 150, 196
Bolsheviks, 5-17; and agriculture,
143; economics of, 5-6; foreign
trade, 147; grain crisis in 1928,
23; industrialization, 5; labor
market, 104-5; Lenin's policy of
defeatism, 21; and managers, 177;
on market, 9; and NEP, 9, 13;
party, 22-23; and peasant private
enterprise, 29; on peasantry, 9-10;
on pecuniary institutions, 9, 61,
196; on planned economy, 16-17;
revolution, second, 21; and
scissors crisis, 10-11; and Tsarist
government, 197; women, 116;
mentioned, 8, 201
Bonds, state, 90, 170
Branch management: defined,
123-24
Brezhnev: conservative policy since
1965, 200; and Khrushchev
reforms, 55; radical reform of

A Note on the Author

JAMES R. MILLAR is a native of San Antonio and a Phi Beta Kappa graduate of the University of Texas. He earned a Ph.D. at Cornell University in economics after special study at Harvard University in Russian area studies. He has held Woodrow Wilson and Ford Foundation fellowships and has traveled and lectured in the Soviet Union. He has also conducted research in the USSR twice for extended periods. Since 1965 Mr. Millar has taught economics at the University of Illinois at Urbana-Champaign, where he is now a professor.

Professor Millar's articles have appeared in many journals in both economics and Soviet studies, and he was the editor of *The Soviet Rural Community: A Symposium* (University of Illinois Press, 1971). He also served as editor of the *Slavic Review*, the journal of the American Association for the Advancement of Slavic Studies, from 1975 to 1980.

The author's wife was raised in the USSR and teaches in the Slavic Languages department at the University of Illinois. They have a son and a daughter. In 1979, the family accompanied Professor Millar to the Soviet Union, where he conducted research for six months at the Academy of Sciences in Moscow.